OUTIN

# OUTIN

## BRANDT LEGG

THE SAGER GROUP

Artifex Te Adiuva

OUTIN

Published in the United States of America by The Sager Group
Copyright © 2013 by Brandt Legg
All rights reserved.

Original poems attributed to Linh written by Roanne Lewis

Cataloging-in-Publication data for this book is available from the Library
of Congress.
ISBN-13: 978-0-9895241-1-7
ISBN-10: 0-9895241-1-6

Cover designed by: Caitlin Legere
Formatting by: Siori Kitajima and Ovidiu Vlad for SF AppWorks LLC
Title page illustration by: Caitlin Legere

www.TheSagerGroup.net
www.BrandtLegg.com

PUBLISHER'S NOTE
This book is a work of fiction. Names, characters, places and incidents
are products of the author's imagination or are used fictitiously. Any
resemblance to actual persons, living or dead, businesses, events or
locales is entirely coincidental.

*For Teakki and Ro*

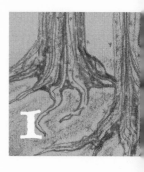

$M$*onday, October 6*
Once we were inside, with the veil closed behind us, the noise from the special ops helicopters and all traces of the regular world were gone.

"I thought this place was a dream..." My brother Dustin's eyes were overflowing with tears.

"Where are we?" Dazed, I wondered if the CIA's secret Lightyear division of psychics could find us here, and I was stunned by the world before me.

"We're there. Don't you see? It's real, we made it back." I could see why Dustin had wanted to return to this place and why he never tried to describe it. I would not have believed him. Even with all that had happened—discovering our dad had been murdered by the government, finding out I was one of my generation's seven souls able to help the world through a great awakening leading to the unlimited power of our souls, and learning many of those supernatural powers myself. Federal Agent Fitts had tried to stop me and almost succeeded, but he died trying, and now, I was wanted for his murder.

We'd been seconds away from being apprehended or killed, when Dustin opened an invisible veil, and instantly we were in this other world beyond imagination. A soft mist cleared from around our feet, illuminating an infinite starry sky in place of the ground. Trees with black, white, or gray trunks streaked with starlight grew out of the darkness. I grabbed Dustin, thinking we were going to fall in, but instead we walked on *something* soft and completely invisible; the chasm of space beneath our feet left me disoriented. The colorless trunks made up for their plainness by growing small colored globes instead of leaves. It was an explosion of saturated hues—purples, blues, reds, pinks, incredible yellows, and oranges set against a sky of aquamarine that moved like ocean waves, an inverted tidal sea. Bubbles floated through the air, some popped empty, others contained what appeared to be water, while the majority was filled with colored liquids.

"Talk about a drug trip. Is this what dropping acid is like?" I asked.

"Acid's chewing bubblegum compared to this. After being here, drugs aren't worth the time." Dustin's gaze was lost in distant awe, like he'd come home from a ten-year foreign war.

"So why'd you do them?" I asked, remembering how his drug use destroyed what was left of our family after our dad's death and helped get him sent to the mental institution.

"Because I couldn't believe this place was real. How could I?" Dustin had almost died after his first visit here.

We were quiet then, taking it all in. A warm gust disturbed the bubbles and brought what seemed like pastel, coaster-sized snowflakes. A few hit us, soft and powdery, and the rest vanished into the infinite below. The wind sounded faintly like the soft gentle laughter of toddlers; otherwise, the sky created a white noise of churning surf.

"Are there any people here?" I inhaled deeply, the air sweet like citrus and honeysuckle.

"I didn't see any when Crowd brought me here before." He meant before Mom sent him to Mountain View Psychiatric Hospital. That was more than two years ago, before Dustin knew Crowd was a mystic and before I knew anything.

"The drugs I did and the meds they gave me at the institution really messed up my memory," Dustin continued. "I think Crowd thought this place would somehow get my mind straight. He was always trying to help, but it must have been too soon or the drugs altered this *altered*-reality a little too much... I don't know."

We kept walking. It almost felt like being back in another Outview, the episodes that took me into other lifetimes. It was too much to believe, I began to mutter to myself, "I'm Nathan Ryder, I'm sixteen, I'm from Ashland Oregon, it's October—"

"I'm Dustin Ryder, I'm eighteen, and you're killing my buzz."

"Sorry, man. It's just... what is this place?"

He shrugged. "It's going to be intense finding out."

"Where are we going?"

"I don't know that either," Dustin said, "but don't you feel great?"

I did. The place was magic, but I was worried. "Yeah, but Spencer told me that anyone can get through a portal. What's to stop those soldiers from showing up and cutting this fairy-tale world in half with their machine guns?"

"Have a little faith, brother. Just because Spencer is like the leader of the mystics, doesn't mean he knows everything. Maybe he's never even been here." Spencer was the mystic who had taught me the most and healed me when Lightyear's Agent Fitts almost killed me. Spencer must have known about this place. He'd told me there is far more unseen than seen, more unknown than known, that there were places we know nothing about hiding from us in the breeze.

There was something in the air, an energy that pulsated; I felt I could do anything. Giddiness gripped me, like a kid at his first carnival. Four or five lime green and orange birds flew nearby, chirping sweet songs. I realized both of us were smiling at nothing, at everything.

Dustin suddenly stopped, extending his arm to block me. He tapped my chest with the back of his hand and motioned ahead. A person was leaning against a stark black tree that was crowned with a kaleidoscope of blue, green, purple, and yellow globes. Although I recognized him immediately, the sight of *anyone* else could not have shocked me more.

"Do you think he's real?" Dustin whispered.

"How could he be?"

He suddenly looked at us. "Hey guys, I wasn't sure you were going to make it."

Before I could answer, he stared into my eyes. There was no mistake; it was me, Nate! I mean we both were. He looked slightly different, a bit older with shorter hair, but he was me.

"Who are you?" I asked, incredulously.

"Don't you recognize me?" he smirked.

"Of course I recognize you, but how can you be…"

"I'm you. I'm just about eleven months older."

"You're Nate from the future?" Dustin asked.

"Sort of. I'm from a different dimension, the closest one to where you just came from."

"If you're me, and from the future or whatever, then you must know that I don't have a clue about 'identical selves' from different dimensions. Maybe you could try explaining it."

"I'll teach you about other dimensions. But first let me tell you what's happened, rather what's going to happen in the next eleven months of your life." His somber tone bothered me.

"You can do that?" Dustin was excited. "Cool."

He nodded.

"It's not good, is it?" I asked, recognizing my own expression on him. It was obvious he/I was about to deliver some bad news.

"What?" Dustin asked, catching the mood. "Where am I? Why aren't I with Nate eleven months from now?"

My "future self" took a deep breath. "You're missing; no one can find you. Mom's in federal custody."

"Christ! How did this happen?" Dustin shouted. "Where am I? How long have I been gone?"

"There's more, isn't there?" I asked.

Future Self stared.

"It gets worse?" Dustin asked.

"Amber and Linh are dead."

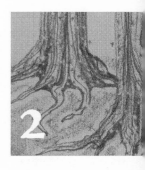

I found myself lying face down on the bottomless bed of stars that served as the ground, feeling as if I'd fallen out of a tree, gasping for air. The view of space was astonishing. I'd never seen the cosmos so stunning except in the Hubble images that hung on Kyle's bedroom walls. I wanted to float away. Dustin pulled me to my feet while I tried to breathe. Amber and Linh, two of my best friends, dead? It was my fault. I'd mixed them up into this. I would rather be dead myself.

"How?" was all I could muster.

"Once you two disappeared on Mount Shasta, Lightyear put Mom, Kyle, and the girls under surveillance, hoping they'd lead to you..."

"What about Kyle?" My head was pounding. My oldest and most loyal friend was also in danger.

"Alive but devastated since Linh's death, but Lightyear seems to be leaving Kyle as final bait for you."

"And where am I?" Dustin asked again.

"Like I said, no one knows, just that you *are* alive..."

"When did this happen?" I was down on the ground again, crouching, shaking, unable to support myself.

"A couple of months after you left Ashland and didn't immediately turn up again, Lightyear's director leaked a story that you were the terrorist who killed Fitts and announced that you were wanted for a large attack in the Midwest. Then they arrested Mom. The next day, the FBI picked Kyle up for questioning. Finally, Lightyear had an assassin kill Amber and Linh but made it look like you did it in order to silence them."

"Oh God! This is a nightmare!" I looked around at the floating bubbles, up to the ocean sky then to starlight depths beneath me. "Tell me this is a crazy dream, none of this can be real. Wake me!" I shouted.

But his glance told me I was awake.

"Did they suffer?" I whispered.

"I don't think so."

"You don't think so?!" I was fighting the urge to vomit.

"But wait," Dustin began, "we just got here and all this horrible stuff happens like two months from now. Can't we prevent it somehow?"

"That's why I'm here. It won't be easy, but we're going to try."

"Really?" I stood up. "Of course, multiple destinies! Where's Spencer?"

"We don't need Spencer now. Remember, I'm from eleven months in the future. You wouldn't believe what I know and… I'm your next mystic."

"Is that possible? Can I be my own mystic?"

"Apparently," Dustin said. "But not a good enough mystic to know what happens to me in a few months."

"Relax Dustin, we're going to find you. Geez, all I seem to do lately is go looking for you!"

"How is it possible to change the future?" Dustin asked.

"There isn't just one universe, as should be apparent by this extraordinary dimension we're wandering in now called 'Outin.' You'll soon learn of Outin's importance, but that's not a good idea to discuss right now." The waves overhead grew louder and more bubbles fell.

"How many universes or dimensions are there?" I asked.

"Impossible to say. Each universe is infinite, and there are an infinite number of them. And mix in the grand illusion…"

"What's the grand illusion?" Dustin asked.

"That solid matter exists. It doesn't. Everything is really just vibrating energy."

"Doesn't everyone already know this?"

"That's why it's an illusion. People think they know, but they don't understand what it means," Future Self said. "I mean scientists have proved that everything in the universe is connected. They split the smallest particle and separated the halves. When they moved one, the other, located thousands of miles away, also moved. It's all one, everything. Individuality doesn't really exist. And these other dimensions are all around us, closer to you than the clothes you're wearing."

"Wait, do *you* really understand what you're telling us?" Dustin asked.

"Barely. Still, just look at Nate and me, we're both here and yet we are one. We only appear to be separate, but we are not."

"Okay, all this new age stuff is really cool but..." Dustin said.

"Most of this comes from the top scientists today, not the mystics," Future Self said.

"The infinite infinities are part of the multiverse, but trying to grasp it can't be done using our limited perception."

"It takes two Nates to figure this out, and I still don't get how it helps us change the future." Dustin said.

"You need to understand the rules we're playing under, and they're nothing like any rules you've ever known. Otherwise there is no hope of saving the girls." He looked from Dustin to me.

"And?" Dustin was becoming impatient.

"Don't you get it? Nothing is permanent or separate, so we can change one thing and everything will be different."

"But how do we know what to do?"

"Well, that's the thing. We have to alter the right event in the correct sequence. It happens constantly; a tiny shift occurs in *any* universe, and our lives instantly convert to something new until a nanosecond later when another modification ripples through the multiverse and transforms everything again."

"Let's get back to our dimension and change something so I won't disappear, the girls will live, and Mom won't get arrested," Dustin demanded.

"It's not that easy," Future Self said. "Cause and effect will continue to push us toward that outcome or variations of it—Mom gets killed or Amber and Linh live a day longer or Kyle gets killed or whatever."

"So how do we stop it?" I asked.

"I don't know yet."

"Oh, come on!" Dustin shouted.

"I just know we can," Future Self responded.

"Then tell us more about what's going to happen, so we can come up with a plan to change it," I said.

"It all started when terrorists blew up the Mall of America."

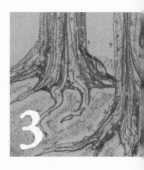

W e stared at him; a sick feeling filled me.

"Mall of America, outside Minneapolis, is the largest mall in the country," he continued. "It's five million square feet, forty million people visit every year, and there are roughly twenty thousand parking spaces. It's enormous. The FBI claims two men drove tanker trucks loaded with fuel into two separate entrances and detonated them."

"Jesus!"

"And according to the official story, you and Dustin hid in the parking lot, and as soon as large groups of survivors gathered, you opened fire with AK-47 assault rifles."

"Are you making this up?" I shouted.

He shook his head. "It was the fire that did the most damage…"

"Does anyone believe those lies?" Dustin asked.

"Six hundred and ninety-three people died. Over twenty-two hundred were injured. The majority were kids and teenagers. Worst terrorist attack since 9/11. People were hungry to blame someone, anyone…"

I pictured the hellish scene; screams choking through thick black smoke, cries of agony across trampled teenage bodies burned and ripped open by bullets. The complete horror and inexplicable cruelty strained my comprehension. My body wanted to shut down. Lightyear couldn't be allowed to breed this kind of destruction and misery.

"The truck drivers were among the dead," Future Self continued. "That just left the Ryder brothers. They claim the guns and other evidence left behind had your fingerprints all over them. They had Dustin's prints from the time Fitts took him into custody, before you saved him. They had yours from the murder weapon you used to kill Fitts."

"Unbelievable. I didn't kill Fitts!"

"That's when they grabbed Mom and had 'you two' kill the girls…"

"What was our supposed motive for the attack?"

"They claim you and Dustin are simply schizo-psycho lunatics looking to create anarchy."

"Nice," Dustin said, sarcastically.

"They kill all these people just to get to me? Why are they so afraid?" I asked.

"The director of Lightyear, a guy named Luther Storch…"

"You know his name? How did you find that out?"

"I've been busy these past eleven months. It hasn't all been running and hiding. But I don't want to tell you too much. No one, least of all me, understands the ramifications of interacting with other versions of the same incarnation and interdimensional time manipulations. So if it's possible to save Amber and Linh, we should avoid changing things too much, or we won't know enough about what *might* happen to be able to prevent it from happening."

"Nate and Nate, I think this conversation is going to make me go crazy for real. That's probably why I'm missing in the future: you guys had to commit me again," Dustin wasn't joking. "Two of you, and the power of the universe in your hands, and still all this death. And I end up disappearing. Whoever decided you should be in charge wasn't thinking clearly."

"It was Dad."

Dustin glared.

"Listen guys, this isn't all about us. We're just in the way. Storch wants the world and makes Fitts look like a Boy Scout. You won't believe what this maniac will do."

"You mean *more* than slaughtering a shopping center full of innocent people?" I asked.

"Yeah, much more. And remember, Fitts may have been the triggerman, but Storch ordered Dad and all the other Montgomery Ryders killed. He also decided Rose, Amber, and Linh should die and that the Ryder brothers should become notorious terrorists. But he's been doing stuff like this for years and not just in the U.S. He's the one Spencer warned us about when all this began. Spencer said he'd kill a school full of children without a thought... Storch is just getting started."

We just looked at each other.

"Back to my original question: why is it so important to destroy us?" I asked.

"Storch knows you possess the ability to stop Lightyear, but if you join them then they *can't* be stopped. But he's no idiot and realizes the odds of you signing up with the dark side are minuscule to nothing. So everyone must believe you're the most despicable terrorist since Bin Laden. That way they'll be justified when you're killed."

"I don't see why it matters what people think of us," Dustin said.

"Being the only surviving member of this generation's seven, Nate can help cause incredible change, Storch knows this and fears he could be cause problems for Lightyear. Storch is fond of the way things are, where control is his," Future Self said.

We were all quiet, grasping for answers as to how we could stop that kind of evil. I watched the bubbles and realized they were a form of rain floating down from the ocean-sky.

"How can we stop all of this?" Dustin asked, exasperated.

"Nate, get Dustin up to speed on the powers you've already remembered."

"I know more than you think," Dustin said. "I don't need Nate to play professor."

Future Self gave me a concerned look. "There's a lot to learn in this dimension. I'll show you where to start. But mostly, we wait."

"Wait?" we exclaimed in unison.

"All we can do is try to get the timing right. Because the moment you step back onto Shasta, you'll be in a race against time."

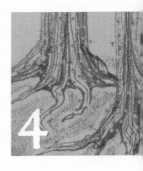

He led us to the first of the four lakes of Outin. The stars liquefied around the lake's edge and flowed into it from all sides, creating a gold and silver sea of light surrounded by sparkling waterfalls, a virtually perfect circle, six or seven miles across and fittingly called Star Falls.

"You should swim in each of the four lakes every day. They affect us differently. This one helps conquer fear. The next one, Floral Lake is for nourishment; instead of eating and drinking, you swim."

"No food here?"

"They don't waste their time."

"So there are people here? Where are they?"

"Remember, we only exist in our own imaginations," Future Self said.

Dustin and I looked at each other and then back to Future Self.

"The beings who live here vibrate at a different frequency than we do. So you'll only encounter them if they're part of your experience or vice versa," he said.

"No food, no people..."

"No distractions," Future Self finished.

"Some kind of spiritual boot camp?" Dustin said.

"The soul is powerful beyond your wildest imaginings. But to find the connections and see what is possible, you'll need time... and Outin has a way of making time something entirely different than you've ever known."

He left us at Floral Lake, promising to return. This one was nearly twice as big as Star Falls. The surface of its water, which was probably ninety square miles, was completely covered with millions of wildflowers—as if Monet's palette had exploded. Upon closer inspection we discovered that these nearly stemless flowers were floating on a crystal clear, shallow body of water no more than ten feet deep. We stripped and dove in. It was bathwater-warm and velvety; the flowers closed in around us but parted easily as we swam.

Our hunger from before was instantly gone, and in its place was the feeling of having eaten the perfect meal. The water was more than nourishing—it was healing. I'd never felt healthier; I could hear better, see farther, and my arms and legs were lighter.

"Is this the freakin' fountain of youth or what?" Dustin asked.

"Can you imagine if this was a spa back in our dimension? I mean anybody can get through the portal... What if someone discovered it and started advertising for visits to an interdimensional spa? They could charge a fortune for this treatment."

It was impossible to know how long we were in the water. Time was a mystery in Outin because our cell phones didn't work and there certainly weren't any clocks or anyone to ask. As soon as we left the water, our bodies were dry. We dressed and started for the next lake. Future Self had given us a layout of the immediate area. The four lakes of Outin were arranged roughly like the leaves of a four-leaf clover. We would spend most of our time between them. There was a small structure, called the lodge, built entirely of black clay and stars, so that when you were lying inside on a cloud-like cot it was like camping under the night sky. Future Self had told us this was home during our stay. There were two small rooms and a tiny entrance hall that separated them, no doors or windows and no bathrooms; they weren't needed. He said our packs would be safe. "Everything is safe here" were his exact words. The trees around us were home to more birds than seemed possible, the bright mixed hues of their feathers made them blend perfectly with the colored-globe "leaves." They sang continuously, an extraordinarily beautiful sound that I imagined would be difficult to live without.

The skywaves started turning orange, which Future Self had told us meant the day was coming to an end. We were almost to Dreams Lake, the smallest of the four; its shape impossible to define since it was literally a sea of bubbles with even more bubbles rising several feet above it like fog. The water was almost too hot, but icy currents occasionally flowed through making it bearable. This lake's purpose was to show us our dreams and fantasies. I was looking forward to seeing what was going on in the dark corners of my mind. Dustin was less enthusiastic, saying, "I already know what's in my brain—chemical spills mixed with shattered pieces of funhouse mirror—it's a mess."

I lost him in the bubbles and realized in this water no swimming was required; it wasn't even possible to dive below the surface. I floated, surrounded by images. A fantasy version of Amber, which seemed redundant, joined me. She was naked too, and we tumbled together in the water laughing, kissing, and then finished what we'd begun in San Francisco. It was a dream, so the sex was perfect. And because this lake was all about dreams and fantasies, Linh showed up next. She hid among the bubbles playfully. I chased and finally caught her in a kiss; it was the sweetest thing imaginable. Having kissed Amber in real life enough, I could tell the difference. Amber was sultry hot, leaving me burning in passion; Linh was a drop of dew. I breathed her in deeply, lavender. She smiled and whispered, saying beautiful things I couldn't remember. I asked if she wanted to have sex, Linh nodded, but her soft words contradicted. "Let's wait Nate. There's time, a better time." I didn't know which one I *really* wanted. But that was second to the desperation I felt to somehow change the future and keep them alive.

The skywaves went from orange to brown. It was getting dark, and I reluctantly found my way out of the lake. I heard Dustin calling. We made it back to the lodge and fell asleep quickly. I woke up in the night terrified. I couldn't shake the panic that Storch was going to succeed in killing the girls and all those innocent people at the mall. It had already happened in the future, so what chance did we really have to change that? Human life meant nothing to him. He and Lightyear had done so much damage to the world and to my family. Amber and Linh were next. A lump grew in my throat, and my palms were sweating. His terror just wasn't going to end. I fidgeted with the gold box from my dad's desk. There was something about it that gave me confidence. If I could just get it open, I just knew there was an answer inside. What did the inlaid jade pattern mean? There was a reason I found it with the list of nine names and pages of code, but what was it? My head was aching when the birds woke me again.

In the morning we found Rainbow Lake, which offered a glimpse into the future. From the surface to as far down as we could see, there were pockets and bands of bright Kool-Aid colored water—reds mixing with yellows, blending to orange, yellow overlapping blue turning green. What kept it from becoming one big stew of cloudy water?

I landed in between primary red and blue in a purple splash. Suddenly, I was at the Mall of America on a Friday night, months into the future, watching in horror as flames exploded to inferno. Just as Future Self had said, hundreds of teenagers who had escaped were caught in a hail of bullets. But I saw the real shooters, paramilitary types with cold hearts. How did Storch convince these guys that killing kids is okay? Their escape routes had been planned, backups ready. It was a precise operation, and the guns they left behind with our prints on them weren't even the ones they used.

I met Dustin back on shore. "Did you see the mall attack?" I asked.

"No. I don't want to talk about it."

"Why not?"

"Because you don't get to know everything, psychic-golden boy. Let's just get to Star Falls and see what fun overcoming our fears is like."

I left it alone.

Star Falls had to be one of the most beautiful sights in this or any other dimension. But as soon as we were in the water, I was engulfed by terrors and tortures I thought would kill me, that I wished would kill me, things that rivaled my lifetime when I died at Dachau and surpassed it, horrors that I could never speak of—to anyone.

After the cruel nightmares of Star Falls and Rainbow Lake's tragic future view, Floral Lake brought us back to life while the joy of Dreams Lake helped disperse the morning's traumas. As the days passed I grew stronger, and Star Falls wasn't quite as difficult to face.

For the next eight weeks we practiced our powers and rotated through the lakes. Future Self showed up one other time, and we argued with him about when we could leave. Dustin and I were so worried about what was happening in our world that we tried to find the way out even after being warned against it. We were trapped in Outin.

Before coming to Outin, I'd learned so much from Spencer and the other mystics about life and death, but the five great powers were the only things that had kept me alive. I wrote a list to help Dustin remember.

1. *Gogen*—(many forms) used in manipulating space and moving objects.
2. *Vising*—to transform energy and read people.
3. *Timbal*—deals with time, Outviews and prophecy.
4. *Foush*—for enhancing the senses, including Sky-climbing and Lusans (healing light orb).
5. *Solteer*—controls consciousness, such as putting people to sleep and making them see things.

All the natural soul abilities, which we thought so amazing, were part of the five great powers... and we hardly knew any of them yet. Teaching Dustin proved far more challenging than expected. It was the first time I realized how important being one of the seven was. He was good on the astral but mostly because our Aunt Rose, an astral projection expert, had spent a year and a half working with him. We both missed Rose; Dustin credited her with keeping him in touch with reality while locked up at Mountain View Psychiatric Hospital. Lightyear killing her took away our most trusted teacher... which was likely why Storch had ordered her murder.

Reading thoughts was Dustin's strength, and he helped me develop my own abilities there. But he couldn't create a Lusan no matter how many times he tried, and healing with hands eluded him. Moving things with Gogen frustrated him, and although he once got a small stone to wobble, nothing ever lifted off the ground. And Skyclimbing was no better. Solteer baffled him, planting a thought or vision in someone's mind or putting someone to sleep he considered impossible, but he was making some progress on the various Vising disciplines, reading trees, rocks, me, and even notes I wrote him without his looking. And parts of Foush he could manage, seeing auras, color pops, shapeshifting animals, and Outviews but not nearly as often as I, and those were things he could do before Mountain View. I was interested to know if teaching others was going to be this hard or had he been irrevocably damaged by his time in the mental institution.

Star Falls' torments were showing me that once you remember what your soul is capable of, only one thing can steal your powers—fear. I tried discussing this with Dustin because he was having great difficulty in those waters. It was possible his fears were slowing him down.

"Dustin, what are you afraid of?"

"I don't know man. That hellish lake is like a stew of post-traumatic stress disorder, horrific deaths from past lives, Mountain View, bad drug trips, and all kinds of karmic payback. It's not making me stronger; it's breaking me." We considered having him skip the Star Falls swims, but he wanted to continue. "I've got to do it. It's like I can't get my powers or find my purpose until I walk through the Valley of Death."

I, on the other hand, was improving swiftly and now understood what Spencer had tried to tell me a month earlier, about learning too much at once without taking time to master any of it. And, just as the danger warning that made my body temperature rise and enhanced my hearing came to me without training, now I had a photographic memory. From then on, everything Dustin said was recorded in my head, and what I saw became part of me, ready for instant recall.

In between our time in the lakes and practicing, we took walks around the enchanted woods. I never lost the feeling that we were going to fall into the stars below. Occasionally we would step into what could only be described as a puddle, not much bigger than our feet. I don't know how deep they were but when we dropped a rock into one, it fell through space and became too tiny to see anymore.

"How in the hell is all this time here, this endless waiting, going to help us stop the mall attack? Do you realize you and I have the power to actually make a difference? We could be heroes..." Dustin said.

"I don't care about being a hero. I just want Amber and Linh to live."

"Don't you mean all of them?"

I didn't answer.

"What if you have to make a choice? A thousand dead at the mall... or saving your two girlfriends."

"The universe isn't cruel enough to force me to make that choice."

"You forget."

"What?"

"Earth is the cruelest place in the universe."

"How do you know?"

He shot me a look. "I know. And you know I do. Up until a couple of months ago you've led a pampered life little brother, while I've been battling demons you know nothing about."

"Stop getting so hung up on the past. We're in the present together now and the future is frightening. Let's worry about that."

Perhaps the most interesting things we encountered in the fascinating world of Outin were the Windows. They appeared randomly and weren't permanent. When we tried to return to one we liked, it wasn't where we'd seen it before. Most were the size of a regular bedroom window, ripped into irregular shapes that peered into other times and other worlds, including our own.

We discovered the first one when Dustin noticed a torn section of contrasting ocean-sky ahead. Through it we could see a busy Manhattan street, the jumble of yellow cabs was a giveaway. It was probably the mid-seventies judging by the make of the cars and a theater marquee that advertised *All The President's Men*. I stuck my hand through and was pretty sure we could have crawled in but it seemed very likely there would be no way back.

Other Windows showed alien worlds, ranging from paradise to cruel wastelands. Most were versions of Earth. One Window showed my dad still alive at Dustin's high school graduation, in that parallel universe Dustin never went to Mountain View. Another showed our parents divorcing years before my dad died, with us trading households on weekends. There was one where Dustin was drafted into the army to fight in the America-China war—a scary conflict we were losing as it entered its eighth year. The Windows were captivating, like watching alternative endings to a favorite movie, yet disturbing at the same time because somewhere this stuff was really happening.

It was a surprise when a portal appeared one morning on our way to Star Falls. As incredible as Outin had been, we were desperate to return to our world. We weren't sure if Future Self sent the portal or if Outin somehow knew we were ready to leave, but it didn't matter. We weren't going to miss the opportunity to escape. I was suddenly flooded with fear and looked at Dustin.

"We can do this," he said, with a nod.

"At least we know there are many futures out there, but most of them still wind up with the mall attack and the girls dying."

"We have to try."

"But, we may fail." My voice trembled. "I'm afraid we'll screw up and get everyone killed."

"Remember what we're capable of. We're going to kick some ass!"

We stepped through the portal.

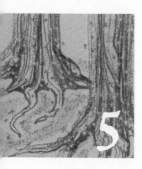

M onday, *October 6*
After Outin's dreamscape, the first few steps on Shasta's hard ground felt insulting.

"Nate, Dusty!" Crowd's voice startled us, as if slapped from a vivid dream.

"Crowd, how'd you know we were coming out today?" He was the coolest and funniest of the mystics and had saved my life in San Francisco when Fitts pushed me off the cliff. Crowd was somehow gristly, hip, wise, laidback, and powerful all at the same time.

"Because you haven't gone in yet. It's the same day as when you went through the veil."

"How can that be, we were there for like two months?" I asked.

"Time's a funny thing…"

"Hysterical," Dustin said sarcastically.

"So what happened to the helicopter and the soldiers that were after us?"

"They'll be here soon."

"Are you kidding?" It wasn't registering.

"Right now it's about two hours before you went through. An Outin month is equivalent to about an hour in *reverse* time in our world."

"That explains some of the 'confusion' I was dealing with before Mom sent me to the loony-bin," Dustin said.

"You're telling me we just turned back time?"

"Righto."

"Then we could return to Outin and stay long enough to prevent Lightyear from killing Aunt Rose… or even my Dad… we can get them back! This is—"

"Slow down, Nate," Crowd held up his hands. "It isn't as simple as all that. They got Rose ten days ago, that's 240 hours, which means you'd have to stay there for 240 months, that's *twenty years*. I can't even begin to do the math on your dad; he's been dead four years. You'd have to stay in Outin for something like forever."

"Two thousand nine hundred and twenty years," I sighed.

Dustin gave me a look expressing awe and boredom at the same time.

"We need to get y'all out of here now, before the other 'yous' and the feds show up," Crowd said firmly.

"Where?" Dustin asked.

"It's your life," Crowd said.

"Yeah, well, you're the guide," I said.

"If you're asking… You are asking right?" He smiled.

I nodded.

"Then it's probably a good idea to get in your truck as quickly as you can and head to Cervantes Island to meet Spencer."

"And if we decided to go back to Ashland…"

Crowd shook his head.

"Maybe head deep into the mountains to hide, or a few days lounging on the beach?" Dustin asked.

"Not a good idea," Crowd said.

"What about multiple destinies?" I asked.

"Yes, yes to be sure, you two, the dynamic duo," he made quote marks with his fingers, "could go anywhere, do *so* many different things, but it's a matter of your *optimal* destiny. That, and well… not getting your heads blown off."

"Cervantes sounds cool." Dustin said. "Where is it?"

"In the Pacific off the coast of Mexico somewhere. Know anyone with a boat?" Crowd winked.

"As a matter of fact, I do. Let's go. I'm turned around. Which way to the truck?" I asked.

"Allow me to *guide* you," Crowd bowed theatrically.

As we sprinted through the woods following him, I asked, "So if we haven't gotten here yet how is Dustin's truck here?"

"I had someone bring it from Ashland."

"What happened to the two hours that we just erased?"

"The hours are still in there somewhere. Time is like a deck of cards, not linear; it's a stack, an endless stack that can be shuffled every which way. The Nate and Dusty that were in Ashland this morning will cross into a space between cards falling in a shuffle, and that's that."

"That's what?" Dustin asked. "And who's shuffling?"

"Come on, do I look like some genius? Time has all these wrinkles, folds, and stuff. Nothing's as definite as you think. Laws of physics are really more like guidelines."

"Good. We're counting on things not being definite, timewise that is," I said.

We arrived at the truck. "You're in California now, so you ought to have new plates," he said, pointing to fresh tags. "Less attention if you're 'in-state.' Lightyear had a GPS tracking device attached, I took the liberty of removing it. Didn't think you'd mind."

"No," my mouth went dry.

"You guys need to realize the feds aren't as dumb as you think. When it comes to police, spying, war, anything with guns, the government is pretty damn good at that kind of stuff. Don't make the mistake of underestimating them."

I felt dumb.

"Don't sweat it," Crowd saw my regret. "You're playing out of your league, a couple of teenagers against the entire military-industrial complex. But I left a handful of books on the front seat that will help you—survival skills, military training, intelligence manuals, that type of thing. It'll give you some good ideas; just take you a minute to read them with your Vising.

Dustin smiled. "Can't wait to try out my new skills."

I still felt more a part of Outin. Getting into the truck seemed like a strange dimension, but the reality of what was going to happen at Mall of America and to Amber and Linh sobered me up. I was back on earth.

"Hey Crowd, why is Outin here at Mount Shasta?" I asked, leaning out the window.

"It's not just here, it's everywhere. Shasta is just *one* of the entry points. Now you guys need every minute to get ahead of Lightyear, so shove off."

"When do we see you next?" Dustin asked.

"Depends on which road you take." Crowd smiled and waved.

"Which way?" Dustin asked.

"Head toward I-5, hopefully I'll have an answer on north or south before we get there."

I went onto the astral and found Trevor. In a past life we'd been married but died in a Nazi concentration camp. I knew he could be trusted *and* he had a boat. Communicating with him didn't work, but I knew where he was. "We're heading to San Diego."

"South it is then. Shouldn't we call our Ashland fan club right now?" Dustin asked.

"Yeah, but as much as I've thought about it, I don't know what to say or who to call first." Crowd assured us that the cell phones still weren't traceable but warned that in the days to come that could change.

"Call Mom last, she'll just frustrate you. You're in love with Amber and Linh, too emotional there, so that leaves Kyle. Call him first."

"I'm not *in love* with Amber and Linh."

"Why not? You should be. I am," Dustin said with a laugh.

Kyle remained typically calm, even when I told him what the future likely held. "So the multiverse is real? That's reassuring since humans are totally screwing up *this* universe. I've read enough of the theories to know that tweaking forward time is definitely possible given that the multiverse exists." He didn't speak for a few moments. "We'll figure out a way to save them. We have to. In the meantime, I think we should get Linh and Amber into hiding."

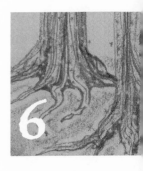

There was no way I was ready to talk to Amber or Linh. I couldn't call Mom because Outin's reverse time meant Dustin and I were still at the hotel in Ashland with her, and hadn't even been to Outin yet. I didn't want to find out what a telephone call back through time could do to our present mess. After about an hour on the road, the strange sensation of hunger returned after having not eaten in two months. All I wanted to do was have a Cinnamon Caramel Catastrophe from the Station, Mom's restaurant. But we were farther from Ashland than mere interstate miles. Dustin spotted a sign for the Wonderland Diner; we couldn't resist the name. And it didn't disappoint us. The food was fantastic and the waitress was a mystic.

At first we didn't notice. Kirby, an attractive girl who couldn't have been more than nineteen, took our order; Dustin was practicing his flirting. Then a lady, most likely in her seventies, brought the food. After three or four alternating encounters with them I realized they were the same person and Dustin agreed it was possible. Their identical nametags were the first giveaway, but they shared mannerisms and the same smile.

"Which one is the real you?" I asked the older one, as I finished my fries.

"Afraid it's me, dear," she smiled wide at our discovery.

"If I was still that pretty young thing, I bet you'd like to take me along... and I suppose I'd want to go too."

"So you know who I am?"

"Of course I do, Nate. But let's talk outside," she looked around as if Lightyear agents could be lurking in neighboring booths. She took care of our check and met us in the parking lot.

"Do you shapeshift for all your customers or was that special just for us?" I asked.

"I bet it's great for tips," Dustin said.

Kirby laughed. "This was my first day waitressing, so I practiced a bit before you boys showed up." Right in front of us she switched back to her youthful form as we made our way to a worn path that led to a river. "The trail is easier to navigate with young legs," she said with a wink at Dustin.

Once down by the river, she morphed back to the old lady. "I've got two things to show you today... Hmm, how to do this? Dustin, let's start with *Kellaring*. It means to block and conceal, but it's a form of Vising. When someone is trying to find you on the astral—remote viewing, reading your mind, using some type of Solteer on you, things like that—you can use Kellaring, which will prevent them from succeeding in *almost* all cases. However, if you use another soul-power, the Kellaring will be interrupted and you may be located or susceptible."

"What if you start Kellaring again?" I asked.

"It will work. But keep in mind even a brief opening of seconds can allow a skilled individual to find you."

"Okay."

"This is a very useful ability, especially given your current predicament. Now Dustin, get an image of your eyes into your mind, then surround them in a white light until your eyes are no longer visible."

"Okay, I think I'm there," Dustin said.

"You did it. Congratulations. You're now invisible to anyone searching the astral. Lightyear's remote viewers will not be able to locate you as long as you refrain from using another soul-power. If you need to use Gogen or something do, then after, get the Kellaring back in place quick or they'll be able to zero in on you."

"Should I try it now?" I asked.

"I don't expect you'll have any trouble but you need it in place anyway, so give it a go."

"Great," she said, after a minute. "No trace of you on the astral either. Good boy. Now it's time for shapeshifting."

"How is that even possible?" Dustin asked.

"Think of it this way; your body is made up of fifty trillion living cells, and they join together in a specific order to form tissues, which form organs, and so on... it's all energy, you're just going to change the order." She looked at me. "Now picture a football player on the San Francisco 49ers." She went on about how we were moving energy and rearranging atoms. It took a while but I transformed into a 265-pound, six-foot-three, wide receiver in full uniform. The shocked look on Dustin's face made me laugh.

Dustin was going to need weeks of practice to get this. In my excitement, I forgot how sensitive he was and made fun of him.

"Sure Nate, I'd like to see you do it if you weren't one of the chosen seven. One day you'll have to do some real work."

"Boys, save your energy, the enemy is out there," Kirby said, pointing away.

I changed back to my regular form and was left with a throbbing headache and a sore back.

"The side effects will ease up in a few hours," she said, seeing me grimace. "And it can be done instantly. Once you get better at it, you'll hardly feel a thing unless you depart radically from your current form, like trying to be a five-year-old or something."

"Or like a football player?"

"That's why your back hurts," she chuckled.

"It's a drag not being perfect, huh, Nate?" Dustin said.

"Now, I'd love to spend the whole day with you two handsome boys, and originally I did, but if things are going to turn out different this time then, well... you need to get back on that road."

After a hundred miles or so Dustin said, "You better call Mom."

"You call her."

"I don't think so."

Once she was on the line I didn't waste time. "Mom, I need to know once and for all if you trust me completely? Do you believe in me?"

"What is it Nate? What's happened?"

"Yes or no? Or I'm hanging up now."

"Nate... okay, yes, I do. I'm your mother, for God's sake. Now tell me what's happened."

"It's not what has happened; it's what is going to happen. I've seen into the future, and it's some scary stuff. Sometime in the next eight weeks you'll be arrested..."

"What? I've done nothing..."

"That doesn't matter. Quit acting like we live in a free country."

"But..."

"Think of Dad, Rose, and what they did to Dustin. You're next. Get prepared. Gather as much cash as you can and stash it in several places, keep a bunch on you, and don't put it in banks. If you have to run, don't use your credit cards once you're out of Ashland. Keep your car filled with gas, a backpack of clothes and packaged road food."

"You're really scaring me!"

"Good! It's about time."

"Nate?"

"Mom, Aunt Rose told me Dad fell in love with you because you were so smart. Show me he was right."

She was quiet before finally asking if Dustin was okay.

"He's fine. He's driving. Mom, I'll call when I can. It may be a few days. Try not to worry. And remember, always assume your calls and computer are being monitored. I'm not staying on long. Crowd claims the phones we're all using are random and untraceable as long as we don't say certain things, but I don't think anyone knows how good the government has gotten at monitoring its citizens." Mom frustrated me constantly—I was a teenager after all—but I needed her to believe and support what I was doing, and her safety was a big concern.

After that, I reached Amber. She was just driving home from school and pulled over to take the call. Before I could explain the future, she told me Kyle had already filled them in.

"Nate, why are they doing this?"

"It's beyond any reasonable understanding. These kind of *people* have existed throughout human history and have committed horrible atrocities. The repercussions echo through time, affecting lifetime after lifetime directly, delaying the awakening."

"I want to be with you right now."

"It's not safe."

"It's not any safer without you."

"I know. I just have to meet Spencer and try to sort everything out. We're fighting time."

"I need you."

"I miss you. We need to go. Watch yourself."

"We're really up against some kind of evil," I said to Dustin. "A mall full of teenagers, just to make us look like terrorists. Storch wants us dead so badly, it's amazing we're still here."

"We wouldn't be if not for our escape to Outin and the Kellaring that's not letting their remote viewers locate us. Like Crowd said, we're just kids against a whole army of super cops."

"Hey Dustin, you're the positive one, remember? We haven't made it this far on our own. There are powers far greater than Lightyear. And if we can expose their corruption and the murders, their own system will hang them."

"Are we smart enough to pull that off?"

"I'm working on it."

Several hours later we were getting tired and hungry again. A chain restaurant roped us in with a billboard promising New York style pizza.

"I'd rather be eating pizza at the Station right now," I said.

"Forget the pizza, I'd kill for a Vanilla Volcano."

It became uncomfortably warm. Then my prepaid cell phone rang. It was Kyle. "Where are you?" his voice tense.

"I don't know, still north of LA."

"A story just broke on the evening news and all over the Internet. Two brothers wanted for killing a federal agent. The FBI is asking for the public's help in locating them. They're believed to be traveling south on I-5 in a silver Toyota pickup..."

"Damn, I'll call you back" I looked at Dustin. He read my face. Without a word he left a twenty and a ten on the table and grabbed his pack. I followed him toward the entrance. As soon as we stepped outside we saw the California Highway Patrol car next to the truck.

"How'd they find us so quick?" I asked. "Those are new plates..."

"He's checking the VIN number through the windshield. They'll know we're here in minutes!" Dustin said.

My body temperature was uncomfortably high. We were in a big interstate travel plaza with a major gas station, several fast food joints and a truck stop. Without thinking we moved around the side of the building away from our vehicle and toward a long line of semis.

The driver of a giant red Kenworth truck noticed us. "You kids looking for a ride?"

"Yeah," Dustin answered. "You got room?"

"Where you heading?"

"San Diego."

"I'm headin' into Mexico via Tijuana, so I can get you there. Got twenty bucks to help with my diesel?"

"Yeah," I said, reaching into my pocket.

"Each," he eyed Dustin.

A few minutes later we were heading up the ramp to I-5.

"You boys runaways?" He asked, gazing at our packs.

"No. Nothing like that," Dustin began. "We've got friends in college down there."

"Ah," he nodded.

It was small talk for the next hour or so, as we tried not to act nervous. I was glad we always kept our packs with us because, aside from a change of clothes, mine held Rose's journal and the gold box from Dad's desk.

Around San Clemente he pulled off into another truck stop. "Bathroom break. Those chili dogs didn't work out too well with all the coffee." He laughed gruffly. We decided not to go in for obvious reasons and after about ten minutes became worried. Dustin climbed out of the truck to get a view inside the windows. Then I felt the heat overtake me.

"Nate, he's in there talking to a couple of guys, and they're pointing out here."

I was already getting down from the truck.

"He seemed suspicious from the start," I said, following Dustin to the back of the truck. I was sweating. We had been stupid thinking we could just drive down to San Diego and hop a boat. Luther Storch was ruthless and wanted us dead. I was all that stood in his way to achieve his diabolical goals.

"Dustin, how are we going to get out of here?" I whispered loudly.

"Maybe you should shapeshift."

"Then we'll lose the Kellaring and they'll know exactly where I am…"

He raised an eyebrow, "A little late for that, wouldn't you say?"

I heard a helicopter in the distance.

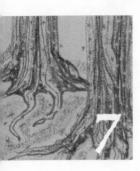

7

We crossed through another line of parked trucks, then at the fuel islands for regular-sized vehicles, a Mexican guy in a dirty green pickup made eye contact.

"We're looking for a ride," I said.

"Get in," he answered in Spanish.

I looked at Dustin. We had no choice. Once we were southbound. I asked in Spanish, "Where are you going?"

"I'm taking you to San Diego Harbor," he answered, smiling.

I translated for Dustin.

"Cool." Dustin relaxed.

"Mystic?" I asked.

"Sí," he answered, saying his name was Baca. He could have been mistaken for a prizefighter. For the next twenty or thirty miles we spoke Spanish, as he filled in the details we weren't able to get from Kyle. Once we disappeared on Shasta and Crowd discovered the GPS tracking device, Luther Storch contacted the FBI and it was made public that I killed Agent Fitts. There was, of course, no mention that this sadistic bastard had killed Dad, my aunt and tried to kill Mom, Dustin and me. Suddenly the Ryder brothers were on the "Ten Most Wanted" list and being hunted along the I-5 corridor in California. Storch probably wasn't too happy about getting law enforcement and citizens involved, but he needed the story out in order to convince Lightyear's remote viewers I was an enemy of the state. And once we started using Kellaring, the public's help was crucial.

There was construction up ahead. I wasn't surprised to recognize the flagman.

"Just a short detour to get you off the interstate for a while. Gonna be a roadblock set up twelve miles south of here in about five minutes," Crowd shouted as we slowed to head down the ramp. I looked back and saw him pulling up the orange traffic cones.

Baca went on. "That trucker you were riding with saw you on TV when he went inside. I hustled on out to my truck and waited for you."

"How'd you know we'd be coming?"

"There are friendly people all over California right now who want to help you."

"Why? Don't they know I killed a federal agent, and we're armed and dangerous?"

"There are many who don't believe what they see on TV, not enough yet but it's growing."

"What's growing?"

"The Movement." I thought about that while we drove south over the next hour.

Baca told me he was currently a migrant worker but once owned a farm in the mountains of southern Mexico. A few too many drought years pushed him north of the border in order to make money for his family. The conversation veered toward what he used to grow, and then before I knew it we were discussing my favorite foods.

"The soul needs a decent vehicle to navigate this life in, and you fill yours with garbage—Coca-Cola, French fries, cheese pizza, bacon, eggs…"

"You're making me hungry," I joked, but Baca was serious. Dustin was lost in his own thoughts, staring out the window because he didn't speak Spanish, but he did glance over at the mention of a Coke.

"The cleaner you keep your body the easier it is to find your soul."

"It really makes a difference?"

"You could keep eating junk and still get there, but it will take much longer. For those of us who aren't one of the seven, we need every advantage we can get and eating well is a major one."

"How well?"

"Organic plant-based foods. And French fries don't count as a vegetable," he said with a smile.

"Oh man!" Dustin interrupted, hitting my shoulder and pointing. There was a police roadblock just ahead.

"Damn, where's Crowd?" I moaned. We had just come over a rise and there was no way off the road.

"Shapeshift!" Dustin yelled.

"What about you? They'll have photos of you too."

"Maybe if you're a Mexican chick or something they won't notice me…"

"It's too risky," I said.

"Got any better ideas? Anyway, Nate, you're the important one. You should just let me out here…" Dustin unlocked his door.

"What are you talking about?"

If we U-turned now they'd see us and catch up in minutes. We were going to have to go through. I took an inventory of my powers and quickly made two invisible Lusans; I put one in my lap, and the other at my feet just in case. I knew my Kellaring was blown. Kirby had been clear, if I used another power while employing Kellaring then the remote viewers could find me. I just had to hope it would take more than a few minutes. The heat warning caused my temperature to climb to unbearable levels. I quickly shapeshifted into a fourteen-year-old Mexican girl.

"Tell me you have a green card?"

"Sí," Baca nodded.

"What about me?" Dustin asked.

"I'm going to use Solteer and make him see you as a teenage Mexican boy. Here put on Baca's hat," I grabbed the green John Deere cap off Baca and passed it to Dustin.

"I don't know, it's pretty weak," Dustin said.

"It's all we've got."

As we pulled up, a trooper approached each window.

"I can't do them both," I whispered, clutching the Lusan in my lap.

"I'll use Solteer on this one, you get the one at Dustin's window," Baca said.

The patrolman asked Baca for his license.

Baca never stopped staring at him as he handed it over and his green card over. I watched the female officer on Dustin's side who, after a quick glance inside, started looking back toward the vehicles behind us. The patrolman gave Baca his cards back and after a last look at us, waved us on.

No one spoke until the checkpoint was no longer visible, "We did it! We did it!" I yelled.

Baca exhaled deeply.

"Well that certainly wasn't relaxing. Nate, get your Kellaring back in place," Dustin said.

"I did but they probably already know where I am."

Eight miles later, Crowd flagged us onto the shoulder.

"Where were you?" I asked, annoyed.

"They're moving fast, and your Kellaring is making my job more challenging since I can't find you either." His face was stressed. "You and Dustin need to get in there." He pointed to a rectangular concrete drainage tunnel going under the road.

"What about Baca?" I asked.

"Go now!" Crowd shouted.

Baca gave me a silent nod. I waved and then ran, following Dustin under the road. The tunnel was only about four feet high and not as wide. We stooped inside and stopped around the halfway point. A couple of long minutes later Crowd joined us.

"What's happening?" I demanded.

"Lightyear found you. The highway patrol is on their way."

"And they know we were in Baca's pickup truck?"

"Yes."

"So how's he going to get away?" I asked.

"He won't."

Suddenly, we heard the echo of sirens as several cruisers raced overhead. Not long after that Crowd led us back out just as a carpet cleaning van pulled over. We jumped in and almost twenty minutes later passed Baca's truck edged off the road, front door wide open. Police were leading him out of a nearby field in handcuffs.

"What's going to happen to him?" Dustin asked.

"I don't know," Crowd said quietly.

"Can we help him?"

"We'll see."

We never said a word to the driver of the van. Crowd told us that as soon as Lightyear identified our vehicle and location, they disbanded the roadblock. Baca was supposed to go as far and as fast as he could so we'd have time to slip through before they realized we were no longer with him. The van eventually dropped us at a house in a suburban neighborhood. Crowd motioned for us to get into the front of a blue sedan parked in the driveway. He knocked on the door of the house and a man let him in. Two minutes later he came out with the keys and directions to the harbor. It was less than an hour from the house.

"They have no idea where you are at this moment so let's try and keep it that way," Crowd said.

"Thanks, man," Dustin said, and we pulled away.

8

It was almost midnight when we found Trevor sitting on the deck of his boat, the Ninth Wave, sipping tea. "I had a feeling I might see you tonight," he said, smiling. Even though it was too dark to see his eyes, our connection was strong, and now it was more than our dying together at the hands of the Nazis. He also helped keep me safe and alive on this very boat after Fitts shoved me over the cliff in San Francisco.

"Been talking to Spencer?" I asked.

"No, just had a feeling."

We climbed aboard and I introduced Dustin. Then I hugged my oldest friend, who I'd only known for a few days. I explained where we needed to go, and Trevor located the island on his charts. He wasted no time showing us what to do to help get the boat to sea. As soon as we were out of San Diego Bay and in the open waters of the Pacific, Dustin and I found my old room and crashed.

It was close to ten when I awoke. Dustin had eaten breakfast a couple of hours earlier. I found them on deck, land nowhere in sight. Trevor, lean and tan, looked like a sailor; one might be surprised to learn he was a serious artist with paintings selling for thousands of dollars. He was continuing his lesson from the night before, teaching Dustin all aspects of operating the yacht.

"Good afternoon," Dustin joked.

"I love sleeping on this boat."

Trevor smiled. "I've got some sodas left over from your last visit. Hard to believe it was only a few days ago."

I thought of Baca. "Got anything healthier?"

He tilted his head and squinted against the sun. "Do I know you?"

"I want to clean up my diet, anything wrong with that?" Later, we had vegetable soup along with several slices of dark bread. It was perfect.

Trevor told us we were going to be on the boat for a few days, which was fine with me. I felt safe. After we filled him in on the future view, he was horrified and would talk of little else.

"I read a story about you online when I was in port yesterday. The feds are really making you guys out to be dangerous."

"They're setting the stage to blame us for blowing up the mall," I said.

"We can't let that happen," Trevor said firmly.

"How are we going to stop it? Nate's Future Self said there was a chance, but all we're doing is trying to take a different path into the future and hope that produces a different outcome," Dustin said.

"Spencer…" Trevor and I said at the same time. He smiled and let me continue.

"He'll know a way, if there is one," I added.

"So have you finally decided to let Spencer help you fulfill your destiny?" Trevor asked.

"Well, as Spencer would say, it's complicated. I don't even have a choice while Lightyear is trying to kill me. And besides that, my greatest priority now is to prevent Amber and Linh from getting killed and stop the mall attack. "

"It's all the same problem. Destroy Lightyear and everything's good," Dustin said, as a warm salty breeze massaged us.

"Right. So maybe after I save myself, our friends, and all those kids in Minnesota, I'll figure out if I'm up to saving the rest of the world."

"Great change comes with great costs," Trevor said, eyes looking forward.

"If you're saying what I think you're saying, Trevor, then I'd have to say you've been floating alone out on this ocean too long."

"I'm not suggesting you sacrifice your friends. I would be the last one to *ever* say something like that." His stare pushed me back to Dachau. We listened to the water lapping against the boat, looking back at the wake. "What I'm trying to point out is we don't win every battle."

"Battles? I didn't agree to a war."

"Who does? Just because you didn't start the war doesn't mean you don't have to fight in it. Remember, choosing not to decide is still making a decision."

"Trevor, we're in," Dustin began. "There's no going back to normal after everything we've seen. I think Nate is saying that we may not be able to control the order of things, but we'll wind up in the same place you and Spencer want."

"Yeah, I guess that's what I'm saying. The only difference is how we get there," I said.

"And when," Trevor added.

For the next two days we discussed philosophy, time, space, and reincarnation while soaking up the sun and healing sea air. We ate only good food, although Dustin wasn't ready to abandon sodas yet. There were a few odd shapeshifting incidents, like when a herd of buffalo, a thousand strong, ran across the ocean. No one else saw them. And the second morning when seven giraffes swam by with only their necks out of the water. But none of it compared to the Outview that came on the last night.

I was hiding in an old Indian village in the mountains of northern New Mexico, sometime in the early 1800s. The powerful Catholic bishop had orders from Rome to have me killed. With all their missions and converts, the Church's influence was widespread throughout the Southwest. Even the Native Americans were converting, but there were still some resisters. They hid me for a time, at great risk to themselves. I toiled in a dark pueblo room, writing my story and beliefs by the light of a small piñon and cedar fire. Smoke escaped through a hole in the low adobe roof. Tagu, my protector, came in the middle of the night and said I must go. He led me into the forest where we met another man I recognized as my old friend, Thomas Mercer. He believed in my cause and had proved his deep loyalty to me many times. We followed a narrow river miles into the mountains to a shimmering blue lake. There was a shelter, and we slept under an elk hide for several hours. It was light when Tagu woke me and said that the Church had raised a small army to find me and they were not far. I gave my writings to Mercer. "You're from back East. Get them out of the Southwest, away from the Church's power. Hide them until it is safe to publish them."

"No," he said. "We'll get you out…"

"But what if we don't? If I'm taken, it all dies with me."

"You will live," he said.

"The only way to be sure I survive is to separate me from my papers and protect them. These papers *are* me, so if I do escape then there will be two copies."

Mercer nodded his understanding.

He left immediately, heading toward the Cimarron cliffs. Tagu and I started for the tiny village of Arroyo Seco. Our plan was to make it into Colorado where the Church was not as entrenched. We were in Arroyo Hondo when the posse spotted us. I woke up from the Outview, gasping as I remembered the final moments, diving into a ravine above the Rio Grande gorge.

Cervantes Island was a three-mile wide, six-mile long paradise of white sand and lush forest. We docked in one of several empty slips next to two other boats. A casually dressed man greeted us, and we followed him to a dark green four-wheel-drive golf cart. He drove around the gorgeous island past the main home, a two-story, terra cotta roofed, white hacienda surrounding a courtyard of exotic gardens, tiles, and fountains. Whoever owned Cervantes had enough money to make every detail perfect. I was glad someone so wealthy was on our side. The tour ended at a compound of resort-like private cottages sprinkled in the trees. The man showed us our bungalows and explained where various paths led and that Mr. Lipton would be arriving in the morning.

"Booker Lipton?" Dustin asked.

The man nodded.

Dustin's eyes widened, thinking the same thing I was. Why would Spencer want to meet on an island owned by one of the most despised corporate raiders in the world?

Each place was elaborately decorated. Closets contained freshly laundered clothes in assorted sizes. Dustin and I changed; Trevor was already in shorts and a T-shirt.

"Let's check out the beach," Dustin said.

Down a short narrow trail, weaving between tall palms and giant green plants, we found a sweep of virgin sand and endless ocean. It was interrupted by only one thing: a primitive gazebo constructed of old whitewashed faded boards. Inside a lone figure stared out to sea expectantly.

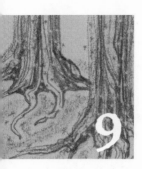

9

I ran toward him. "Have you seen it? Amber and Linh? The mall attack?" I asked breathlessly.

Spencer's face was warm as he turned, his turquoise eyes squinting in the sun. I took a deep breath. "Yes, I've been watching those tragedies floating out in the future since before you were born."

I steadied myself on the gazebo's railing. "Did you see my father's death before it happened?"

He closed his eyes and exhaled slowly, "It can never be simple between you and me, can it?"

Trevor and Dustin reached us. "What's going on?" Dustin asked.

"Spencer knew they were going to kill Dad and did nothing to stop it!"

"It's not anywhere close to that simple," Spencer said with a sigh.

"Tell us then!" I demanded. "How do you stand idly by and watch people you care about suffer?"

"Nate, surely your experience at Outin showed you firsthand that the future is a murky place shrouded in fog." He gazed out to sea and continued more softly. "Where storms blow in and out like the ocean's tide, changing and rearranging with each falling wave."

"If you know, then you can do something," I said.

"It's all but impossible to know what even a trivial change here and there will do to the outcome. And death is *very* difficult to change..."

"Then we can't save Amber and Linh?"

"I didn't say that..."

"Then what are you saying? Why can't you ever give a straight answer?"

Trevor grabbed my arm. "Let's go for a walk," he said, holding my gaze like he was Rachel talking to Erich in our past life back in the concentration camp. I couldn't say no.

Dustin stayed in the gazebo with Spencer while Trevor half led, half pushed me down the beach. The hot, midday sun was countered by a steady breeze off the water.

"Nate. Remember me?" He stared.

"Yes." I knew he meant Rachel.

"Do you? Because for someone trying to get back to their soul, you're pretty detached from it most of the time."

"I'm not trying to get back to my soul. Spencer wants that. I'm just trying to keep my friends and me alive."

"You need to stop thinking and acting with your sixteen-year-old emotions and start being your ancient self... your true self."

"You want me to be perfect. Who can be that? Not everyone can just drift through life on a boat, dodging the realities of this cruel world. Why don't you try living in this lifetime for a change?"

He wanted to slap me, I could tell by his look. I crumbled, realizing that hurting him sent me back to Dachau. "I'm sorry."

"I know," he took a deep breath. "But this is a defining moment... not just in the life of Nathan Ryder, but in the existence of your soul. We're at a critical crossroad in human history, and *you* are the difference."

I stared at him with tired eyes.

"You need to let yourself feel your destiny flowing through you. This hasn't been thrust on you, Nate. You keep acting like someone is making you do something, but *you* set this up."

"I wasn't conscious when I cut that deal," I said quietly.

"That's why Spencer's here. You need to trust him. Stop fighting him. Do you really believe he would have let your dad die if he could have stopped it?"

"No."

"Then stop misplacing your anger and realize Spencer's the best surrogate father you'll ever have... or friend, or whatever. Trust him. His whole purpose in life is to save you."

"So I can save the world?"

"So you can help wake it up. No one is going to build monuments to you or worship you, and you don't have to worry—they'll never make your birthday a holiday. But you have a job to do. It's not a mission, it's just a job, okay? You work at the front desk of a big hotel, and you need to make wake-up calls."

"Okay, I like that. Maybe you should call Luther Storch at Lightyear and tell him I'm no big deal so he can let me go."

"I oversimplified?" He laughed.

"Yeah. Someone needs to keep me in line. You're a good friend."

"Then it's safe to go talk to Spencer?"

"I'll play nice."

We walked back across the beach, the sand scorching my feet.

"Spencer, I'm sorry I've been a little difficult..."

"A little?" He winked. Before I could respond, he added. "Your youthful enthusiasm keeps this interesting, reminds me to focus on the human realm. You've got nothing to apologize for."

He had been watching my life unfold since before it all began, and if I was better at controlling my powers, the answers to my questions could be found in his ancient eyes. "Good, then we should get to work. Give me a straight answer, okay?"

Spencer nodded.

"Is it possible to save Amber and Linh and stop the mall attack?"

"Yes."

"But we're fighting time?" I asked.

"No. Fighting time is a fool's battle. *Playing* with time is the way, and someone with youthful enthusiasm is the perfect person to do it."

"How?"

"Time is just another place to visit, and even though you've been there before doesn't mean you saw it," Spencer said.

"I kind of see why Nate keeps getting frustrated with you, Spencer. I mean with all due respect, get to the point," Dustin said.

"Some are better than others at doing that..." Spencer began.

"Okay, but at Outin, Nate from the future showed up and told us all this horrible stuff about what's going to happen but that we could change it. And you say we can too," Dustin said. "But no one is telling us how... we're wasting time."

"Don't worry about wasting time, there's plenty of it... it's unlimited really. It's all in how you relate to it," Spencer said.

"How come Lightyear is suddenly able to find me with remote viewing?" I asked.

"While Fitts was alive they were convinced they had you cornered and there was no need to divert valuable resources to track you psychically," Spencer said. "Storch was trying to keep you on a short leash, using informants, tracking devices, monitoring, and agents, hoping you'd lead them to me."

"You?" Dustin asked.

"Yes. Lightyear doesn't like me too much. For many years, I've been the only person who knew what they were up to. And the only one who might know how to stop them."

"Fitts told me before he died that they'd been after you. But a few weeks ago, you didn't even know who was in charge at Lightyear," I said.

"I didn't," answered Spencer. "But turmoil is increasing, and there have been many parallel occurrences merging in the multiverse. So information has been simultaneously in flux and becoming more readily available. For a while they believed there was a good chance they could recruit you."

"Did they ever think that was *really* a possibility?" I half laughed. Something in the way Spencer looked at me made me shudder. "You don't mean it *was* possible?"

"Worse. In some parallel dimensions you did join them."

"Oh my God!" Dustin wailed.

"I'm surprised you didn't see it in Rainbow Lake," Spencer continued. "You were undoubtedly distracted by the mall attack or Amber and Linh. But in one case you joined to try to break them from the inside. Not a bad idea in some ways. Then in another you actually decided that with so many alternative realities it wouldn't really matter if you went with them. At least the girls and you would be safe. And Nate, you may find that a tempting solution if we can't stop the mall attack and the girls are about to get killed."

"Join Lightyear? They killed my dad and Rose!" I protested.

"I'm not saying it's a good idea. But I've seen a future where you justify joining by deciding that saving your friends in the present is more important than what Fitts did in the past."

"Here's a question *I'd* like a straight answer to," Dustin began. "It's bothered me since I first saw Outin. Which reality is the real one? Which universe or dimension are we really in? I mean, if you saw a future where Nate joins Lightyear, how do we know that's not the real one?"

"You're not going to be happy with this answer." Spencer answered meeting Dustin's eyes and then mine. "They're all real."

Trevor, who'd been standing off to the side, spoke. "So Spencer, is there a universe where Hitler won the war?"

Spencer nodded.

"What happened in that world to the Jews?"

"Like anything else, there are multiple outcomes."

Trevor leaned forward, slightly trying to pull the answer out of a reluctant Spencer.

"In one, a small number of Jews survive in the world and eventually they work to build and lead a coalition to successfully overthrow the Nazis."

"And is there one where Hitler succeeds completely?"

"Yes."

Trevor walked away.

"I should go," I said.

"Let him be alone with his demons. He needs to overcome them on his own," Spencer said quietly.

"We're all wired differently," Spencer continued. "Trevor has spent much of his recent years focused on Dachau, while you've been focused on your dad, Dustin, and friends. One day you may want to search every last universe, and alternate future, for surviving Nazis."

"That's possible?"

"Anything is possible."

There was a small pile of fantastic seashells in the corner. I wondered who had collected them.

"Right now, in *this* time in *this* universe, we need a plan to change the outcome of our world," Dustin said.

"How do we change time?"

"Ah, that is the great question, isn't it? Our first problem is Lightyear's remote viewers. That's, of course, one of the reasons we're on Booker's little island. They really can't see you here even when you aren't Kellaring."

"Are they looking for me all the time?"

"Yes. They now fully realize you're a far more substantial threat to their plans than I could ever be." He gave his words extra punch, and I felt them. Lightyear was the most powerful group on earth, and I was their greatest enemy. My palms sweated and throat tightened, imagining the real possibility of dying before this was all over.

"Leaving Outin when you did and some of your steps getting here have already changed the future but not enough to alter the major events we care about. You need to stay on Cervantes longer than you'll like."

"How long?" Dustin asked.

"Hard to say. It'll change constantly, but months."

"Months?" I whined.

"There are worse places," Dustin said.

"That's for sure, I could show you if you'd like…"

"No thanks. But when does the mall attack happen?"

"A few days before Christmas. But that can obviously change too."

"I feel like we're always waiting. What are we supposed to do all that time?"

"We need to get Kyle, Linh, and Amber down here for their Thanksgiving break."

"Really?" I was excited about that idea.

"Yes. Originally, you two were only here about a week before you went back on the road with a plan to expose Lightyear. The chain reaction led directly to the mall attack and the girls' deaths. But the longer we keep you here in a controlled and somewhat eventless environment, the easier it will be to see what the future is becoming."

"Then what?"

"We still need a plan to expose Lightyear, and I have some ideas."

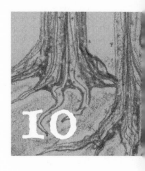

B reakfast, like dinner the previous night, was a gourmet vegan affair. Trevor had set sail mid-evening with a promise to return in a few weeks. Spencer, Dustin, and I continued our conversation until very late, as we walked the beach under a starry sky, shimmering more silver than black. It made me feel insignificant, yet part of something great. Spencer retired to the main house, but Dustin and I weren't sure he ever slept. After breakfast the three of us borrowed one of the golf carts and drove to the far end of the island where Booker's plane was due.

Booker Lipton was famous, I knew a lot of his story from media accounts, but Spencer filled in more details. Booker, an only child, was born to an African American father, a successful car salesman, and a Caucasian mother. His father died when he was only nine. Devastated, the family lost their home in an affluent Philadelphia suburb and for several years bounced around low-end rental units until his mother passed her real estate exam. At ten, he began buying collectibles at garage sales and resold them to antique shops, through classified ads, or to a growing list of clients. If he found a Tiffany lamp, he learned all there was to know about them. If he stumbled across a first-edition Scarlet Letter, he researched Nathaniel Hawthorne. He dropped out of school a couple of years later, saying he didn't have time "for fill-in-the-blank busy work and soda-pop history." By thirteen, he was submitting materials to auction houses and soon paying half the rent on a four-bedroom house in a nice neighborhood. One room was his office, another, his showroom. He bought and sold almost anything except drugs and guns. He told a friend once, "they may be profitable but the downside is so steep you can't see up." He bought a crate of microcalculators and paid high school kids in four districts a commission to pedal them to students.

Before he turned eighteen, he had three full-time employees, paid under the table of course, and an army of part-time workers. He got into art as the market was getting hot, and his cash began to pile up. Then he started buying real estate, using his mother as the exclusive broker. It wasn't long before Booker's companies filled an old ten-story downtown building. He played the stock options market, and by twenty-one was worth nineteen million officially—and twice that if the IRS wasn't looking. The press loved him, and he was a folk hero in the African American community.

It was then that he got serious about money and began buying and selling companies. He was tough, made millions—tens of millions—and the press turned on him, as he closed factories and sliced up businesses. The deals kept getting bigger, and, at thirty-five, his estimated net worth was $2.8 billion and Booker was hated. Then the tech boom hit, and he put his cash hoard into venture capital for dot-coms, made it out before the bubble burst, and by the time the second wave hit, he was sitting on more than $30 billion in assets, but many suspected his worth was much higher. He retreated from public view but his legend, like his power and wealth, continued to balloon. Although the public saw a ruthless tycoon, an air of mystery grew around him; there was another side to this complex individual. This was the side that Spencer knew.

"Why Booker Lipton's island and not some other secluded island paradise?" I asked, as Spencer navigated the narrow jungle roads with familiar ease, ferns and palms sweeping the sides of the cart as we passed.

"There's far more to Booker than what you've read," Spencer began. "He's the leading financier of the Movement."

"What Movement?"

"There's an awakening going on. I know you've been concerned with the attacks on your family, and now you're all caught up in the possibility that your friends and many other people will be killed but... how do I say this without you screaming at me—"

"Those are just distractions," Dustin interrupted from the backseat. "In the grand scheme of humanity's awakening, hundreds or even thousands of lives ultimately don't matter."

"Well said," Spencer agreed.

"Where did you get that, Dustin?" I was astounded. "Are you saying it doesn't matter if Amber and Linh die, the kids in the mall, even Dad?"

"That's not what he means. But Nate..." Spencer stopped the vehicle and looked straight at me. "No one *really* dies. Do you believe that?"

I thought of Dad giving me the matches across time, all the past lives I'd seen, the soul-powers I possessed, Rainbow Lake and the Windows of Outin. Of course, I knew no one really dies.

"Spencer, you know what I'm talking about. Just because their souls reincarnate or they continue to exist in another dimension doesn't negate the pain and the fact that they're gone from the here and now!"

"You don't know what their destinies hold," he said.

"Do you?"

"Life needs to be lived—the good and the bad. Human existence *always* ends in death."

Dustin put his hands on my shoulder from behind, calming me as I was about to erupt again.

"We will try to save them," Spencer began softly. "But you must prepare yourself Nate. The complexities of one life in one universe are astounding, multiply that by trillions of lives within infinite universes floating in a multiverse, and the repercussions of one seemingly trivial decision are astronomical. We are nothing, yet we are everything."

In the ensuing silence he started driving again, and a couple of minutes later we arrived at a surprisingly modern runway located on the southern end of the island. The Gulfstream jet approached.

I had never met anyone famous before, and Booker was way beyond your average celebrity. Once the plane came to a stop, Spencer pulled up next to it. Booker came down the steps, dressed in a cream-colored linen suit, followed by an assistant. A handshake with Spencer turned into a hug before he extended an arm to Dustin and me.

"The notorious Ryder brothers, how wonderful to meet you both."

"Thanks for putting us up," I said.

"More than that," Dustin said. "Thanks for aiding and abetting."

Booker laughed deeply. "I'm not a big fan of governmental laws, too easily manipulated. Don't worry; I don't think they'll find you here…" He glanced at Spencer. "And hell, if they do, I've got a handful of other islands we can move you to."

"Why are you helping us?" I asked.

He looked at Spencer again.

"I started to tell them, but our conversation digressed," Spencer said, as he and Booker got in the front seats and I joined Dustin in the back.

"Let's talk about it at the lagoon."

Ten minutes later we stepped onto a pier, which led to an elaborate, floating gazebo in the middle of a stunning lagoon, a small waterfall cascading on one end. There was a lush spread of fresh fruit.

"You boys lost your father at a young age. We have that in common. Although mine wasn't murdered, it was no less tragic to me. As a kid, I asked my mother and anyone else who might know, what happened to him after he died. You know the answers I got... 'heaven,' 'a better place,' 'with Jesus,' but none of it was believable. Then one day while I was in a bookstore, looking for something about an odd antique I'd acquired, I noticed a book on life after death. From that day on, the topic fascinated me. And as my fortune grew, I discovered a great many things about the human world and those who control it."

Inside the gazebo, I listened to an impassioned speech on the darkness of Lightyear. "It's beyond what you've seen, beyond the worst you dare to imagine."

"You're like the richest guy in the world. Why can't you stop them?"

"My billions are no match for the trillions they manipulate. Their corruption knows no limits. Their reach is everywhere."

"So how can they be exposed?"

"I've been waiting for you."

"Me?"

Booker glanced at Spencer then back to me. "You're going to wake everyone up."

"So I've heard, but no one has bothered to tell me how."

"Lightyear and its backers aren't just seeking power and riches. There's a conspiracy in place to prevent the shift. They know an enlightened population means an end to their plans," Booker said.

"Many will see you as a fraud; some, the messiah; and others, the devil," Spencer said.

"That sounds like high school," I said sarcastically.

"Lightyear has already begun the campaign to discredit you. But people are working to get your message out," Booker said.

"What message? I don't have a message," I said.

"You are your message," Spencer said.

"Just concentrate on staying alive, and it'll all come out."

"Yeah, one, don't get killed; two, save Amber and Linh; three, prevent the mall attack. Find out what's in the mausoleum, the gold box, locate Calyndra portal..." My dad had carefully hidden several thing for me behind a false panel in his desk. But I still didn't know what they meant: a list of nine names; pages of code, a key that led to an ornate mausoleum outside Washington, DC, and an antique, jade-encrusted gold box. I needed to know what he'd stashed in the mausoleum and why these things were so important to him.

"You'll be able to do all those things more easily if you stay here and study," Spencer said.

I scoffed.

"Your list depends on destroying Lightyear," Booker said. "And if they get you first, it'll all be lost. Think of your time here as training and strategizing."

"Okay." For some reason it was easier to agree with Booker than Spencer. He was commanding and had nothing to prove.

"Pretty high stakes," Dustin said.

"Fate of the world..." Booker said gravely. "But defeating Lightyear doesn't solve all our problems."

"Let's not get ahead of ourselves," Spencer said, immediately. "You're going to have to meet with Luther Storch."

"That's not funny."

"You think Storch is going to agree to meet with Nate?" Dustin asked.

"He'd like nothing more," Booker smiled.

"Will Nate be safe?" Dustin asked.

"Will Storch be safe?" I asked.

Booker roared with laughter.

"I could kill him. Why not rid the world of that if I had the chance?" I asked.

"Let's see where we are when that time comes. You may feel differently then."

"When do I meet him?"

"Early December looks most likely."

"Won't he know Nate might try something? Why would he leave himself open to that?"

"We're talking about seven or eight weeks from now. A lot can change. Let's not waste time speculating," Spencer said.

Booker and Spencer went on to the main house after dropping Dustin and me at our bungalows.

"Having Booker Lipton involved takes this to another level. Between his cash and our soul-powers, we've got a real shot at beating those Lightyear bastards!" Dustin said, as he left me at my door.

"Fate of the world," I whispered incredulously to myself. "He's been waiting for *me*."

I sat by the window, alone in my room, letting the humid salty breeze satiate my senses. Through the trees, the Pacific mirrored the starry night. Despair overtook me. If Booker couldn't defeat Lightyear, what chance did I have? Was I really safe here? How long until they tracked me down and finished the job Fitts had started?

I was suddenly looking at Kyle's loft. His hands were working the impossibly massive all-white jigsaw puzzle that drew him in when he was most troubled. His usual unlit cigarette dangled. If only I could talk to him now, I thought, as I said his name out loud.

"I thought you agreed to stay out of my head?" he said smiling.

"Kyle, you can hear me?"

"Either that or I should start packing for Mountain View."

"Spencer says I need to stay here for a while. Try to change the future by not doing anything. It doesn't make sense to me. And I feel like I'm getting swallowed."

"Meditating?" Kyle asked.

"Not enough."

"Listen man, if you lose it, then Linh and Amber are dead. You need to meditate as much as you can. And do what Spencer says."

"Got any new advice?"

"Federal agents were at school the past two days. They dragged in everyone who knew you, anyone who might know your whereabouts—students, teachers, even a janitor and a couple ladies from the cafeteria. They kept Linh, Amber, and me the longest."

"Damn. I'm sorry." With that, Kyle faded out and all I could see were soldiers running through trees—horribly unsettling, but Kyle returned.

"They threatened to indict us," Kyle continued. "Aiding and abetting a fugitive. Even suggested Amber and I could be implicated in crimes because they know we drove you around at the times of your alleged terrorist acts."

It was all so unfair, so unreal. I thought of the Kafka book I'd read somewhere with my Vising power. How deep did the corruption go? Would we be able to bring down something as big as Lightyear before we were silenced?

"My uncle called the principal, school superintendent, and even our congressman to complain," Kyle began. "He and Amber's mom have hired the same top criminal defense attorney for the three of us. Now my uncle is under surveillance just like the rest of us. It's totally out of hand." Then he was lost again. Images of police surrounding an RV on a busy street appeared before he, abruptly, came back.

"You all should be in hiding with me," I suggested.

"Nate, you're the only chance we have to save Linh and Amber. It's too risky to lead Lightyear to you."

"Maybe if I turn myself in the girls will be safe."

"I hope you never have to make that choice."

The following night I was able to communicate with Amber over the astral. "What a rush having you inside my head."

"Sounds like you're holding up under all the pressure."

"Why shouldn't I be? We're going to win. Lightyear doesn't know what they're dealing with."

"That's the problem. I think they do," I said.

"I saw on the news they released your mother an hour ago."

"What?"

"You don't know? Haven't you talked to her? Homeland Security picked her up this morning. Held her all day for some kind of interrogation. Her attorney issued a statement and said your house was also ransacked."

"Jesus! I have to talk to her."

"No phones are safe. Can you get her on the astral?"

"I'm going to try now. I'll find you later."

But for some reason, even after meditating for an hour, I couldn't reach her. I went to Dustin's room and told him about Mom, and he suggested talking to Booker and Spencer. They must know something.

They were on a wide veranda overlooking a gorgeous section of beach.

"Nate, she's all right." Spencer stood.

"When were you going to tell us?" I tried to remember what Trevor and Kyle had said about trusting Spencer, but he always seemed to be keeping things from me.

"I've been monitoring the situation and would have informed you in the morning."

"Informed me?"

"Nate, what could you have done?" Spencer asked.

Booker raised an eyebrow at the question.

"Spencer, do you know everything I can do? And even if you do, it needs to be my decision. The other day you asked why it always has to be so difficult between us. It's because from the day we first met on Tea Leaf Beach you've been telling me only part of the story. It's hard to trust someone who keeps so many secrets."

"Just because someone holds secrets doesn't mean they're being deceptive or have something to hide."

"Did you hear what you just said?"

Dustin laughed.

"Listen to me, Nate. Will you admit that this is a lot for anyone to handle? That a sixteen-year-old has little life experience to be able to deal with this kind of situation? And if I told you everything at the beginning, you might have either not believed me or run away?"

"You underestimate me, Spencer. Do you know the extent or limits of my power?"

He looked past me. His gaze stretched beyond the ocean. No one spoke.

"Are you going to answer?" I pushed.

"There are no limits. You *can* do anything." His eyes focused back on me. "But that's the broad answer. The difficulty is in the details."

"If I can do anything, then details don't matter."

"Everything matters. It's one of the truths of our human experience... Everything matters."

Silence returned until Dustin asked, "What about our mother?"

"She was taken into custody for questioning. Your home was aggressively searched. Your mother was put through a punishing interrogation, but was released unharmed—"

"And she has a top attorney representing her now," Booker interrupted.

"Did you hire the lawyer?" Dustin asked.

Booker nodded. "We've put undercover security on her round the clock."

"You may be able to do anything, Nate, but you don't know how yet. You couldn't have stopped it, and she's fine."

"Since they took her into custody, does that mean we've changed the future?"

"We're constantly changing the future. There's been progress made toward avoiding the mall attack. Even Amber's and Linh's deaths have been pushed back, but they're still happening."

"How can you be so sure that waiting on this island can change anything?"

"I know it's frustrating, but it's the only control we have."

"Don't I have any say in the decision making? I can't take this hurry up and wait. If I'm the chosen one, why can't I choose?"

Dustin looked at Spencer. "One of these days, Mr. Copeland, you may find that the Ryder brothers aren't so easily controlled."

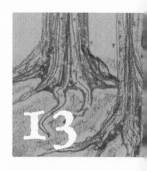

The next few weeks passed slowly, as time does in the tropics. Spencer and Booker both left the day after Mom was questioned. Dustin taught me to drive in one of Booker's nine beautifully restored convertibles he kept on Cervantes. In turn, I worked with Dustin on powers. Spencer had told us it was as important for Dustin to learn them as it was for me to practice teaching. "The Movement is filled with people ready to learn," he said. But whenever I pressed for details about the Movement, the conversation seemed to slip away. Spencer had also warned to limit astral communications with my mom and friends as Lightyear's tracking tactics were advancing fast.

The small staff Booker kept on the island was friendly but they weren't interested in much conversation. They did, however, keep us well fed with healthy gourmet-style food. "We have to be the luckiest fugitives in the world," Dustin said, almost daily. But that was when he was happy, usually after a great meal. As the days crawled, he struggled with horrific Outviews and painful micro improvements in his powers.

"Where's Aunt Rose?" He demanded one day, after spending an hour trying to get a book to float.

"Dead."

"You know what I mean. How come she hasn't spoken to us? She would come to me in a dream, a vision, a voice inside my head, something. Dad's gotten through to us."

"Yeah, but nothing major."

"Dad speaking to me from beyond the grave, telling me to forgive Mom, is a big deal to me. And it's pretty freakin' major to get a tin of matches through time from your dead father when you were about to freeze to death."

I nodded.

"So where the hell is Aunt Rose, Nate? She was part of all this. She was helping us."

"I don't know. I still try to contact her every few days, but there's nothing."

"Maybe Lightyear figured out a way to obliterate a soul. Or maybe they found some corner of the universe to imprison souls that can't be reached by your powers. Even dead, she's a better teacher than you," Dustin complained.

"I don't deny that, but you have to take part of the blame for your problems. Maybe if you hadn't done so many drugs."

"Maybe if they hadn't forced so many pharmaceuticals into me."

"Which came first?" I paused. "Let's just get back to practicing."

"You practice, Golden Boy, I'm done for the day."

Dustin ran off down the beach and was soon swimming through the surf.

I headed in the other direction. The warm, soft, white sand caressed my feet. A storm churning hundreds of miles to the west echoed in the ocean. Its mood matched mine while I sorted the fears, tension, and anger fighting for dominance in my mind. As the sun came through the clouds, I was reminded of the painting, the Ninth Wave, which was the namesake for Trevor's boat. Its depiction of shipwreck survivors clinging to debris had inspired me since Trevor first described it, and suddenly I felt hope and excitement. My powers were real, and in my growing comfort with them was the realization that not only could I survive but that defeating Lightyear was possible. Perhaps I could help the world find enlightenment, or whatever being one of the seven meant.

I wandered back to the bungalow and pulled Rose's journal from a drawer. It was the first time since I took it from her

Merlin home that I'd done more than flip through its pages. After a couple of paragraphs, it was obvious this wasn't Rose's journal. The words were definitely written in her handwriting but they described a life that was not hers. By the third page I knew this book was meant for me. The mention of Taos, New Mexico, and a posse raised by the bishop to hunt the man whose story Rose had transcribed were identical to the Outview I had the night before we came to the island. It was filled with details of Thomas Mercer, Tagu, and the Indian village where I hid in that lifetime. It was called Taos Pueblo and my name was Clastier. Rose had carefully copied his/my writing at some point. Did she know I was Clastier reincarnated? Who was he, and why was the Church so against him and his beliefs? As questions continued to ricochet, I absorbed the rest of the book using my Vising power. More information and images came through than were contained within the pages, and Clastier's words would become a constant inspiration— and distraction—to me.

14

Over the next few days the tension between Dustin and me grew as we continued working hard to advance our powers. Every session ended in an argument, and I didn't know what to do about it. Meditation didn't help, although it kept me calm and focused. That infuriated Dustin even more. I began taking long walks alone instead of practicing with Dustin.

Exploring the far end of the island, I wandered down a narrow trail of thick jungle and came upon a small hut, on a slight rise, with a commanding view of a dramatic and rocky section of beach. It appeared to be a place Booker might come to meditate. As I walked around looking for the entrance, an incredible sight halted me. A bone-skinny brown man wearing only faded gray shorts was levitating three feet off the ground. He seemed oblivious to my presence. His hair was shaved close and matched the color of his shorts. I couldn't take my eyes off of him. Suddenly he spoke in a deep and steady voice that shattered the sound of surf unexpectedly.

"Can I do something for you?" He remained floating, his gaze not leaving the ocean.

"I'm sorry to disturb you," I stuttered.

"I am not disturbed." For some reason this made him laugh.

"I'm a friend of Booker's. My name is Nate."

"I am also a friend of Booker's, so you and I must also be friends. Please. I am Wandus."

"Do you live here?" I asked, peeking into the empty hut.

"I'm present at this place."

"Are you a mystic?"

A broad yellow smile stretched across his narrow face. "Booker calls me a sage, but I am merely a seeker." He spoke without moving and his humility would not allow him to admit he was a mystic. He was older than anyone I'd ever seen.

"Will you teach me to levitate?"

"You think I am too old because you are young now, yes?" he said in an accent, which confirmed he was from India. While still smiling, he floated slowly around. "But you are older than me too. Perhaps you teach me, perhaps I teach you." Another laugh, his eyes reflecting light. I wanted to stay with him and listen to anything he had to say. His energy was so pure that being in his presence left me felling better than I had since the Lightyear ordeal had begun, better than I had since before my dad died. Dustin needed to meet Wandus. Dustin needed to live with him.

"Come old-and-young Nate." He unfolded his legs and they touched the ground, or at least I think they did. His steps were light and left no marks in the sand. He led me down to the beach and quickly was levitating again. "You'll like this. I call it, 'wave-o-tating.'" He laughed several beats under his breath. His eyes widened and his yellow teeth lit his wrinkled, leathery face. He floated just above the water until he was out above the rolling surf. Then as waves broke and crashed, he somersaulted with them, inches above the water—body-surfing for gurus. Wandus even whooped a few times.

He floated back to shore. "Now you try."

Twenty minutes later I felt heavier than ever and thought this was impossible without years of study and contemplation.

"You think you're not skinny enough?" He pointed at my stomach. "This is not what makes me float. It is true I do not eat, but that is for purity of thought."

"Wait! You don't eat?"

He shook his head and smiled. "Not for many decades, I think."

"How is it possible to live without food?"

"How am I here if it is not? I am here, yes?" Wandus put his hands together. "I am alone much of my life, and it becomes difficult to know if I *really* am here sometimes." He looked puzzled. "Yes, see the air is full of life. As energy, all we need is energy. Food keeps us in the physical."

"But how?"

"It can only be done by creating a life that is more spiritual than physical."

"How long does that take?"

"A day… ten thousand days. More or less. This depends on the concentration, the contemplation…" he said, his eyes brightened wide, "and the imagination." He said the word as if it was brand-new.

"My world has quite a few distractions right now."

"What if the world was run by imaginations instead of separate nations?"

"That sure would help."

"Let me show you again." And he rolled above the crashing foam, smiling.

After he came back to the sand, I Skyclimbed, running on top of the waves, the water falling away with each step. Breathlessly, I returned to him and fell to the sand, exhausted. His wav-o-tating didn't tire him at all.

"Your body is tired from all the food." He winked.

"You have seen the Mayan runner, the imprisoned martyr, the fleeing slave, defrocked priest, a betrayed soldier, a child in the plague, wealthy banker, the terrible holocaust—"

"You know about my Outviews? You can see my past lives?'

"Oh, so young in this life. They are not *past* lives. All those experiences are happening to you at this moment."

"This moment?"

"This very one. Those incarnations of your soul are all in your eyes, in your aura, radiating from within you. The energy that's in Nate on this island is all of them."

"How do you see them?"

"It is not hard to see once you know how to look. The difficulty, my friend, is knowing *how* to look. Many years I have quieted myself to remove distractions. The more we look within, the more we know that is where we are."

"I don't have years to learn all this."

"You can learn everything in an instant."

"Because I'm one of the seven? Great, how do I teach Dustin and my friends and the whole world? They'll never give up food and devote years in solitude to learn."

"The more who awaken, the easier it is. This is true you are one of the seven, but we are all one of the one, therefore we are all one of the seven." His face showed he was pleased. "How long does it take to learn that which we already know? Have you forgotten something and then found it back in your mind, suddenly remembered? Yes, this is the same."

"I don't understand. You're just like Spencer and all the mystics. It's all riddles and mysteries."

"This is not a course in mathematics we're speaking of. You are not trying to memorize dates of historic battles. This is the core of all existence."

"Then how can I teach?"

"Every day, without Nate, people are awakening to their souls in every different way. As the days follow, it is therefore easier. You will show them so that even more, so many more, more than you can believe, will can see. And it is your Outviews where your understanding is, where it must come from. I cannot tell you, Spencer cannot, voices of your dead and lost cannot. It must be understood through your own experience to be authentic. This is why the experience occurred, so that you could feel it, could be it, could know it. So you could share it."

Suddenly we switched places, and I was in Wandus's wiry and wrinkled body and he was looking back from my young frame with a huge grin. "You try it in Wandus and see." Effortlessly, I glided just above the water until I began to roll in the air, rising and falling with the waves. It was a roller coaster ride without the safety bar—or even the car! I laughed and flipped, but beyond the thrills was a profound feeling of oneness with the air and water molecules. I experienced the crashing waves as if I was them. No greater thrill could exist, and with that realization I was back in my own body. I looked out at Wandus, the body I'd just occupied, and his eyes were brighter than the sun's sparkle on the water. Without thought or struggle, I was wave-o-tating next to him and in that exhilaration knew, with certainty, that all things were possible.

Just before sunset on another beautiful island day, Spencer found Dustin and me on the beach.

"When did you get back?" I asked.

"Just now. The arrangements for your friends have been made. They'll be here in a few days."

"I was hoping you came to tell us we could leave," Dustin said.

"Actually, you're going to be late." Spencer looked at me.

"Where are we going?"

"The future."

"What are we going to do there?" Dustin asked.

"Just Nate is going."

"What?" We asked at the same time.

"Two of you would multiply the risks."

"I'm not going without Dustin."

"This is the best chance to save Amber and Linh."

"But not the only chance," Dustin said.

"No. But as I said, it's the best chance."

Dustin and I exchanged glances.

"Our window is closing," Spencer said.

"What do I have to do?" I asked.

Dustin walked away. I wanted to go after him.

"There's no time. Not everything can be fixed, not everyone saved," Spencer said.

"What's that mean?"

He just looked at me. After a few seconds, I understood. Dustin needed to work this angst out himself. His attitude and feelings certainly weren't as important as saving the girls and the others.

"The mall attack is still happening?" I asked.

"In about three weeks."

"So we haven't done anything to stop them? We've been wasting our time on this damn island and nothing has changed!"

"Everything has changed. But time is not that simple when life, death, and destiny are mixed in."

"Tell me where I'm going."

"You're going one year into the future to see Amber and Linh."

"They're still alive?"

"Hopefully. The idea is that if you can get to them in one year by leaving before Lightyear kills them, it will strengthen the time continuum to the dimension where they remain living and therefore increase the probability that they will survive."

"How will I find them?"

"Because when they come here in a few days, you're going to tell them where to be in a year so that you'll be able to find them today."

"This is incredibly confusing."

"You have no idea. I've spent years working on this problem and still don't understand a fraction of it."

"So it may not work?"

"It may not be permanent, but it will give us more time. And if you don't go, I think we'll lose them for sure."

Spencer drove us to a small prop plane. Once airborne, Spencer filled me in. We would fly to a spot over the ocean out of view of land where one of the Pacific's vortex portals was located. This one would allow me to travel forward in time to a specific spot and date of my choosing.

"There are significant risks that you need to be aware of," Spencer began. "If you're there for more than an hour, you will not be able to return to the present time, at least not without major consequences."

"Shouldn't be a problem if I'm just going to make contact with them."

"You also must note exactly where you come out of the portal so you can return. And if you stray out of sight of the portal, it will seal. Remember, it's not a permanent opening, just a flexible exit point."

"Anything else?"

"You won't be able to use Kellaring. Lightyear will be able to see you."

"Jesus! Even if they don't get me in time, I'll be leading them straight to the girls."

"Yes."

"Have you seen past that point in the future? Do you know what happens?"

"We're going that far out for a reason. Shorter periods of time usually leave you, them, or all of you, dead. And longer doesn't seem to hold the connection to this present."

"What are my chances of making it?"

"Nate, I don't want you to go."

"Then why are you doing this?"

"Because you won't realize in time that the Movement is more important than the girls' lives. You won't know that they would gladly have given their lives for the advancement of the Movement until it's too late. You're too important to the future, and the only way you'll be any good is if they live. So we have to risk your life or there'll be no point to your life."

He was right that I couldn't see anything worth letting Amber and Linh die for, but his words made an impact because, if nothing else, I learned that Spencer valued me above everything. And if he was willing to risk my life to keep me happy, then the Movement must be more than I could imagine.

"Just remember that because you can't use Kellaring, you'll have all your known powers at your disposal to defend against any Lightyear attack."

"Will there be one?"

"I think you should assume there will be."

"This is it," the pilot announced, a few moments later.

I looked out the window and at first saw only open sea, but after a few seconds the familiar shimmer of a portal entrance was visible. "I guess I'm jumping out of the plane?"

"We'll get you as low as we can but if we get too close it'll take the plane in."

"Seriously?"

"Ever hear of the Bermuda Triangle?"

"Yeah."

"It's riddled with portals."

The plane banked. "You'll have to go on the next pass. Ready?"

I shook my head.

"Remember who you are." He patted my back as I leapt out of the open door five hundred feet above the water.

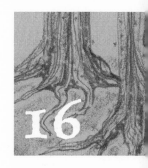

The portal was a painful burning blur that lasted no more than half a minute before I rolled out onto soft-forested ground in the redwoods. One of the giant trees made up a side of the portal's opening. I memorized it. Amber, now eighteen, and Linh, seventeen, ran toward me. In spite of the strain on their faces, they had both grown more beautiful.

"Are you okay?" Linh asked.

"I just came from the past."

"We know," Amber said. "You told us to meet here when we were on Cervantes a year ago."

"Nate, we've been on the run for months," Linh said. "I drove up from San Francisco where I've been with family friends."

"We stay apart for safety. I've been all over," Amber added. "Kellaring, you taught us on Cervantes, worked for a long time, but someone at Lightyear must have figured a way around it and started to know where we were."

"How?"

"I don't know but it's only sporadic, like they might only have one person able to break through the Kellaring, and they're looking for so many of us, but mostly you."

"That explains why we aren't meeting at a place surrounded by water. This is a pretty good spot. It would take a while for them to get a large force in here, and helicopters are useless in these trees."

"Not to mention the trees are so massive their thermal imaging would be all screwed up."

"How do you know that?" I asked.

"You've taught us a lot in the past year."

"When I left Cervantes, you hadn't come there yet."

"But when we got to Cervantes you already knew about this. You'd come and gone many times into the future trying to find the right time and place that didn't get us all killed," Amber said.

A sick feeling overtook me. "You mean they've found us. Why would Spencer—?"

"It's an impossible mission, trying to change the future," Linh said quietly. "He never wanted you to come. You even died on a few attempts."

"You're only here to save us," Amber said. "This doesn't stop any of the other bad stuff."

"There are only so many chances to get in and make changes, and there are infinite variables. It's quite remarkable we're not all dead already," Linh said.

"I'm not afraid of death," Amber said.

"But Amber, it's more than living or dying. It's what Lightyear does to everyone who's left," Linh said. "We all need to live in order to stop them."

"No one knows for sure," Amber said. "Spencer may be brilliant, but even he can't calculate the entire multiverse."

"You know about the multiverse?" I asked.

"You told us about it when we were all at Outin."

"When were we all at Outin together?" I asked. Before they could answer, the heat hit me so hard, I gasped for air. "Run!" I was shocked to see Linh Skyclimb up a tree across from the one I was going up. I wondered when she learned that.

Two small black drones negotiated their way around the ancient pillars with stunning speed. In the confusion, I lost sight of Amber, but I was pretty sure she was still on the ground. The Special Forces filled the area like ants overtaking a garden.

At least four drones were now buzzing around the trees, firing at Linh and me. It was as if I knew where the bullets would be just before they came, although I didn't consciously remember how. Something told me I'd been in this fight before, and hiding in the tree wasn't my best choice for survival.

I flew down with such soaring force that two soldiers were knocked unconscious as they broke my landing. I came off the ground making tennis ball-sized Lusans as fast as I could throw them into the faces of my attackers. A drone came at me shooting laser-machine gunfire far more advanced than a mere year in the future warranted. I uprooted a thirty-foot spruce with Gogen and sent it into the drone's path—instant fiery crash. Fifty-feet away, I spotted Amber in the custody of four soldiers who shouted for me to surrender. Two of them had weapons trained on me, and the others were pointed at Amber.

I sprang through the air, somersaulting toward them. At the same time, Amber brought large branches smashing into two of the men. I collided into the others. Laser bullets were coming from all directions as we dove behind the nearest tree, more like a fortress, with two redwoods growing unusually close together.

"We might win this." Amber smiled. Her expression quickly changed. "I think they hit me." She rolled over. Her pants were oozing blood where the laser bullet had burned through. I pushed a Lusan into her hands and started her in the motion of moving it back and forth across the wound. I tore her pant leg off and saw a deep gash just below her waist to her knee. She wasn't going to be able to walk for a while. I quickly moved some branches and brush around her and left a pile of Lusans. "Anything moves, throw one of these at them."

"Where are you going?"

"If we wait here, we're dead."

She grabbed my shirt and pulled me close. Our lips were almost touching. "If I die, don't forget I'll still be with you... always."

"You're not going to die." I kissed her quickly. "I've got to go." I Skyclimbed back into the trees.

"Nate," Amber managed to scream. "You can make fire and rain with your mind."

"How?" I shouted above the growing noise.

"I don't know. Same as everything else."

From up in the redwood I could see the wreckage of the copter I'd brought down with the spruce tree. I used Gogen to fling it into a second one coming down on me— another fantastic crash. A dozen soldiers were just twenty paces away from discovering Amber. I concentrated on fire, and almost instantly everything flammable around them ignited. Their screams of terror were horrendous as the flames engulfed them. The fire expanded, creating a new problem—smoke, heat, and the possibility of destroying a huge swath of the last surviving redwoods, not to mention the girls and me. I communicated with Linh over the astral and she told me there were only six soldiers remaining. The last two helicopters were covering a lot of ground trying to find us in the dense woods, and now the growing fire and smoke was adding to their difficulties. I asked Linh to get to Amber and help move her away from the fire while I dealt with the surviving enemies.

Linh had given me a general idea where the six soldiers were, in two groups about 150 yards apart. The fire was spreading alarmingly fast. If I couldn't make it rain, we'd all be trapped in an inferno. It was harder than I expected, mainly because I needed to be calm and that's not easy while choking on smoke and trying to endure blinding heat. I forced myself to put the soldiers, Amber's injury, and the flames out of my mind. Finally rain came, fast and heavy. The forest embraced the moisture, and the smoke changed to mist as the rain extinguished the fire with the power of a tropical storm. I nearly fell out of the tree, as the wood, moss, and leaves were instantly slippery. There was no way a drone could fly in the deluge, but seconds later, its light pierced through the fog straight toward me. I was about to leap from my perch but used Gogen to push the drone into the nearest tree. Done. Where was the last one? I needed to stop the rain as the ground was running with small streams. I tried everything, but it continued to pour. I Skyclimbed above the soldiers. My plan was risky. I came down fifty feet in front of them, got their attention, and as they turned to fire, I simultaneously levitated using the wav-o-tating method and pushed the middle soldier's weapons with Gogen. His shots killed the other two, and then I quickly turned the survivor's gun on him.

Gunshots and screams. I grabbed a gun from a dead soldier and ran toward the trouble, I was too late. Amber and Linh were both down. Linh wasn't moving. Amber was still screaming. I shot two soldiers almost in half with the advanced weapon, but the third took cover behind a tree. I was able to use Gogen to hold him paralyzed against the massive trunk.

I reached Amber first. She hadn't been shot again but must have fallen out of a tree as both her arms were broken. But her shrieks hadn't been from the pain. She screamed because Linh was badly injured. When I got to her, she was barely conscious, blood everywhere. Psychically I was able to tell she'd been hit just below her heart and to the side of her stomach. She didn't have much time. I cradled her in my arms and made a Lusan right on her chest.

The alarm Spencer had given me went off in my pocket. The digital rings told me there were three minutes to get back in the portal. I looked up and saw the shimmering seam thirty feet away through the rain. It would take hours to save Linh, if it was even possible.

Amber limped over. "Oh God, Nate. Is she going to die?"

"Not if I can help it." Pushing the Lusan against the wound, trying to staunch the blood, I silently begged my guides for help.

"We're not safe here."

"I know."

The heavy branches provided some shelter from the unrelenting rain, but we were still wide open to more troops. Amber gritted her teeth through blinding pain, pulled the gun from my hand and shot the soldier I'd left pinned to the tree.

"What's that ringing?" Amber yelled.

"I have to be back in the portal."

"Or what?"

"The world ends. I don't know! It doesn't matter, I'm not leaving her."

"Nate, look!"

I turned ready to fling the Lusan at more soldiers. Instead saw the unmistakable figure of Dustin moving through the downpour.

"Nate, you have to get in the portal," he yelled.

I looked down at Linh and back to him.

"We'll take care of her," he shouted. "You have to go... Now!"

"What happened to him?" I asked Amber. The tanned and fit guy I'd left on Cervantes an hour before now looked far worse than he did at the institution.

"Long story. No one's even seen him for months."

"Dustin, I can't leave her." The rain grew heavier.

"You have to. If you're not in that portal in about sixty seconds it all ends right here, right now."

"Why would Spencer have risked that?" I yelled, even though he was now only a few feet away.

"Don't you get it? This is all a risk. Even the great Spencer Copeland doesn't know what's going to happen for sure. Can't you stop this damn rain?"

"I've tried."

"Nate. Go now!"

"Listen to him," Amber cried. "We'll stay with Linh."

"If I leave her, she'll die."

"She'll die if you stay," Dustin said, staring straight into my eyes. "Lightyear will napalm this place. Go right now or everything is lost."

I stared back trying to make him understand that there was no way I was going to leave Linh. He understood. I saw it in his eyes just before he picked me up half with physical power, half with Gogen and threw me into the portal. The last thing I heard above my cries was the clear sound of drones returning. I was still screaming when, seconds later, I landed in the Pacific Ocean with no land in sight.

I alternated between treading water and levitating for twenty minutes trying to find a way back in the portal before I spotted the Ninth Wave, Trevor's boat.

"Need a ride?" He smiled when he finally reached me.

Not in the mood for humor, I climbed aboard and started yelling. "Do you know how to get back in the portal? I have to get to Linh!" I yelled.

"I'm sorry," he said softly. "I don't know anything about portals. I'm just supposed to take you back to Cervantes."

I nodded and didn't speak again until we reached the island. He had fresh clothes and a warm blanket, I was grateful, but all I could think about was Linh. I kept replaying every second in the redwoods, trying to figure out how to do it differently next time. Surely Spencer was going to send me back.

Spencer and Dustin were waiting at the dock.

"When can I go back?"

"I can't let you go back," Spencer said slowly.

"You can't *let* me?" I exploded.

"Nate, calm down," Dustin said trying to get his arm around my back. I spun around and swung at him. I was aiming for his jaw but hit his neck instead. He recovered and pushed me to the ground. I flew up in a Skyclimbing move. "You're the one who sent me back here! Back to this forsaken sunny paradise where I can't do anything to save Linh. She's bleeding to death right now. I need to go, damn it! I have to."

"Nate, she isn't bleeding now. You will see her in the morning. What just happened to you is a year into the future. Linh is alive and unharmed. She'll be here soon," he kept repeating.

I took a deep breath. He was right. There was time to figure out how to save her. "Why are they going to be here in the morning?"

"The hour and two minutes you were in the future has to come from somewhere," Spencer began. "It's a complicated equation similar to when you're at Outin. You've actually been gone from Cervantes for over a month." Nothing was simple anymore, and trying to understand it all left me feeling anxious. "Nate, this was your thirteenth attempt and the first one where you didn't die. You can't go back."

"The hell I can't. I'm obviously getting better. I'll find a way. Don't you see? If I don't get back there, Linh will die in a year."

"All of that can change."

"Stop pretending you know. You don't know. I won't tell them to meet me there. If they don't meet me there, then she won't get shot."

"Nate, listen to me. This is all about trying to save Amber and Linh and the people at the mall. But I have to be honest with you, even with everything we've done these past weeks and after your mission today, I've never seen a future with Linh alive more than eighteen months from now."

I stared at him, fighting tears, squeezing my fists. All I could see was the blood pumping out of Linh's chest. I lunged at Spencer. He anticipated and moved with a breeze. I tumbled past him to the ground.

"Nate, calm down," Trevor yelled.

I Skyclimbed, this time clipping Spencer's elbow with my foot.

"Nate, don't do this," Dustin shouted, coming toward me. "Get a hold of yourself!"

I went right over him and caught Spencer in a half tackle, which he easily rolled out of. For the next ten minutes we danced mostly in the air with occasional dashes on the water or ground. Trevor and Dustin watched as Spencer played sage-like defense to my angry offense. I was exhausted but determined to beat him. Suddenly, just as I was charging him again, he vanished.

"Wow, he disappeared," Trevor said.

"How. Did. He. Do. That?" Dustin asked.

"He didn't really disappear. He's right here somewhere. It's just some kind of shapeshifting trick, or he's used Solteer to make us think we saw him vanish," I said, catching my breath.

"Either way, it's freakin' cool," Dustin replied.

"He just knows I was going to win."

"Nate, it's not a contest," Trevor said.

I walked away.

Dustin came to my room that night. "Listen, Nate. I may not be Spencer's biggest fan, but the guy is doing his best and has managed to keep us alive this far."

"A lot of people have been keeping us alive. There's a whole 'movement' out there trying to keep us alive or hadn't you heard?"

"Yeah, well, you're the great leader."

"If I'm the leader then why don't they listen to me? Or at least tell me what's going on?"

"I don't know what this whole movement thing is, or about you being one of the seven, but I do know that whatever it is, you're not ready to lead anything."

"Oh, what makes you so sure Mr. Burnout?"

"Because a real leader wouldn't attack his brother and start a fight with his teacher. Face it, Nate, every day you keep proving you're just a punk."

"You don't know what you're talking about. What have you done for the month since I've been gone other than lie on the beach?"

"Hanging out with Wandus."

His answer surprised me. "Has *he* been able to teach you anything?"

"Working on it. He's a lot better teacher than you, and he's not even one of the seven."

"Do me a favor, Dustin. Don't bother showing up in the redwoods next year. Because I'll knock you out as soon as I see you."

"Sure thing. All that matters is what Nate wants."

"Linh was bleeding to death in my arms, Dustin! I was the only chance she had to live, and you threw me in the portal. You threw her life away."

"Grow up, Nate. Everyone dies."

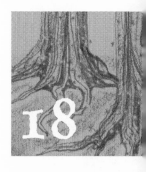

18

The plane landed as the sun was setting, turning the small jet's white fuselage pink. For a moment, as my three friends emerged from the plane and descended the steps, they looked like awed tourists landing on a resort island. But time was attacking us from many sides, and the seriousness of our situation could be seen on each of their faces once they were close enough to hug. I held Amber, we would have four days together; after that there was nothing but uncertainty. My mind was wild with desperation to save her and Linh. A minute later Linh came into my arms and I nearly collapsed; it was overwhelming to see her alive and healthy. But she had been condemned because of things I had done in this and other lifetimes, and although I knew death wasn't real, the thought of a world without her was unbearable. At that moment I realized that losing her would, more than anything else, kill me.

"If you have to live in hiding," Kyle said looking around, "this is the place to do it."

"Believe it or not, you do get tired of it after a while, but I've got no complaints as long as we're all still alive," I said.

"Your mom sends her love," Linh said. "She's still a little upset she couldn't come."

"It was too risky. You all coming was dangerous enough, but we had to try and throw off the time-path-destiny that gets you killed."

"How's that coming?" Kyle asked, hugging me. I counted on Kyle's special brand of calmness; his presence gave me strength. But since my time on Cervantes, I wondered at what cost to Kyle was his composure. He wasn't born acting forty, so when did it happen? His parents' death? The only time he crumbled was at the sight of police or soldiers, and there was sadness in his eyes even when he was joking.

"Thanks for coming," I whispered to him, before announcing "let's go talk to Spencer. He has a better grasp of our progress than I do."

The girls seemed so young and innocent compared with the ones I'd left bleeding in the redwoods the day before. I didn't know how to tell them about what was ahead, but Spencer would have already worked out how to handle this. I hadn't seen him since his disappearing act, but Trevor reported a sighting not long after our fight. He had been sitting on the beach, typically staring out to sea. In spite of my anger, I found that reassuring.

We found Spencer at the lagoon on the floating gazebo. He greeted me with a warm look before hugging Kyle and Linh. "And Amber, I'm happy to meet you at last."

"Likewise," she flashed a Hollywood smile and hugged him. After everyone was done marveling at the splendor of the place, including a fancy dinner spread, Spencer asked us all to sit down.

"I wanted you all here for more than just an attempt to change the future," he looked at our questioning faces. "I want to explain it to you."

For an hour he told us about the many different futures he had seen, including the ones when we all die in various ways and in different combinations. It was a depressing conversation in which the five of us learned that the odds of our survival were slim. "The people behind Lightyear are attempting to take complete control of the world. The only thing that can stop them is a mass awakening, and they will do anything to stop that. This is about trillions of dollars and control of virtually all the major assets in the material world."

"How do they think they can get away with something so huge?" Kyle asked.

"They've almost done it already. Their trick is that no one knows they're doing it. Little by little they've gained control, but that is a discussion for later. Right now, you just need to know that they're doing it and that anyone in their way will quickly be killed. As we've discussed, the future is bleak, but there is hope. A small but growing force, known as the Inner Movement, or IM, has evolved from many groups that have recognized various parts of the takeover plan and want to stop it."

"Can the Movement succeed?" Linh asked.

"I believe it can."

"But have you ever seen a future in which IM actually does win?" I asked.

He hesitated and then shook his head.

Amber sighed.

"Great," Dustin said.

"But that doesn't mean it's not possible," Spencer said. "Something could change today with all of you here that makes it possible for the Movement to triumph."

"Really?" Kyle asked. "Like what? How can we make that happen?"

"Nate needs to teach each of you how to connect to your soul and tap the power of the universe. The more who are aware, the greater chance we have."

"Let's get started," Amber said.

"In the morning will be soon enough. Enjoy the beautiful evening."

It was hard to relax and "enjoy the beautiful evening" after all Spencer had told us. Dustin didn't stay but promised to come to the training in the morning. The four of us sat around a fire on the beach under a gazillion stars.

"Tell us more about when you went into the future to try and change things," Linh said. "Spencer said we died. What was it like?"

"Apparently there were many attempts, but so far I remember only one. It was awful, but I didn't see you actually die." It was all too fresh, and I couldn't bear to talk about it. "But what I learned from that and from everything else that has happened is that time's a strange thing."

"How so?" Kyle asked.

"All our past lives, history itself, dimensions... they're all happening simultaneously. There is no past and no future. There is only one instant—now."

"Right on," Kyle said.

"What does that even mean?" Linh asked.

"We've always been taught, always believed that time is linear, but it's not. A mystic told me it was like a deck of cards, but from what I've experienced it's more like a single card. You know what I mean?"

Linh shook her head. Amber's expression told me she was almost there.

"It's all right here," I said, waving my arm in a circular motion.

"What?" Linh asked, exasperated.

"The multiverse," I whispered.

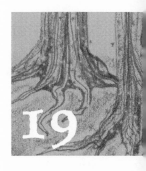

## 19

I woke the next morning in Linh's bed. Unable to sleep, I had wandered over to her bungalow just to look at her. I was having a hard time dealing with the bloodbath in the redwoods. We talked into the night and finally fell asleep. Being with her after knowing the future made the present seem more like a dream. She needed to be protected and hidden from that future. I wanted to do that, not just out of the obligation I felt in having caused so much of the danger, but because, although they said I was one of the seven special people, Linh was truly the special one.

After breakfast we all met on the beach, including Dustin. Everyone was happy. Dustin and I needed the new energy and company on the island. Kyle, Amber, and Linh were relieved to be safe at a secluded resort. But it didn't last. Dustin was exceptional at mind-reading, but once the newcomers easily passed him in all other abilities, he became agitated and angry. His interruptions and outbursts were making it difficult for each of us, and finally he stormed off.

He didn't show up for dinner, and I hoped he was with Wandus. Everyone was excited about actually being able to use soul-powers. At the same time we were exhausted from the work and the drama of Dustin. We arranged for breakfast to be brought to the beach the next morning and went to bed early. I woke from a deep sleep to muffled arguing.

"Dustin no. Leave me alone. No!" It was Amber.

I burst into the room to find him on top of her. They were wrestling on the sofa. He was pulling at her clothes. "What the hell are you doing?" I grabbed him. He turned and shoved me hard. I stumbled. Amber took the opportunity to escape. He caught her blouse and ripped it off. She fell at the same time. I tackled him before he could reach her again. He came up fast and landed two strong blows—a punch to the side of my head and another in my stomach. I was stunned.

"Stop it!" Amber yelled.

"What's your problem?" I gasped, dodging a kick.

"My problem? You're the one who thinks he's king of the world with all your powers and adoring girls. Amber's just like her sister. She's an untrustworthy slut and—"

"Screw you, Dustin!" Amber said. "You're jealous of your little brother and can't stand the fact that he's better than you."

"I'll show you who's better, baby!" He lunged at her.

I got between them and used Gogen to send him sailing back onto the bed. He pulled the bedspread off and ran for me. "Can't do anything without your powers, can you Nate? Why don't you fight me like a man instead of being a freak." He threw the cover over me, and we crashed to the floor.

Focusing my energy, I was quickly on the other side of the room leaving my brother holding an empty bedspread.

"Dustin, why don't you go for a walk on the beach before I show what a freak I really am."

He glared at me.

I stared back, trying to understand this latest personality shift. "What's happened to you, man?"

"Do you really want to know, Nate? Why don't you use your fancy powers and read me, and see what I went through at Mountain View."

"Okay."

"Oh hell, don't waste your time, little brother. I don't want your sympathy."

He tossed the bedspread at me. "Yeah, you're the great mystic, and I'm the great mistake." Dustin marched out the open doorway. I would have felt better if he slammed it.

"Are you okay?" I asked Amber.

"I'm fine. Talk about a freak."

"Two years of drug and alcohol abuse while Outviews and voices messed with his head, then two years in a mental institution, two months of Outin lake therapy followed by two months on an island watching your brother do everything better than you. I'm surprised he's not worse off."

"Can't Spencer help him?"

"Spencer is so focused on the future that I don't think he could even if he wanted to. I've got to figure out a way." I wrapped the bedspread around her; she pulled me close.

"I feel like those people in war zones. You know, like there may be no tomorrow so they pour extra passion into everything."

I nodded.

She kissed me passionately. "Tell me about the lifetimes when we were lovers," she whispered.

In the morning, still in Amber's bed, one of Booker's men woke me. I was embarrassed, not because of what he thought but because of what Linh would think, if she found out. She had less than a year to live, and I didn't want to cause her any more pain. But after hearing what he had to say, I had bigger worries. A minute later, I was in a golf cart rushing toward the docks. Trevor was waiting.

20

Leaving Trevor at the dock, I walked back to the others on the beach to tell them what I had just been told because every change was a matter of life and death.

"We saved you some breakfast," Linh said.

"What's wrong?" Amber asked, seeing my face.

"Dustin's gone."

"What do you mean gone?" Kyle asked.

"He stole a boat last night and left the island."

"Where'd he go? Can't you see him on the astral?" Linh asked.

"He's using Kellaring, which means as long as he doesn't use another power, I can't see him."

"Are you going to go after him?"

"It's a big ocean. Maybe he went back to San Diego. Maybe Mexico. Trevor's going to sail back to San Diego, and Brookings, to see if he shows up there."

"Maybe the time alone will help him," Amber said.

"What if Lightyear finds him?" Kyle asked, searching for smokes.

"I don't know." And I didn't. "Spencer is working on it too."

"How'd he take the news?"

"He's very concerned but said that this is so out of the blue, it could end up changing things enough to actually help us. Meantime we've got a couple of days to teach you guys as much as possible."

For two days we laughed, played, and worked hard on powers. Everything was lighter and easier without Dustin. Maybe that's why he left. The girls mastered all the Vising techniques. Kyle, who wanted to absorb books more than any of us, was having difficulty but was great at Solteer. He even made me think I was getting run over by a fire truck. "Paybacks are hell," he laughed.

All of them got the basics of Foush but only Linh could Skyclimb, and no one could do a Lusan yet. Gogen was another tough one. All three could move sticks and pebbles, and Kyle was tossing around large rocks and even moving ocean waves by the end of the third day.

I took them to meet Wandus on the final afternoon. He and I wav-o-tated for them, but they weren't at that level yet.

"You have much filling your head just now," Wandus told them. "Let your new skills settle in and then the rest will follow. Fear prevents much."

Everyone smiled because no one could deny that they were scared of what was to come. Wandus began a lecture on oneness and, at the same time, spoke to me on a completely different topic. I could hear both his monologues, but he said the others could only hear his talk on oneness.

"The Outviews you have seen are not random. This is not like using a television remote and switching through channels. Understand this: your soul is telling Nate a story. Those lives are all about secrets—finding them, keeping them, telling them. But mostly, they are about protecting secrets."

"What secrets?"

"This you need to know."

"So tell me," I said, watching the others listen to him talk about oneness. Kyle asked lots of questions, and Wandus never wavered. It was rather incredible to see. The others had no idea I was having an entirely different conversation with him.

"If I tell you the secrets that I see in your eyes, you will never understand them," Wandus began. "These secrets cross time. You need to learn them from their origin. Understand?"

I didn't really but nodded anyway. He smiled.

21

I secretly stayed with Linh on their last night. We held each other and whispered about things we'd done together over the years and things we still wanted to do. When it was time to meet the others for breakfast before sending them off, I didn't want to go. I was desperately afraid of losing her, of letting her die.

I don't know how Amber knew but she did. "Did you two find anytime to sleep last night?" She wasn't being nasty but wanted me to know she knew. Perhaps she'd come to my room looking for me. I was about to answer but her glance and smile waved me off. Just then Spencer arrived.

"Nate, you're leaving today too. I believe Lightyear's remote viewers will be capable of zeroing in on your location here within the next few days."

"Is he coming back to Ashland with us?" Linh asked, excited.

"No, to DC; you have a meeting with Luther Storch."

"You're going to let him meet the head of Lightyear?" Kyle asked, rising from his chair.

Amber knocked over a glass of orange juice.

"Yes. I know Nate and some of you share reservations about the Movement and have been focused on just trying to stay alive. However, those goals do share one thing in common: the Movement cannot succeed and you four cannot stay alive if Lightyear is allowed to survive." He was quiet for almost a full minute while we all looked at each other. Everyone knew he was right. Lightyear had to be brought down. "Now, this part may give you pause, but Nate is the only one who can stop them. It's part of his destiny."

"I believe you," I said. My words shocked me even more than they did my friends. The only one who didn't seem surprised by my support was the person who should have been the most: Spencer.

"In order to beat Lightyear, Nate has to know who Luther Storch is."

"Don't we already know who he is?" Amber asked.

"I mean his soul. Nate must learn what connection he and Storch share. What is their karma? Without that knowledge, there is no chance to defeat him."

"Isn't there another way to find that out?" Kyle asked.

"I have to look into his eyes," I said.

"It's too risky," Kyle said, pacing now, blowing imaginary smoke from a new cigarette.

"Kyle's right," Amber said. "Nate has been running from Lightyear for three months, and now he's just supposed to walk in and meet their leader? They'll kill him."

"Do you trust me?" Spencer asked me.

I stared at him for a few seconds. "Yes."

"I've seen this tens of thousands of different ways. For longer than you've been alive, I've watched you wage this battle. In every case, when you did not meet Luther Storch, Lightyear has won and plunged human civilization into a darkness lasting farther into the future than I'm capable of seeing—millennia."

"Have you seen him not surviving the meeting?" Linh asked quietly.

Spencer turned his gaze toward her. His face gentle, eyes filled with compassion. "Yes, Linh. His success is far from assured. You deserve to know. I've only seen him survive twice."

"Twice out of tens of thousands of times. What then? You're telling us Nate has something like a one-in-ten-thousand chance to survive?" Amber shouted.

"Probably not that good," Spencer said.

"Listen, if I don't go, Lightyear will win for sure, which means the rest of you die along with me anyway. Let's not waste any more time. I'd rather talk about how it's going to happen and what I need to do to survive."

"That'll have to wait until the flight to Washington. The plane is ready. You'll all fly to an airfield in California together, where you three will pick up another flight to Medford and Nate will continue on to DC."

The plane was richly appointed, with tan leather chairs, a tiny kitchen stocked with goodies and a miniature conference room in the back. Amber grabbed the seat next to me. "About last night," I began.

She quieted me with a quick kiss. "Nate, she loves you too. We're all in this war-zone mentality. It's cool. But can't I go with you to Washington? There's a great place to hide back in the conference room."

"Spencer would never allow it."

"I don't care about him. Would you allow it, if you could?"

"Yes."

She smiled, closed her eyes and leaned back in her seat.

"We've stopped climbing," Kyle called from the conference room. Ever since they came to the island, Kyle had wanted to talk about the gold box and pages from my dad's desk. Something always seemed to be happening, but I promised we'd spend time on the flight discussing them. Kyle was intensely focused on saving the girls above all else. He explored other ideas and wanted to solve the mysteries we'd encountered for one reason: stop Lightyear so the girls could live. I had a million distractions. Kyle grounded me and kept my attention on what was most important. Amber followed me back to the conference room where Kyle and Linh were already waiting.

"See," she whispered, pointing to a narrow cabinet that might be just big enough to hold her.

Ignoring her, I sat down and pulled the gold box and four pages from my pack.

"Shouldn't you have left those on Cervantes where they'll be safe?" Linh asked.

"I won't be going back to Cervantes."

She didn't ask how I knew. Instead she just stared at me, wondering if we'd ever see each other again.

"I've gone over these with Spencer and Dustin. Spencer keeps telling me that I'm wasting my time trying to figure them out and that the answers are in my Outviews. Wandus wants me to study the Outviews, too, but maybe not for the same reason."

"Do you still think Spencer knows what the box is about?" Kyle asked.

"Yes, but for some reason he can't or won't tell me."

"Why not?" Amber asked.

"What I've figured out about him is he can't be figured out."

"Have you gotten anywhere?"

"The gold box has shown up in two Outviews. The first time I was a Mayan about four hundred years ago, and the conquistadors killed me while I was trying to hide it. They pushed me into a cenote, a deep sacred pool, and the box would have been lost except that a friend dove in and retrieved it after they left. The friend was my father from this lifetime. And then about a hundred years ago he and I were together again. We were Americans and went to Chichen Itza, in Mexico, to retrieve the box. I was killed. I don't know what happened to my father."

"Wow!" Amber exclaimed.

"Somehow the box got into your dad's desk in the current time. So for at least three lifetimes, probably more, he and you have been trying to protect this thing."

"Yeah."

"And you've been killed twice, that we know of, doing it," Linh added.

"Is it possible that Lightyear wants it?"

"Anything is possible."

"What about the pages? Are they connected?"

"Well, the one list has nine names, including Spencer Copeland and Lee Duncan. The ninth name is just 'you,' which we assume is me. So who are the other six?"

"Have you done an Internet search?" Amber asked.

"I was afraid to after what happened last time."

"I'll find a way to do it," Kyle said, as he copied the names down.

"The other three pages are a code and Dustin believes they aren't connected to the gold box but to Aunt Rose's journal, or what I thought was her journal. It's actually a transcription of papers written by a man named Clastier, who was me a couple of hundred years ago."

"How do you keep all these different lives straight?" Linh asked.

"It used to be hard, but then Wandus taught me that there is really only one life—that my soul is the true me. All the personalities and human identities are really just expressions of that."

"Even the bad?" Amber asked.

"Even the bad. All of it is part of the soul's experience."

"If the code is connected to Rose, I'd like to work on it," Linh said.

"Okay, if you think you can get somewhere. I've got them memorized," I said, handing her the three pages.

The jet landed at a small airfield in southern California. A car was waiting to take Amber, Linh, and Kyle to a larger airport where they would catch a flight to Medford, Oregon. After refueling, I would fly on to Dulles International outside Washington DC.

The influence of paradise now faded, Amber was careful not to make too much of our kiss goodbye, but I could feel her apprehension. She wanted to come with me, and we both knew she would have been if it weren't for Linh's feelings. I didn't know if Amber was safer with me, or apart.

"You guys keep practicing those powers; we're going to need them."

Linh handed me a poem. I held her a long time. "I'll see you again," I promised.

As we hugged, Kyle whispered to me, "We're standing at another precipice. Save them."

I watched as they drove off. It was like a recurring nightmare: once again we were searching for Dustin, trying to avoid Lightyear, and worrying about the safety of my friends. I read Linh's poem and, as usual, her poetry anticipated my feelings and explained them back to me.

> I am as full as an ocean
> filling the shore, my eyes, my heart
> swelling like a bruise, hit with apprehension
> and fear whose sides penetrate like a drum
> through every fold and shadow
> not dark, nor painful, just full
> like the sun. And it burns to hear
> silence below the surface,
> Can you see this sense of movement
> in our lives? It is a dream
> unannounced, proclamations of dissent
> into emotional depths, like a storm
> quickly it turns and passes
> but destructive and consistent at the ready.
> I am here, always, battered, torn, vacant,
> pungent, like birth.
> Don't indulge, now. Gently, hero,
> step delicately and steadfastly,
> our warrior hands, trigger-happy smiles
> and quick, sensual clips suddenly seem
> to thread the pieces together into
> a scenic overture,
>            listen. I am here.
> Always and time-soaked,
> dirty and oppressed, absent and second best
> but here. Spilling into pools reflected in the
> sky-like worlds available, disclosed and

> naked, and true. True, hero, step through
> this veil, this war-splattered body, this
> crazy sense of living. This is life,
> live the steps like a flower, just open,
> accept the wind, the rain, the hand that
> desires. Your life is cut and adorned.
> It is not up to you, or me.
> It is not up to you, or me.

The need for Kellaring meant I was literally powerless. Spencer told me that if the remote viewers found me during the flight, they would blow the plane out of the sky—it had happened in another universe. There was no way to search for Dustin. That would have to be left to Spencer until I was in a safe place again. When would that be?

I passed the time during the flight talking to Spencer over the astral. For some reason that didn't interfere with the Kellaring. He gave me instructions for the meeting with Luther Storch. It seemed incredibly risky, but he'd seen it too many times for me to bother arguing. Before my meeting with Storch, there was something I needed to do in Washington that I hoped would answer the questions we'd been trying to solve since I first discovered my father had been murdered.

## 22

Booker's driver slowed the car in the B section of the old cemetery that grew out of a parish started in 1712, in what is now the center of Washington, DC. Rock Creek Cemetery was a beautiful place, more a rolling park than a graveyard. There were more than eighty acres filled with the remains of powerful and famous people from the prior two centuries. The Hibbs mausoleum was the most elaborate, built in the 1890s to resemble an English chapel, with arched doorway, imported marble, and stained glass windows. I pulled the strange key from my pocket. Since my hurried visit through the portal from Crater Lake, I knew it would fit perfectly into the antique lock. The question was why my dad had hidden it for me, and what secrets were buried here.

Once inside, a symphony began playing, which startled me. The original builder had installed a sound system that, for a hundred years, would play continuously each time the door was opened. I stood facing a large, intricately carved sarcophagus, and gazed around the body-filled marble walls carved with names and dates long past. Light filtered in through colored glass and an ornate chandelier hung overhead, but it remained dark and dusty. I shivered, feeling a little trapped in the old tomb. Why was I here? Why the key? The Old Man of the Lake had told me the key protected secrets and asked if there were secrets I needed to know. The list was long, starting with the items found in my father's desk: the list of names, the other pages, the gold box, the key. Why wasn't Rose communicating from the dead? What did her "journal" mean? How could I stop Lightyear?

"What am I supposed to do, open every crypt?" I asked out loud.

I knew my time was limited. Lifting the cover of the sarcophagus carved from a giant slab of yellow Italian marble would be impossible without several strong helpers, or Gogen. Because using any powers would stop the Kellaring and immediately reveal my location to Lightyear, I had to start with crypts, but which one? If I could use Vising to read the walls, I could learn where my father had hidden something, but it would also bring Lightyear. I opened my pack and pulled out the tools I'd brought and silently asked my guides where to begin. That's when I noticed the paperclip. It was on the ground behind the sarcophagus and seemed too modern for this place. I knelt down to pick it up and realized there were six cabinet doors concealed in the baseboard. The first one I opened contained plans, registers and details about the mausoleum. The next door was something entirely different. Sitting on the floor in the dim light, two stacks of twenty CDs in crisp white envelopes glowed before me. If the paperclip was too modern, then these were futuristic and the USB thumb drives in the next cabinet might as well have been from another planet. It wasn't until I got to the fifth cabinet and found the files and letters from Lee Duncan that I realized my father had never been here at all.

There was no time to review everything, but it was clear that this was the case against Lightyear, enough evidence to expose and annihilate them. Suddenly, I was more afraid than ever. They would do anything to destroy these things and anyone who possessed them. It wasn't just my psychic abilities they were after; they believed Lee's stash was in my hands, and now it was. I knew the evidence should not remain here. There was no way to know how trackable I was, or even if they were still working to uncover Lee's final movements.

I shoved more than fifty thumb drives in my pack. The remaining files and CDs required three trips to Booker's car. My heart was pounding. I scooped up the tools, ready to make my final exit, when the ceiling began spinning.

The Outview took me fast and my last thought as Nate was to wonder if an Outview would stop the Kellaring and allow Lightyear to find me. There I was, an older man walking through an enormous home tastefully appointed with antiques, fine Persian rugs, and oil paintings. As I passed a mirror in the foyer, I saw the white hair and guessed my age to be early seventies. I stepped out onto an endless front veranda and glanced at an elaborately landscaped lawn. Judging from the automobiles parked along the grand circular drive, it was the late 1930s and I was master of this great estate. I admired a splendid three-story tower overlooking flower gardens and boxwood, and then remembered that if this Outview was like the others, I was about to die. I quickly turned back, as Spencer had shown me. Instantly, I was the same man but younger. It was maybe thirty years earlier. A chauffeur drove me through the gates of the estate. The name on the car was Rolls Royce, and the carved stone column announced we were at Graydon Manor.

There was a woman sitting next to me. It only took a second to recognize her as Spencer. The chauffeur addressed me as Mr. Hibbs. I was William B. Hibbs, the man who had the mausoleum built!

Soon we walked into a spacious library located in a separate building from the main house. Two men were waiting for us. The first I recognized as my father, but in this lifetime he was younger than me. His name was Cavanaugh. We had been together in a prior Outview at the Pyramid of Kukulkan at Chichen Itza, where we recovered the gold box just before an unknown assailant slit my throat. Because I was Hibbs and my father/Cavanaugh was the same person in both Outviews, it was obvious that my soul was incarnated as two people during the same time period. That would have seemed impossible to me a few months earlier but then so would almost every aspect of my current life.

The other guy was an incarnation of Lee Duncan. Both he and my father/Cavanaugh appeared to be working for Hibbs/me. The woman/Spencer and the two men were probably in their mid-thirties while Hibbs was over forty. They spoke in the hushed tones of conspirators even there, in Hibbs' private library.

"It's been nearly four years since our man was murdered on the Yucatan," Lee said. "Yet the Jadeo is still safe." He was talking about the gold box from Dad's desk that I, as Nate, now possessed. That meant my father/Cavanaugh had gotten it out of Mexico after my death.

"I met with President Roosevelt yesterday at the dedication of the new Masonic Temple. I'm quite high and respected in these circles," Hibbs said, with a quick smile.

"Yes, dear, we know," the woman replied, absently pulling one of her blond hairs from my dark suit. "But you must remember, it wasn't just some stooge they killed in Mexico. It was you."

"That part is still too fantastic for me to believe," Hibbs said. "As you know, I became convinced of the corruption and dangers their group posed when they assassinated President McKinley within days of me advising him against supporting the banking reforms. We were friends."

"Friends? You were poker buddies," the woman said.

"It was more than that, but no matter. Now there's talk of instituting a federal income tax and turning our monetary system over to a private central bank. Could our leaders be so incredibly foolish to allow this?"

"It's only the beginning," the woman said.

Cavanaugh, who had been silent until now, spoke. "We're not here to debate what the Masons or any other group is or is not going to do to this country. We're simply here to maintain our oath and keep the Jadeo safe."

"Yes," Hibbs said. "It's time to move it far away from Washington."

"We agreed it should remain in the country," Lee said.

Everyone nodded.

"To the wilds of the Pacific Northwest. It remains the least infiltrated and corrupt territory in the land." Hibbs' choice of hiding place for the gold box was most likely responsible for me being born and raised in Oregon. My father would have to retrieve it in yet another lifetime and make sure I would find it.

"We'll leave tonight," Cavanaugh said.

Hibbs led the group to a bookshelf that, after a few maneuverings, opened smoothly to a lit staircase. We descended the spiral steps, and reached a long curving tunnel approximately six feet wide and eight feet high. The space was furnished with rich carpet, crystal wall sconces, carved mahogany dressers flanked by Chippendale chairs and mirrors in gild frames above each dresser. Hibbs stopped at the second one. Without being asked, my father and Lee lifted the heavy frame off the gray stonewall. Cavanaugh carefully worked a seam between two stones, and after a minute pulled the stone out of its socket. Hibbs smiled at the tiny safe door before dialing a combination. "Your birthday," he said to his mistress, as he dialed the first number. His wife and daughter were at his home in the city. "The day we first met," as he stopped on the second. "The day our son was born," he said as the final click released the lock. Although the door was small, the safe opened to a larger compartment that housed stacks of large envelopes. He withdrew a black cloth bag and from it produced the gold box, the Jadeo.

"These other papers," Hibbs motioned toward the safe, "although irrelevant compared with the importance of the Jadeo, would normally carry enough significance to murder and die for. Their contents and the implications could impact millions."

"I hope you can remember Billy's statement for a very long time," the woman said, staring at Lee.

He nodded.

I was searching Hibbs' memory for what exactly the documents contained when Booker's driver shook me violently, the mantra began in my head, "I'm Nathan Ryder, I'm sixteen..."

"Nate, are you okay?" he asked, pulling me from the floor.

"Yeah, I think." I was still adjusting to not being Hibbs and trying to comprehend the consequences from what he/I did more than a hundred years earlier.

"Booker told us not to stay in one place more than fifteen minutes. We've been here almost half an hour. We're leaving." The sunlight strained my eyes as he ushered me back outside.

"Hey, you're from this area, right?" I asked, as we were turning back onto New Hampshire Avenue.

"Yes, fourth-generation Washingtonian."

"Ever hear of Graydon Manor? It belonged to the same Hibbs buried in the mausoleum."

"No, but I'll bet Google has." Seconds later his iPhone showed him search results of Hibbs and Graydon. It was located in Leesburg, Virginia, and was now a children's rehabilitation center.

"How long would it take us to get there?" I asked.

"Just over an hour, depending on traffic, but there's no time to get there and back before your big meeting."

I wasn't ready for the big meeting. I knew I could die and that I probably would. Then it occurred to me, the answers might only be found in death.

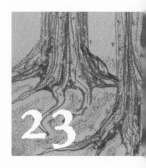

Booker's driver dropped me at the parking lot and drove off. None of us were interested in him being arrested or his identity being known and linked back to Booker. He wasn't followed. Homeland Security had closed Roosevelt Island for the afternoon. The eighty-eight acre island, located in the Potomac River between Virginia and Washington, DC, would be the site of the secret meeting between Luther Storch, head of the CIA's most covert division, Lightyear, and the nation's most wanted terrorist, Nathan Ryder.

The location suited me because, except for a small memorial park, the island had been maintained in its wild form as a bird sanctuary and was nothing but trees. The Nacotchtank Indians who once inhabited it were said to have used the island for rituals, but sometime in the 1930s, after a long series of owners and claims, it was donated as a monument to the twenty-sixth president. Was it just a coincidence that I'd just experienced an Outiew where I, in another life, was friends with Teddy Roosevelt? Not likely, just as it was not likely that I wasn't walking into a trap.

Two agents approached, one already talking on his radio. The escort lasted until the narrow footbridge, which crossed the swift-running Potomac River. Extra hearing and vision allowed me to see and hear everything. After Outin and Cervantes, my powers were at their peak. If they were going to kill me, it wouldn't be easy. I could torch this little island with a blink of my eyes, or engulf it in a hurricane. I could levitate and Skyclimb and rip giant trees from the ground without breaking a sweat. It all seemed a dream but not believing meant it was all a nightmare.

A new pair of agents, more heavily armed, were waiting at the other side of the bridge. They checked for wires and concealed weapons. After a short walk, we reached the center of the island near a giant monument to Teddy Roosevelt. I thought of the Hibbs Outview again. What was the connection? My escorts moved away as a man emerged from behind the marble pedestal that supported the bronze stature.

Luther Storch was not the ogre I'd been expecting. He looked like a movie star and was intensely charming. "Well, Nathan Ryder. My God, I've actually been nervous about meeting you. A legend so young... thank you for coming."

His warmth seemed genuine. As he pulled off his sunglasses I almost expected serpent eyes, but he looked like a guy from a toothpaste ad. How could he have ordered so many deaths, ruined lives, and inspired a movement against him? All my powers were fully at my disposal for the first time since I left Cervantes, and their energy pulsed through me. There was no heat warning of danger. Storch's friendly greeting left me confused, and all my rehearsed preparations were forgotten.

"No need to pretend you like me, Storch. I've been dodging your bullets too long to believe it."

"Nate, no that's not exactly... can I call you Nate?"

"I don't care what you call me. And I don't want to hear excuses about why you killed my father and aunt."

"Please Nate, hear me out. Fitts was out of control. He was not acting on my orders. He was rogue and had an agenda of his own. The Chinese were paying him—"

"Wait, you expect me to believe Fitts was a double agent?"

"Yes."

"And you haven't been trying to kill me since he died?"

"No. No. My goodness, we don't do that sort of thing. That's all in the movies. I understand you watch a lot of movies. Me too."

I stared at Storch trying to see past this façade, wanting to read him with Vising but knew if I tried, they'd shoot me thirty times before even getting my arms around him. Instead I searched his eyes but didn't recognize his soul from any Outviews. Risking this meeting had been a waste. Why would Spencer not have known that? Too late; he was talking again.

"There have been many misunderstandings, Nate. We aren't some evil organization trying to destroy you. I don't know who you've been listening to, but this has all gotten out of hand."

"You're lying."

"No, that part is true. We may be doing things you don't agree with, but evil? Ha! Evil isn't a real thing. Evil is like beauty, it's in the eye of the beholder."

"Storch, I'm not buying this. You seem to have a convenient answer for all the horrible things that have happened, but I know better and it's not working... just tell me why you wanted me here."

He smiled, then pursed his lips. And there was something familiar in his expression. Maybe I did know him, but there was a shield blocking full recognition, like his eyes were masked. He turned away and looked up at Roosevelt. "We do what we want, but we'd like your help. Nate, I'm trying to appeal to you as an adult. I'm trying to save your life... and a lot of others'. Join us."

"I'd rather die."

"I'm sorry to hear that. And be sure, it's not just you who will die."

"Oh, I know that. I know what you're capable of."

"Do you, Nate? Do you really? Because there is more at stake here than you could imagine. And I'm furiously exhausted by the trouble you've been causing."

"You're exhausted? Have you been running for your life? Has your life been ruined?"

"I have pressures you can't begin to understand... but none of that matters. We can help each other. Your gifts are exactly the kind of talents the agency needs. You can stop running; you can begin a richly rewarding career."

"You want me dead."

"No, we want your help. In only a few months your powers have advanced beyond what it has taken some of our people years to achieve. Do you realize what these powers can mean for our country, the war on terror, mankind?"

"I know what they mean to someone like you who controls and manipulates people with the powers. You tell them they're doing good things, and you pay them well, give them health insurance and paid vacations, perks and toys. They sell themselves out and everyone else on the planet for trinkets and cash."

"What are you, some kind of communist?"

"I'm just saying, if the psychics you have working for Lightyear knew what you were really doing and knew the truth about me and what's happened, then you would be the one running."

"So, what's your answer?" He looked at his watch. "I've got a schedule to keep."

"My answer? If you're asking me to come and work for you at Lightyear..."

He nodded.

"My answer is, go screw yourself."

He sighed and shook his head. "If you insist on fighting us, it's not just you who will lose. Your family and friends may die." His threat shook me.

"I'm begging you to leave them alone," I said, trying not to let my voice tremble.

"Nate, I'm going to be honest. You're not just a small problem for me. Either you get on board, or I'll do worse than have you killed."

"What is—"

"You can't be allowed to be a martyr."

"I won't help you."

"What if I said, I'll blow up a mall, or an airplane... and blame it on you?"

"Talk to an evil man long enough, and his mask comes off."

"I'm not evil, Nate. You just don't understand the importance of what we're doing."

"Important enough to kill innocent people?"

"Don't be naïve. People are expendable—do you know how many are born every day? We're sure as hell not running out of them."

"You're insane."

"Really? But I'm going to walk off this island and continue with my work, and you're not. It's a shame, Nate, we could have used your talents. Say hello to your father."

The sniper's bullet hit just as I began my Skyclimb. More shots came as I went higher and dozens ripped into the trees from multiple angles as I reached the upper branches of a hundred-year-old oak. I leapt from tree to tree as the tiny island filled with soldiers. Choppers appeared. It was the redwoods all over again. I had learned from that lesson and began shooting fires.

I sensed there was a portal nearby. Closing my eyes and clearing my mind, I somersaulted into the air. Instead of plunging a hundred feet to the ground, my body was pulled diagonally into a strange translucent portal. I was invisible to them, yet I could see everything happening at once and instantaneously be at any spot on the island. But the portal seemed to offer no escape; it was completely self-contained. Still, it bought me the minutes I needed to heal my bullet wound. Fires were raging all over the island as hundreds of agents scoured the woods. The portal protected me from the smoke but while I was trying to form a plan, it began to disintegrate. They spotted me near the southern edge where the trees met the Potomac River. Their bullets miraculously missed as I ran straight into the river, but instead of sinking, I was running on top of the water. I was close to making it to the trees and high bank on the Virginia side when one of the ever-present news helicopters, always circling the nation's capital, began filming as boats and military choppers closed in on me.

24

I made it to shore and scrambled up a hiking trail under Key Bridge—a momentary respite from the helicopters. There was no time to tend to my many wounds; agents were close behind. Emerging from cover, I summoned my failing strength and Skyclimbed through the thin stretch of trees between the GW Parkway and the Potomac, then maneuvered to the road. Spotting a red pickup towing a large RV traveling at fifty mph, I increased my speed and made a decent landing on the roof of the trailer. The hard part was swinging down, opening the door and throwing myself inside. I was bleeding too much and wasn't sure they had spotted me. I made Lusans and assessed the damage. Miraculously, there were just four bullet wounds and only one serious. After a few minutes, the bleeding was under control and since the pickup hadn't stopped, it was possible my escape worked.

I switched the flat screen on to a cable news channel that showed footage of me "walking on water" and dodging heavy government gunfire. There was also an inset of my Ashland High School yearbook photo with a caption, "Golden Gate Terrorist Loose in Washington." At least the media thought I'd escaped, but Lightyear might send a missile into this poor person's RV at any second. The next image that flashed on the screen was CIA headquarters; according to the map, I was heading straight for it. Defensive preparations were being made.

Commentators were already debating how I managed to escape by walking on water. The anchorwoman actually asked if I was the Antichrist. I changed channels and saw a government expert saying that it was too soon to analyze my stunt, but it was possible I had access to a special combat suit being developed by the Chinese. That would also explain how I started all the fires simultaneously, but he cautioned, some types of pyrotechnics might have been planted on the island in advance by my network of terrorists. How did they get this garbage up so fast? I hoped Spencer was watching and the girls weren't.

How long would it take Storch to find me? Kellaring was not an option because I needed Lusans. It was time to move again. The truck slowed and took an exit at Chain Bridge Road. I was surprised to see an actual sign for CIA Headquarters. Someone in that building was using psychic powers to find me. Many others were probably using satellites and surveillance cameras. I found some clothes, a little loose but better than my blood-stained shreds. The TV said roadblocks were going up at key locations and to expect long delays at all area airports, train and bus stations, and ports. In an unprecedented effort to bring me in, local police departments were visiting hospitals and even doctors' offices.

Breaking through the clutter of cable news reports was my father's voice. "Get out now, Nate. Right now." Just then the truck stopped for a red light. Without hesitation, I opened the door and stumbled out in front of a real estate office. In the large parking area behind a Thai restaurant, a news helicopter sat with blades rotating. I was about to start running when a familiar voice called my name. It was Booker's driver. I ran toward him and he pulled me inside just as the chopper lifted off. "Booker owns this station," he said with smile.

"Where are we going?" I asked.

"Not far. They've restricted air traffic. Just need to get you out of the area."

"Leesburg?"

"Graydon Manor? I don't think they'll just let you stop by for a visit. They have televisions there too."

"I need to go there."

"When I looked it up earlier I noticed it borders a pretty big nature sanctuary. Do you mind hiding in the trees?"

"There's nowhere I'd rather be."

He gave the pilot instructions.

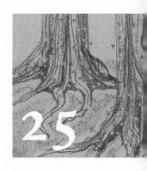

It was a quick and easy landing in a perfect field surrounded by trees bordering Graydon and the Rust Nature Sanctuary. Kellaring had been on since leaving the RV and my wounds were bothering me, but Booker's driver had given me first aid and a great thermal jumpsuit. The sun was setting. It was going to be in the low twenties tonight. He would alert Booker to my exact whereabouts. Spencer was with him, and if they didn't already know my location, I wanted to be sure they had an eye on me. I had no intention of sleeping outside but had to wait for a while before breaking into the mansion.

A stooped man with a cane turned the corner, startling me. I was ready to turn and run but could tell, even at this distance, there was no threat. It was clear he was heading toward me. Maybe this was another mystic; it would be good timing.

"Excuse me, young man." He waved.

"Yes?"

He looked a hundred years old. His hand reached out to touch my wrist.

"Do you recognize me?" he asked.

I stared into his weary green eyes and saw my dad's soul. "I don't believe it."

He smiled.

It was my dad's soul but it was incarnated as Cavanaugh, the man I'd been with at the Pyramid of Kukulkan at Chichen

Itza more than a hundred years earlier. He had killed the attacker who slit my throat and then had escaped. I'd also seen him with Hibbs in the library tunnel beneath Graydon. "How are you still alive? You must be over a hundred."

"A bit more. I'm glad you finally made it."

"How did you know I'd be here?"

"You told me. Or at least the person I knew as you did."

"I'm confused."

"Yes, I should say you are. That makes two of us. Can we sit?"

We found a fallen tree nearby. "I don't know how much you've pieced together of our past lives with Hibbs, but you must know something if you're here," he said.

"I'm not sure what I know."

"Let me see, where to begin... Hibbs had paid for us to go down to Mexico and retrieve the Jadeo. The night before we located it, you told me that I would need to find you in another lifetime and explain the Jadeo to you."

"I don't understand." Obviously Cavanaugh had no idea he'd spent a lifetime being my dad because he hadn't died since the time of Hibbs.

"You had some sort of vision, detailed, very detailed. You gave me three dates and told me we'd meet in the general area around Graydon."

"And this is one of the dates?"

"Yes. The last one."

"Do you know my name?"

"No."

"Then how did you know it was me?"

"You recognized me," Cavanaugh said. "Besides, no one else is around."

"Why did I need you to explain the Jadeo? Do you know Spencer?"

He shook his head.

"Spencer in your lifetime was Hibbs' mistress and was there the night before you took the Jadeo to Oregon. But I know him now. Why can't he tell me?"

"Because he swore to protect the Jadeo and to never reveal its importance."

"Didn't you?"

"Yes, but my first oath was to you."

"Why?"

"You saved my life many times."

"How?"

"It is not important now. Perhaps another time I will tell those stories. I'm old. It has been many years spent waiting since you asked me to deliver this message to you."

"Wait, if Spencer swore to protect the Jadeo, why didn't he just take it from me? I would have given it to him."

"Because he knows that the Jadeo belongs with you. It is your time to carry it."

"What is it?"

His expression became grave, voice hushed, his eyes focused on me. And what he said changed everything. I finally understood Spencer and why it always seemed like nothing really mattered to him other than some mysterious mission that only he knew about. That mission was protecting the Jadeo.

The secrets contained within it were so powerful that they were probably too much for even the purest of people to handle. Did Spencer want it for the Movement? Or did he, too, have reservations about anyone being good enough to handle it? I would ask him the next time we met, but about one thing I was absolutely positive: if Storch got his hands on it, the consequences would be incomprehensible and everlasting. There could be no object more important to humankind than the Jadeo, and it was in my pocket.

26

"Those papers? Oh yes, I remember them, just never knew what they were about. My concern was only ever the Jadeo... but Hibbs considered them critical. You don't think they could still be relevant in this world, all these years later?" Cavanaugh asked.

"Do you think they're still there?" I asked.

"Do you? Only four of us knew about his safe and two of them died before Hibbs. I'm the only one left."

"I'm going in there tonight to check. Will you come with me?"

"I'd only slow you down."

"You could show me the way."

"But you already know the way." Cavanaugh took my hand in his. "Don't be concerned with such old papers. Hibbs himself said they were irrelevant compared with the Jadeo. Your every action should be to protect it." He put a hand on my shoulder and drew me close, our faces inches apart. "Nothing else matters, you must know that."

"But there is a connection."

He looked at me with a confused expression.

"I don't know what it is. But I see things, visions of past lives called Outviews, and even though I don't always understand their meaning, there is one."

His face didn't change. "I trust you know what is best."

I wanted to be as sure as he was. Our talk continued about Hibbs, but it was getting cold. "I'll take my leave dear friend. We'll meet again in the next life. Until then, I'll see you on the astral." I watched him leave, the soul of my father, but not Dad at all.

The worst wounds weren't completely healed, but I couldn't risk making a Lusan. After a couple hours of darkness, I walked carefully to the Graydon library. Night vision was automatic, but I hoped it wouldn't compromise the Kellaring. It was an old door and the lock was easy. They seemed to use the building for storage now. At the shelf, which led to the passageway, my fingers manipulated the latches as if they still belonged to Hibbs. There were no windows in the passage; I found a light switch hoping to stop my night vision.

The tunnel was much as I remembered, but the painting was gone. I managed to locate the gray stone and carefully worked it loose. There it was. I dialed the combination and pulled out the stash of papers. He had lived another twenty-five years after the scene I'd witnessed in the Outview while at the mausoleum. Over that time he'd added to and subtracted from "the proof," as he called them, several times. They were rolled together and tied at both ends by leather bands—maybe a hundred sheets printed on both sides. The safe contained nothing else. My curiosity was charged. I was about to unwrap them when suddenly it became stiflingly hot. Something was wrong. Maybe it was just a school security guard, but judging by the heat, it was more. My night vision must have blown the Kellaring. Loud steps and banging came from the library stairs. I took off toward the house and found two doors at the end of the tunnel. Enough of Hibbs remained in me that I knew one led to a different passage and took it running full speed. It was long, dark and narrow; I was all on night vision. It led to a locked door, which cost precious seconds as I used Gogen. Stairs climbed up to a hatch, taking more time, and Gogen was required to move heavy boxes that had been stacked on top. Finally I emerged at ground level inside the tower I'd seen in the Outview.

Flashing red and blue lights lit the space. I dashed upstairs and breathlessly found my way to the top floor. Agents entered the tower below. The only option was Skyclimbing, not easy without trees. I made it onto the roof just as a helicopter approached, and was about to jump when the TV station's call letters became visible. It was the same helicopter that brought me here. It hovered close and a door opened. I made the risky leap and Skyclimbed toward it. As I crashed inside, Booker's driver yelled at the pilot, "Go, go, go!" The agents on the ground started shooting, but it was too late. We were clear.

I restored Kellaring and thanked him. "This time you don't get to decide. Booker wants you out of the country."

"Do I get to know where?"

"He's got an island near Bermuda, but it'll take a while to cover our tracks. This helicopter was reported stolen about twenty minutes ago. We'll be landing soon."

The chopper came down on a dark deserted back road where a car was waiting. A few hours later we were at a house somewhere in the country. The driver and I wandered through the yard until he found a path that took us to a dock, where another Booker employee waited in a speedboat. He navigated the Chesapeake Bay all night and around dawn pulled next to a small yacht manned by several more of Booker's people. Once aboard, a gourmet breakfast was served, and a woman handed me a *Washington Post*—I was the headline. I clung tight to my pack, which contained the bound roll of documents from Graydon, and checked that the Jadeo was still in my pocket.

That evening we made it to an island about half the size of Cervantes but no less beautiful. I'd slept most of the day and was feeling pretty good when Spencer met me at the dock.

He smiled as we embraced. "Good to see you alive."

"We have a lot to talk about," I said.

He nodded and told me it was safe to use Lusans and finish my healing.

Booker was waiting in a golf cart. "Do you buy these things wholesale?" I asked.

"I own the company that makes them. Want one?"

"Don't know where I'd put it."

"We'll find somewhere. Have to be in a very secluded place though, based on how famous you are."

"I saw the *Post*."

"Oh, it's not just the *Post* Damn near every paper in the country has your picture, as well as the Internet and television. You're public enemy number one. There's a worldwide manhunt for you, kid."

"Am I going to get out of this?" I asked Spencer. "I mean not just stay alive but prove my innocence?"

"They're one and the same, Nate."

"For all the good he's doing for the universe, he's getting damn little help from the other side," Booker said.

"But my dad did help. If he hadn't told me to get out of the RV, I would have been arrested minutes later."

"I asked him to intervene," Spencer said.

"Why can't I talk to him like you do?" I asked.

"Practice and patience."

"Have you talked to my Aunt Rose?"

"No."

"Why hasn't she come through?"

"Souls don't always act as we expect. There are different destinies playing out. Our agenda isn't the single one." He stared off into the distance at something only he could see.

"Speaking of destinies, we need to make a plan for keeping you safe," Booker said.

"You mean there isn't one already?" I couldn't hide my surprise.

"The future changes so damn fast with you that every time we think we have it figured out, the deck gets reshuffled and we have to pick another card." Booker laughed.

"Then let's get figuring."

"I need to deal with a few unrelated things now so I'll have to say goodnight, but I'm here for a few days," Booker said, walking away. "We'll continue this at breakfast."

The change in tempo was jolting. The safety of Cervantes shifted to the turmoil of attacks and pursuits around

Washington, and now, on another Booker island, it was seemingly safe and relaxed. How could anything wait until tomorrow?

Spencer read my mind. "Time's a funny thing."

I stared and shook my head.

"Let's walk," he said. "Your path in this life is not an easy one, Nate."

"Based on my Outviews, most of my lives have been a nightmare."

"Life isn't supposed to be a vacation. Life is hard. But you've had easier ones... Hibbs."

"You were my mistress."

"Yes, we were very close," Spencer replied.

"And we were protecting the Jadeo." He must have assumed I'd learned the name of the Jadeo through my visits to Graydon and the mausoleum.

"The Jadeo has never been more important and never more at risk."

"How many times have I died protecting it?" A floral breeze warmed my face.

"It is a difficult question to answer."

"I'll do it again if needed," I said.

"Then you know what it is?"

I nodded, with long eye contact, letting him read me to see how I learned its secret. "It's hard to believe, to comprehend such a thing exists, and that I've had it all this time."

"I imagine it could be overwhelming when one first discovers what power the Jadeo holds, but your soul has been occupied with this object for almost a thousand years, maybe a hundred lifetimes."

"All of it in an instant, all of it now."

He smiled. "Your soul is beginning to show through. Not just in the powers you use but in thoughts and words. The soul I've known so long is becoming stronger than your personality."

"It's a great relief to you, I can see it on your face."

"It might be just in time." A flight of gulls swooped nearby, reminding me of Tea Leaf Beach.

"I don't feel sixteen anymore."

"You never were."

"But I understand the importance of stopping Lightyear. At least, as much as it's possible to understand something that could so dramatically alter the future of civilization."

He nodded.

"It's funny. I always thought it was about our souls and I just couldn't connect with the mission. But that wasn't it at all. Our souls will be fine, it's the human race that loses if Lightyear wins."

He smiled again. "Our odds get better every time you find understanding."

"Speaking of finding, any sign of Dustin?"

"Nothing."

"Is he all right? We'd have heard if he'd been arrested or... killed, right?"

"I don't know. If they picked him up it might be better for them to keep that secret."

"Will he survive this?"

He looked at me for a moment. "Nate, let's make a deal. Stop asking me about the future because you know it changes all the time anyway."

"Okay, what do I get out of the deal?"

"You get to not hear about a future you won't like."

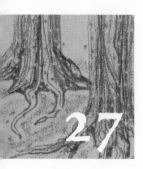

At breakfast Booker was all about making me memorize faces of his employees, men and women, he insisted, who would die to protect me. These were people who could save my life, as long as I could recognize them among the agents and "traitors." He also shared a lengthy list of properties and businesses that he owned around the world, which could be used as refuges. Between my photographic memory and Vising, it was all part of my growing arsenal of knowledge.

Spencer explained that a set of circumstances, as yet unknown, was going to force me back into the world. "This time, the whole world of law enforcement, military and intelligence communities will be hunting you."

"Why can't I stay on the island?"

"They'll find you, even here, sooner or later," Booker said.

"Nothing can be changed while hiding out. You have to engage them, or they win," Spencer said. We strategized for hours, and the end result left me feeling uneasy.

"It's me against the world."

"It's Lightyear against the universe," Spencer said.

Later, Booker lent me a scrambled satellite phone so I could call Mom. She was frantic with the news. "People on TV are talking about taking you dead or alive. Reporters, news trucks, and police have surrounded our house and the restaurant. It's awful. They came in with search warrants and took boxes of I don't even know what. I'm staying at Josh's, but the media will probably find his place any minute. I don't know what to do."

"Sorry, Mom, maybe you should get out of town for a while."

"A while? A while?" she yelled. "Nate, this isn't going to go away in a while. They say you've killed federal agents, that you and Dustin plotted to blow up buildings, bridges. And every channel keeps repeating a video of you walking on water! Are you mixed up with the Chinese government?"

I tried to calm her, but the more I talked, the more wound up she got. "If your father was alive, he'd be so disappointed."

"Why would Dad be disappointed in me?"

"Not you, sweetie. In me. It's my job to keep you safe. He always worried about you and Dustin, overly concerned something would happen to you."

"Mom, it's not your fault. Dad would know that. He does know it. These are the same people who killed him." That sent her into more tears and words I couldn't decipher. Finally, mercifully, Josh took the phone. We spoke briefly, and he promised she would be okay.

The next few days were endless video recording sessions of me describing the truth of what happened since Lightyear first came after me. We left out the supernatural aspects of the story, knowing they would use it to discredit me. With the help of one of Booker's assistants, we added slides and data from Lee Duncan's documents. It ended up being a ninety-minute presentation. The hard drives and discs from the mausoleum contained enough data to help our case against Lightyear, but Booker warned that Lightyear—and the government in general—were masters of propaganda and media manipulation. "In the end, we're going to need nothing short of live TV, Internet feeds, and a massive crowd on hand to get these guys," Booker said. We made numerous copies of all Lee's material and our new video. Booker set a plan in motion to distribute them to multiple points around the world.

Booker returned to the mainland. It was my first chance to bring out the roll of papers from Hibbs' safe. Discussing things from this lifetime with Booker was fine— Lee's stash, Lightyear, even portals and mystics. But for some reason I wasn't comfortable talking to anyone about the Jadeo or Hibbs documents unless they had been there too. Spencer could remember a large number of his past lives without interruption, as if all his incarnations had been one long life. Thanks to Wandus, I was developing the same ability. It made our conversation easier.

"I assumed you went to Graydon for these," he said, when I laid the roll on the table.

"Why didn't you ask?"

"They're yours. And just as I said a hundred years ago, it's the Jadeo that matters, nothing else."

"But these papers are connected."

"To the Jadeo? Impossible."

"Not to the origin of the Jadeo but to the preservation of it. These documents will unlock secrets. They'll give us the way to protect the Jadeo."

"You haven't even opened them."

"I read them on the yacht using Vising and it all came back. I should have taken action in my lifetime as Hibbs."

"They're a distraction."

"Why do you always say that? Just listen."

"I know what's in them."

"Then you know that we can use this information to bring the world's most powerful group to help stop Lightyear," I said, hitting the roll against my hand.

"No."

"Why not?" I was exasperated.

"Because they already control Lightyear."

I looked at him, completely deflated. The implications were seismic, our situation more desperate than ever. "Then we can't win."

"You keep forgetting; the universe is where the power is."

"But the battle is on earth, in the human realm, with humans," I shouted.

"Remember what you've learned," he said quietly.

28

M ost of my time on the island was filled with meditating, wandering the astral, and trying to penetrate the veil that separated the living and dead. I needed to communicate with Dad and Aunt Rose. Spencer worked with me, but his teaching method had always been too much lecturing and not enough practical demonstration. Still, we were getting along better than ever.

It was late morning on the seventh day when a vision of Amber, Kyle, and Linh came. Federal agents ambushed them. It was violent, bloody, and only hours away. Linh was going to die; the others would be arrested. For some reason they were unreachable over the astral. I had to get to Oregon. Instead of arguing, Spencer arranged with Booker to have the jet fly me to Medford. Since soul-powers would alert Lightyear to my whereabouts, hope was my only companion during the uneventful flight. The timing meant it would be possible to just stop the arrests. A car, driven by another one of Booker's men, was waiting for me. Spencer said Booker had four people in Ashland, and there would be three more before I got there. That meant seven against however many government agents showed up to arrest my friends.

There was about an hour of daylight remaining when the plane landed; the vision showed the attack occurring at night, so there was time. Still, it would take twenty-five minutes to get to the Shakespeare theater in Ashland, where my friends were meeting. I told the driver to drop me off at the plaza entrance to Lithia Park. It meant a couple of extra minutes, but agents might already be watching the theater. The door was a problem; the lock was too sophisticated to pick without Gogen. There wasn't time to think. If the agents weren't already here, they would be in the next twenty minutes. As soon as Gogen got me in, I reinstated Kellaring while running into the cold open-air theater. Kyle, clearly startled, was the first to notice me racing down the steps.

"Oh my God," Amber said, following Kyle's gaze.

Linh looked up, smiling, but her smile quickly fell away when she saw my face.

"We don't have much time. Agents will be here any minute," I yelled. "Follow me. The park's our only chance."

But it was too late. A helicopter rose over the center tower of the Elizabethan stage and entered the opening in the roof. This hadn't been in the vision.

"Run!" Linh screamed.

The helicopter spun and fired a small missile as we scattered. I ran toward them, but agents entered from the side. The missile hit as I dove behind some seats. The explosions and screams melded into a horrific noise. I flung Lusans blindly until, thinking there might be enough cover, I peered up and sent flames to roast two agents. Another one fell across from me; four of Booker's mercenaries had arrived. I Skyclimbed to the stage while shots hit all around, and then I quickly scrambled backstage.

Amber and Kyle were across the room huddled around Linh; she was injured. I panicked, but even before reaching her with a Lusan, it was obvious this wasn't the fatal blow I'd seen in my vision. I pushed the healing sphere into Linh's hands. Amber had escaped unharmed altogether; Kyle had some scrapes but would be fine.

"How do we get out of here?" I asked Kyle.

"The best way is back up the way you came because they entered from the street side."

"Let's hide in the tower," Linh said, having spent more time in the place then all of us combined. "There's a way out onto the roof and a concealed ladder down to the street."

"Get on my back," I said.

She hesitated for only a second before allowing me to carry her up the steep steps. Amber was behind me, and Kyle came last. From the top, we were able to see the battle coming to an end. I had no idea where the helicopter was. Among the fires and crater, I counted nine agents, and five of Booker's guys, down. This was a disaster and would bring massive attention and reinforcements soon. We had to get out fast. Kyle helped Linh down the outside ladder. Amber wanted to wait for me, but because our tower location offered a great advantage, I wanted to take out a few more agents before leaving.

"Go. I'll be right behind you."

She stared.

"I need to make sure no one follows us."

"I'm staying with you this time. We don't need to be apart."

"Let's talk about that when we're not trapped."

"Then come down now." I sent flames into two more agents then ran to Amber. "Hurry!" she cried.

She climbed through the hatch that led to the ladder. Everything suddenly vibrated; rotating blades forced a windstorm. I turned back and saw the helicopter deploy another missile and shoved Amber ahead. Then pushed through after her. "Jump!" I yelled, an instant before the rocket hit.

Everything exploded. The tower was obliterated. Steam pipes burst. Splintered wood, metal shrapnel, and glass showered down on us as I bounced off the exterior wall of the theater and hammered onto broken concrete and debris below. Unable to move, blood blocking one eye, I saw Amber crumpled in the grass ten feet away. Kyle ran toward me, his mouth was moving, but I couldn't understand what he was saying. He used Gogen to pick me up and, while draped over his shoulders, pulled Amber up as we passed. She was scoured black and limping, but moving nonetheless. "Where was Linh?" I tried to ask, but all that came out was blood.

I awoke lying across the back seat of a car I'd never been in before. My head was on Amber's lap. Her hands and my face were soaked in blood. She was using Foush, trying to heal me, but time was running out. I was going to die. My last thought was of Linh.

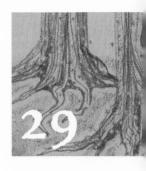

It was dark, the kind of blackness that swallows everything. There was a wisp of breath in my lungs. Human life still existed for me, it seemed. The pain was worse than before, but in fewer places, which scared me knowing that could mean paralysis. With labored breath, people carried my mangled body on a stretcher without using Gogen. The smell of sweat, pine sap, earthy mulch, and moss filled the cool air. Trying to speak only brought a choking cough. A distant voice penetrated my haze. It may have been Amber or it could have been a guide from another realm, even Aunt Rose.

It was maybe a day later, or maybe just a minute—time's a funny thing. Life, if it still existed in my body, was slipping. No other pain remained except an icy burning in my fingertips. The depths of darkness were split by erratic stingings of light. My eyes closed, and when they opened again I knew I was dead. Swirls of colors blurred past while I drifted through space, almost able to touch the stars. It was different than my near-death experience after Fitts had tossed me over the cliff and I had awakened blindfolded on Trevor's boat. This was final.

Amber pulled my body from the tangle of wildflowers, bringing me back to a conscious state. We lay there on the grassy bank of Floral Lake for quite a while before my brain caught up and realized that we were at Outin. I was alive and safe.

"Are you there?" she asked in a gentle whisper, full of hope.

"I think so." My voice sounded strange. I sat up, remembering the attack. "Where's Linh?"

"With Kyle."

"Alive... how bad?"

Amber laughed. "Linh didn't get hurt. She did the hurting. If it weren't for her, we'd have never gotten out of there. Skyclimbing, Gogen, even a few well-placed Lusans—she was a superhero."

"Wow." I shook my head.

"If she hadn't made a Lusan for you to hold, we never would have made it to Outin. It kept you alive, just barely, until Floral Lake could work its magic."

I shivered. I'd come to save Linh and instead she saved me. Something was changing; maybe the mall attack and the girls' deaths could be avoided. "How did you guys find Outin?"

"Crowd."

"How did you find Crowd?'"

"After Linh's performance at the theater, we escaped to Lithia Park. When Linh saw your injuries, she lost it. Kyle got her calmed down. I still don't know if he was using Solteer or if he's just Mr. Meditation and was talking her into some sort of Zen state." She paused and lightly moved her hand through my hair. "Are you up for this story right now?"

"Yes. But I'm a little cold."

She draped a blanket over us. "Better?"

"Yeah."

"So Linh pulled herself together and made a Lusan. It was enough... I mean, Nate, you were minutes from death." She hugged me close and kissed the back of my head. "We had to keep moving. Kyle knew a guy who didn't live too far. Someone from the university, I don't know who, but he lent Kyle a car. Linh and I waited in the trees while the helicopter did flyovers. We could see all kinds of flashing lights in the distance and started hearing cops, agents, soldiers, getting closer. It was intense."

"Yeah, can you just get to the good part?"

She laughed. "The good part isn't until now."

"Crowd?"

"Okay, so while Kyle was gone, I had the idea of getting you to Outin. I remembered your story about Floral Lake being so healing and figured it was your only hope unless Spencer showed up, but he didn't. Anyway, the car was some big Buick or something; we weren't sure it would make it to the edge of town but we got onto I-5 and headed south. I have no idea how we beat the roadblocks, but somewhere around Yreka we saw a hitchhiker. I'm the only one who knew Crowd, and it wasn't until we passed him the third time, in like five miles, that I looked close enough to recognize him. He jumped in the front next to Linh and started giving Kyle directions. Once we got to the parking area on Shasta, he pulled some canvas and straps from his pack and quickly found a couple of downed trees for posts."

"He made a stretcher?"

"Yeah, said we couldn't use powers. We had to carry you."

"What about the Lusan?"

"Apparently that's only traceable when it's being made. Once it exists, it's just energy, like everything else."

"How long have we been here?"

"Three days."

"I must have been just about dead if it took three days in Floral Lake to bring me back. This makes twice that you and Crowd have saved me."

"It's Crowd and Linh. In San Francisco I didn't do anything other than scream. I would have made you a Lusan, but I still can't get much more than a marble-sized one going."

"It'll come. Don't worry."

"I know."

"Where are Kyle and Linh?"

"Looking for Dustin."

"What do you mean?"

"Dustin's here. We haven't found him yet, but he's at Outin somewhere."

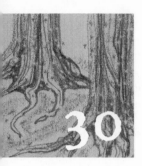

**30**

Crowd hadn't come through the veil when they came to Outin, but he did give them a hand-drawn map showing the four lakes of Outin and the lodge. Between the map and my stories, they had a pretty good sense of the place. Once they had me floating in Floral Lake and could do no more, they took shifts staying with me while the other two went exploring. As soon as they got into the lodge, they saw Dustin's stuff. No wonder no one could find him. He must have come straight here once he left Cervantes.

"Amber, he could have gone through a Window and be living in Paris in 1922, for all we know, or another reality altogether."

"I know. We don't have any idea what's possible here."

"It's Outin, everything is possible... things we can't even dream of."

Linh and Kyle ran up.

"I knew you'd wake up today," Linh said, hugging me.

"So you acted like a great ninja warrior at the theater."

"No, I didn't do much."

"That's not what I heard. You kept me alive... thanks."

"I just did what you taught me."

"We found something," Kyle said.

"Dustin?"

"Not him, but a note he wrote."

"Is he okay?" I was suddenly concerned he might end his life.

"I don't know."

"He went through a Window," Linh said. "At least that's what he says in the note."

Amber eyed me.

"Let me see it." I read silently then handed it to Amber. Dustin found a Window that might allow him to fix some mistakes in his life, made by him and others. He thought, at the same time, he could do some things to help our cause.

"Oh, Dustin," I said. "We've got to find Spencer. Dustin's wandering around some other dimension trying to change things. He'll screw everything up and get us all killed."

"But it's another dimension. How can it affect us?" Linh asked.

"All the dimensions, all the universes, all times are all connected. They ripple in and out of one another."

"It's confusing."

"It's actually very simple: there's really only one thing, it's just that it's infinite."

"That clears it up." Linh laughed.

"What Window did he go in?"

"No clue," Kyle said. "They move you know. There wasn't a Window near where we found the note."

"What's he mean by fifth lake?" Linh asked.

"Maybe he's trying to distract us. All it says is, 'Don't look for me. Instead, go to the fifth lake of Outin.' He really is crazy to think I'd fall for that."

"I didn't know there was a fifth lake," Amber said.

"There isn't. It's his way of trying to throw us off. He has no idea how serious this is." None of them really did. Only Spencer and I knew the truth about the Jadeo. It wasn't safe to tell the others yet.

"How can you be so sure?" Kyle asked. "Dustin was here for a long time. Maybe he found something."

"Why wouldn't Crowd have told us about it?"

"Maybe you weren't ready for it then," Amber said. "Time's a funny thing."

They were right. I was too angry with Dustin to think clearly about his motives or his struggle. "Okay then, we need to find the fifth lake and Dustin. We're safe here, and with Outin's reverse time dynamic, there's no rush. So let's figure out the best way to track down which Window he went through. And if Dustin found a fifth lake alone, then four of us ought to be able to locate it together."

After another dip into Floral Lake under my own power, I felt strong and ready to face the mirrored world of Outin. We drew a grid on Crowd's map. Linh and Amber would stay together but Kyle and I would go out on our own. They still couldn't use Solteer to initiate a conversation over the astral, but I could keep in touch and coordinate all of us.

"Why were you meeting at the theater anyway?" I asked, as we walked toward the lodge.

"I had a breakthrough with the coded pages," Linh said.

"And I found two more of the nine names. Only three to go," Kyle said.

"You guys have been busy."

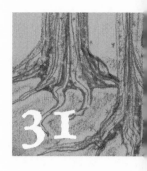

**31**

"The pages each have a separate topic," Linh began. "Because you thought they were connected to Rose, I asked her each night before bed to show me the way to unlock their meaning. On the third night I had a dream about Travis Curry, some kind of expert on Mayan culture and mysticism speaking at the university, but someone assassinated him during a dance. We did a search online, and he really exists and has a book out about Mayan mysticism." She looked at me like I should be shocked and amazed.

"A few months ago, that would have impressed me—"

"Yeah, yeah. Anyway he wasn't really speaking there, but in the dream he was. We saw him and—this part might amaze you—he was Kyle. You know what I mean? Same soul. He and Kyle are the same."

"In the dream or real life?" I asked.

"There's a difference?" Amber asked.

Kyle laughed. "She swears he's me in real life, but we haven't met him in person so speculation would be futile. But the crazy thing is—"

"Travis Curry is one of the names on Dad's list," I interrupted.

"Yep," Linh said.

"So we now know who six of them are: Spencer, Lee Duncan, your dad, you, the Mayan book guy, and some world-famous archeologist."

"But that's not even the best part. In my dream Curry helped us figure out the code. It's based on the old Mayan language, and they used a Trimethius tableau."

"A what?"

"Your dad or someone wrote the pages using a Trimethius tableau," Kyle began. "About five hundred years ago a cryptographer named Johannes Trimethius developed a matrix in order to write coded messages. They laid the alphabet out in a grid, A through Z, across and down with each subsequent row using a Caesar Shift."

I stared blankly.

"It shifts the letters one character. It's complex enough by itself but your dad's sheets aren't just based on our normal alphabet. The twenty-six by twenty-six matrix also uses a key from one of the thirty living Mayan languages. It's like a Vigenère cipher only a million times harder."

"What are you talking about?"

"I told Kyle the details from my dream and his brain, along with a little research, did the rest," Linh said. "Then he got Curry on the phone. But none of that matters right now. The point is, we know what the three pages are." Linh said. "They're all instructions. One addresses the Clastier papers. Rose must have worked on them with your dad. Her journal is only a portion of Clastier's work. The papers have been hidden for hundreds of years, waiting for the right time to publish them. Your dad's sheets say the time is now."

"Another reason for people to be after you, Nate," Amber said, patting my back.

"The next page is about a roll of papers that documents the formation, existence, and activities of a powerful secret group, but not Lightyear. The roll is hidden in a tunnel 'between knowledge and wealth,' But there isn't much more to go on other than the initials W.B.H."

"I have them."

"How? We just found out about—"

"I saw them in an Outview. They were my papers in a past life as W.B. Hibbs."

"You were Hibbs and Clastier? You do get around." Amber said.

I nodded.

"It says the time for their use is soon," Linh said.

"I knew it. Spencer is just afraid."

"If he is, there's probably a good reason," Kyle said.

"What's the final page say?" I ignored his question.

Kyle squinted his eyes. "It's a bit more difficult. It describes what I think is your gold box and calls it 'the Jadeo.' It doesn't say what it is, just that 'all' depends on its safety and continued concealment."

"That's a lot of hidden stuff," Amber said.

"But I'm starting to see…" My body tingled. "The four pages are like a key, a guiding letter from my dad. Three secrets: one's time is now, one is waiting for the right time, and one is not yet time. Wandus explained how it's all totally connected. And even the list of names, they're the people who will help." I was excited.

"Explain it to us slowly," Linh said.

"The pages from Dad's desk, Rose's journal, or what we now know are really a portion of Clastier's papers. Lee's hidden evidence from the mausoleum, the roll of documents from Hibbs' safe, the Jadeo—they are all secrets from the past, revolving around the same thing. It's all about bringing knowledge forward to now. Wandus called it 'many tracks with the same message.'"

"What are they revolving around? What's the message?" Amber asked.

"Our soul."

"That simple?" Kyle asked.

"That complicated?" Amber asked.

"Okay, we're all trying not to get killed… and Nate, we've killed people." Linh's voice dropped. "All this fighting… there must be more to this than just our souls."

"Is there anything more than our souls, really?"

32

The search for Dustin's Window and Outin's fifth lake began when we reached the lodge. For the next few days we were busy discovering and cataloging twenty-nine Windows, each location carefully noted on our expanding map of Outin. A list was made putting Windows into past, present, or future times, some appeared more than once, miles apart. In one, Amber reported watching a ship being built hundreds of years ago. Linh witnessed a spacecraft landing in Peru a thousand years earlier. The glimpses into the future included toxic wars and another one where everyone used soul-powers.

"It's pointless," I said one evening, when we all met back at the lodge.

"Even if we find the Window he went in, he's not going to be just sitting there waiting for us," Amber agreed.

"Then, what do we do?" Linh asked.

"Find the fifth lake," I said.

"So, now you believe it exists?" Kyle asked.

"Yeah. The whole time we've been looking for Windows, I kept having the feeling I'm going to turn around and see the fifth lake."

"Hey, Nate," Linh began, "do you think Spencer knows we're here?"

"Crowd must have told him."

"Why hasn't he come?"

"He probably wants us here. Lightyear's remote viewers can't see us, and because of how Outin affects time in our dimension, what better way to stop the mall attack and save you and Amber?"

"Then why didn't he just leave you here the first time?" Amber asked.

"Impossible to know," Kyle answered before me. "Nate probably needed to do something in the interval, like meet Wandus or Booker."

"Or Luther Storch," I interrupted.

"You know, I've been thinking about that. If people could see what happened at your meeting with Storch, it would expose Lightyear and the public would demand prosecution of Storch and the others," Kyle said.

"Yeah, next time I'll take a video camera."

"But you did. I could use Vising right now and see the whole scene by reading you."

"Great. Then go tell everyone what happened, I'm sure they'll believe you."

"What if I could use Solteer and place the scene, like you did to me with the fire truck that time?"

"I see where you're going. Are you good enough with Solteer to do that?"

"Not yet, but I'm working on it."

"You think it's possible to place the scene in the minds of millions of people?"

"Why not?" Kyle smiled. "But imagine if we could somehow project and record it digitally, like you had a hidden camera. If it's in there and someone else can see it with Solteer, then there must be a way to get it on video."

"Wow," Amber said. "That would shift the momentum to our side pretty fast."

"Everyone would know how evil they are and…"

"It's a great idea Kyle, but until we figure out how to actually do it, let's not get too excited."

"It can be done. I'll find a way," Kyle said. "It's all energy."

In the morning, we practiced. My teaching methods were improving quickly. I checked the map and was showing them which grids to tackle when Amber asked if just she and I could go for a short walk.

"Why do you need to go alone?" Linh asked.

"I just want to talk privately. We don't always have to be together," Amber said.

"Privately? There is no more 'privately' between us anymore," Kyle said.

"They're right, Amber. We've all been through too much together," I said.

"I know, but there's never any time. Don't you see? We're not safe. Any number of things can happen here. This isn't our world and…"

"Amber, what are you talking about?" I asked.

"She wants you to herself," Linh said.

"No, that's not it. But Nate and I were going to find the Calyndra portal. And I think that's what we should be doing. Calyndra can take us to the past. The past, Linh. That's where we can fix things—Rose, Dustin, the whole Lightyear mess."

"We don't even know if Calyndra is real," I said.

"What *is* real?" Kyle asked.

"It's real," Amber said, quietly.

"What do you want, Amber? Should we all stop looking for Dustin and leave the safety of Outin? Or would you prefer Kyle and I stay here, while you and Nate look for Calyndra?"

"It doesn't take four of us," Amber said.

"Unbelievable," Linh scowled.

"Listen, like it or not I'm the leader, so we're going to stay here and keep studying, practicing, and looking for Dustin and the fifth lake. Maybe when we leave Outin we'll go look for Calyndra… together."

"While we're here doing the Yoda-like training, studying soul instead of school, my chances of getting in MIT are vanishing."

"Remember Outin's reverse time, Kyle; you haven't missed any school yet."

"Where does all this time come from?" Linh asked.

"It's hard to understand, but we think of time all wrong. It's a dimension not a line of dates," I said.

Amber laughed. "Kyle, we're not going back to high school. Are you joking? This is way past that. Think about it—all those agents dead at the Shakespeare theater in the *middle* of Ashland. Who do you think they'll pin that on? Nate, for sure, but this time, we were there too, and they know we know everything he does. They'll kill us. We're wanted terrorists. Our lives, at least as we knew them, are over." She walked away toward Rainbow Lake, yelling back at us. "The fate of the world's at stake, and Linh's worried about who Nate's girlfriend is, and Kyle's worried about getting into a good college. High school is over kiddies!"

"What is her problem?" Linh asked.

Kyle put an unlit cigarette in his mouth. "Amber's right." He walked into the lodge.

Linh looked at me pleadingly.

"I'm sorry. It's probably true," I said.

"I guess none of us wanted to talk about it, but our chances of living through this pretty much vanished at the theater. I killed people." Linh burst into tears.

I held her. "We'll survive this, Linh. Remember the future is changing every minute. You were supposed to die that night in the theater, but you didn't."

"I was?" She pulled back, wiping her eyes.

"That's why I came to Ashland because I saw you die in a vision."

"Maybe we really *are* dead, Nate. Maybe we all *did* die that night, and everything since is some kind of illusion." Her voice quivering, "I mean, Outin, what is this place?"

"What, you think this is heaven? Death is the only illusion, Linh. We're totally and completely alive, and we're going to win this."

She surprised me with a kiss, soft and lasting. "I love you, Nate."

At that moment, I believed any response could lead to pain. Instead, I looked away and said, "Let's go check on Kyle."

She tried to hide her disappointment. "What about Amber?"

"Don't worry about her. She's tougher than any of us," I said.

Kyle was leaning against the back wall of the lodge, looking out toward Star Falls Lake.

"I should light this thing," he said, biting down on the filter of his cigarette.

"Kyle, you'll make it to MIT."

"You don't know."

"Neither do you."

"What about Rainbow Lake?" Linh asked. "Amber is heading there. She's been in a few times since we've been here."

"It's always different," I said. "I'm not even sure it always shows you the same dimension."

"Let's go," Kyle said.

"Will you be happy if you see yourself at MIT?" I asked.

"I'll be happy if I see us all alive in a few months." He glared at me.

"If you're so worried, why haven't you gone in yet?"

"He wanted to," Linh said. "But I'm afraid of what we'll see. I asked him not to."

"It's not like a movie of the future. It's contradicting glimpses."

Amber was bobbing in a lemon-yellow-cherry-red-electric-orange swirl when we arrived at the bank. "See anything good?" I asked.

"At least we have sex before I die." Amber smiled. "Other than that, it's no picnic."

Linh mumbled something I couldn't hear.

"Come out and then return in a few hours, it'll change," I said.

She swam to the edge and stood up. I saw the bright colored water dripping off her naked body before turning abruptly. Kyle looked away as well.

"Why so shy, Nate? You've seen me before."

Linh's eyes met mine for only an instant.

"I've changed my mind," Kyle said. "We'll find out the future soon enough."

## 33

W e split up then. I told the girls to stay together but knew
it was unlikely. Each day our grids got farther apart, and
Amber and Linh were now reaching points beyond Crowd's
map. Outin was seemingly endless. I wandered alone among
the most glorious trees that stretched higher and thicker than
redwoods, coal-black bark and tire-sized globe-like leaves
were hundreds of shades of the same color. Each tree came in
different colors—one all in reds, the next all blues, then reds
again, and yellows, oranges—it was breathtaking. They bordered an area we called the "great open." As far as we could
see, the sky-ground rolled into deep canyons and low hills,
filled with blowing sands of glittering black and white stardust, ever shifting into dynamic patterns. So far we hadn't
ventured into the great open because there were no visible
Windows and it appeared as dangerous as it was wondrous.

My thoughts were tense—arguing girls, Kyle's frustration, my mom. Was she safe? After the carnage at the theater,
Lightyear probably picked her up. Wandus had really made me
understand that we have a fairly good idea about what we're
going to encounter in our lifetime prior to being born. Our
souls map out complex possibilities intertwined with everyone else's. I'd been too hard on Mom. If her soul knew that
she'd live a life where her husband would be murdered, that
she'd send her firstborn to an asylum and that her youngest

would become a hunted terrorist, then Mom was a saint. It was time to check on her. I needed Spencer. How much longer could we remain at Outin? And then there were Cavanaugh's warnings about the Jadeo that cursed me, like a thief constantly stealing my thoughts from anything else.

The only thing that could hold my attention was the image of Amber wrapped in nothing but a rainbow sheen of water. She wasn't going back to Ashland—even if it was safe— I wanted her with me. As pastel powdery snow fell, I realized, or admitted for the first time, there was a connection between Amber and me that needed to be explored.

My three friends were my first students. It wasn't fair to count Dustin; neither of us stood a chance in the roles of me as teacher and he as student. Linh had learned the most, but Amber and Kyle were doing well. People in the future wouldn't have that familiarity, and a different approach to teaching might be necessary. At the moment of that thought, I heard a distinct voice, thick with an Indian accent. I turned expecting to see Wandus, but just his words were there. "Outviews hold the key to teaching. Each of your past lives has a lesson. If you can find that meaning, together they will help you understand so others understand, understand?" Aside from levitation, Wandus had taught me two things that had turned my thinking around: all the secrets are connected and the Outviews were more than just random flashbacks.

I tried to teach like Aunt Rose. Whether that would work on a larger scale was in my teetering stack of unanswered questions. Through a dream, Rose may have helped Linh see the key to deciphering the pages from Dad's desk and finding Travis Curry, but Rose had yet to appear to anyone else. She was the queen of the astral, yet I couldn't reach her there. What was I missing? What lesson of hers had I forgotten?

We had to find the fifth lake and somehow yank Dustin out of whichever damn Window he went into. How was I going to help the Movement, teach people to connect to their souls, and defeat Lightyear if I was hiding in another dimension?

I came upon a Window and saw an Orwellian future where uniformed people performed menial tasks endlessly in a life of repression and sadness for the masses, while a privileged few lived in luxury and decadence. I watched and recalled something Spencer had once said: "Imagine a future where you don't need to keep photos or videos, music or movies, books or newspapers, financial or medical records—it's all available online, on the cloud. All monitored and controlled. And all easily taken away."

Amber had seen something in Rainbow Lake. Something kept calling her back to Rainbow Lake, a future she needed to know more about or an incident that she wanted to change. I'd give her that walk alone when I saw her next and find out what of our coming lives she had witnessed.

A muffled shout broke my thoughts, Kyle was charging toward me. "Someone's here!" he shouted.

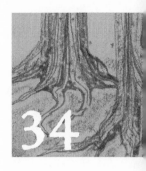

## 34

"What did you say?" I yelled back.

"They're coming." He screamed, gasping, moving his arms, and pointing behind me. I turned and saw nothing, then sprinted toward him. "No," he yelled. "Run, Nate, run!"

Then, emerging from the trees, pursuing him, were six Special Forces soldiers. How did they find Outin? There was an instant to decide—run or fight. Kyle was telling me to run, so I Skyclimbed into the upper branches. Kyle's powers were much more basic than mine, but he'd been practicing and was able to reach me moments later. The soldiers quickly took up positions below.

"Are you okay?" I asked.

He nodded, trying to catch his breath.

"How did they get here? Did someone follow you that night?"

"No. I mean, we were careful. Crowd was with us. If they followed us close enough to see the entrance, how come they didn't kill us that night?"

We were high in Outin's tallest trees, but no doubt these soldiers had come prepared and could use ropes without any trouble.

"It's been five days, that's about ten minutes in reverse time in the regular world. Man, how many ways can they play with that? If Lightyear has access to Outin, we're in serious trouble."

"We're in serious trouble either way."

"Yeah but..."

"Let's get out of here and warn the girls."

"We have to stop them. I counted six. Are there more?"

"I wasn't doing math, I was trying to get to you! Now we need to get to the girls."

"You go. I'll take care of these guys."

"Nate."

"The girls are still looking for the fifth lake. They should be somewhere past the outer Windows. Go."

"You're asking me to choose between helping you and helping Linh."

"It's the same thing. Now go before they attack."

His expression was a ten-minute lecture in a second. He disappeared down through a hundred shades of yellow globes, floating bubbles and chalky black branches. My plan was not very original nor very soulful. But they were here to kill us, there was the Movement to consider, and I had the Jadeo. They didn't know what they were doing, yet they were doing it. Five fires vaporized all but one of the soldiers within minutes. The survivor ran until I pinned him on the ground with Gogen while still seventy yards away.

My first interrogation, and thankfully I was on the right side of it. Reading his past with Vising was necessary because we needed the absolute truth and because he refused to speak a word. What his mind revealed to me was very bad news.

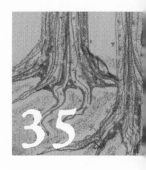

It took more than an hour to catch up with Amber, Kyle, and Linh. They were hiding in a grove of "light trees" we discovered a few days earlier, and because they were visible from a great distance, the grove became our meeting place. The trees shimmered with cosmic light from the stars below. There was a second benefit: it was impossible to see people hiding in them because of their brightness. They'd seen me coming for ten minutes.

I marched my prisoner and used Gogen to pin him to a nearby tree, then I tossed his four weapons on the ground.

"What's going on?" Kyle asked.

"We have a problem."

"Looks like it. What are we supposed to do with him?"

No one spoke.

"Kill him," Linh finally said.

We all looked at her.

"He was sent here to kill us," she said defensively.

"And he knows where Outin is," I said.

"The other soldiers?" Kyle asked.

"Dead."

"He should be too," Linh insisted.

"Killing in the heat of battle is one thing. Executing an unarmed man is another," I said, looking over at the man. He still said nothing.

"I don't believe in killing," Kyle said, "but realistically, what are our choices? We can't let him go. He'll report everything to Lightyear."

"It's unclear whether Lightyear already knows about Outin. The soldiers' mission was to locate us. They had intelligence we fled to Shasta from the theater."

"Where did they get that?"

"Who knows, but our friend over there doesn't even know how they found the veil. He wasn't with the lead group that located it and was the last one through."

"You read him; that's why you let him live?" Amber asked.

I nodded.

"So, do they know or not?" Linh asked.

"Hard to say. They sent a message out with GPS coordinates at the entrance but didn't describe it exactly."

"How would you?" Kyle said.

"So it's possible they may just think we were sighted at that spot and not understand?" Amber asked.

"It's worse than that. They left a man outside, and we need to go out there," I said.

"We're dead," Kyle exhaled.

"Then we have to kill him," Linh motioned to the soldier. "We have no jail, and if we leave him, one of us would have to stay behind."

"Amber, what do you think?"

"I think we should continue this conversation away from him."

I told the man to lie face down, then used Gogen to hold him there. He would have the sensation of floating through space.

"I agree killing is wrong, but we also know no one really dies so there's that. I don't know what to do. We need Spencer," Amber said.

"Spencer would see this as a major threat to the Movement and kill him in two seconds," I said.

"Are you sure? He might have a whole different way to deal with it that we don't know about. Maybe Outin has a portal that just suspends a person or one that sends him to a dimension that makes him a kid again. I don't know. You yourself said anything is possible here."

"Hey, why don't we find some crazy future Window and shove him through?" Kyle asked.

"Who knows the ramifications of—"

Two rapid gunshots—we all hit the ground. I looked up and saw Linh holding an automatic weapon. "We're wasting time. I'll deal with the karma."

"Damn," Amber said, unable to hide her shock.

"The entire U.S. military may be on the way to Outin, and we're debating the life of one soldier. If he could have, he would have shot us all." Linh shook her head. "Now, let's go get the one at the entrance."

Kyle stared at the dead soldier. Blood puddled under his body then seemed to vanish into space. I put my arm around my friend. "You all right?" He didn't answer.

Linh shook her head. "Amber, you want to come with me and get the other one or stay here with the boys? How long do you think he's going to wait there?"

"We do have Outin's reverse time to play with. To the guy out there, they've hardly been gone yet. If we're not careful, we could wind up getting there before they went in."

36

We left the body and headed toward the entrance through a new section of forest. Fearing a possible attack, our steps were slow and cautious. Everyone ignored the Windows we passed except Amber, who tried to get a glimpse into all but the most distant ones. I kept stopping to make sure she didn't fall too far behind. It wasn't surprising when Amber called my name from a Window two hundred feet away, but there wasn't time for any more sightseeing, and I'd given up on ever seeing Dustin again. I waved her off.

"Nate," she repeated. "Come here, now."

"What?" I shouted trying not to raise my voice too much.

"It's Dustin."

Even Kyle began running toward her. The Window was big enough for all of us to see inside. Dustin was walking back and forth across a narrow railing like a gymnast on a balance beam. Near as I could tell, the balcony was at least a hundred stories up.

"Past or future?" I asked Amber.

She shrugged.

"Dustin, can you hear me?" I yelled into the window.

He turned, not more than ten feet from us, laughing, at the same time tears running down his face. "I told you not to look for me. Go do something else."

"What should we be doing?"

"The future isn't all it's cracked up to be, little brother. You might—" He teetered on the railing. Kyle grabbed me before I could leap into the Window. Dustin managed to right himself. "You should concentrate on the past, Nate, cause it's a mess here."

"Where are you? When in time?"

He turned his back and stared down at whatever was below.

"You can actually understand him?" Linh asked.

"What do you mean, of course I can. Can't you?"

"Dustin is hardly even speaking words," Kyle said.

"Huh?"

"I'm in Hong Kong. Nate, America isn't safe anymore." He laughed hysterically, almost ran down the railing, then turned and came back like a circus performer. "There's a portal here that goes to Dubai a year away."

"What year?"

"Nate, how are you talking to him?" Linh asked.

"What?" I repeated.

"It's just the ramblings of a madman," Amber whispered.

Dustin wailed with laughter. "Amber, you're already dead where I am. You and Linh both, but don't worry, there are lots of others dead with you." Tears and laughter.

I was grateful they couldn't understand him. "When is it where you are, Dustin?"

"It doesn't matter, tomorrow, six months, three years... time's a funny thing."

"Help me, Dustin."

"Go jump in a lake." Screams of laughter. But after settling down a little, he explained how to find the fifth lake of Outin and why we needed to go there.

"Come back through. Come back to Outin." I reached my hand into the Window.

"I can't," he sang. "I sailed across an ocean of shame. I waited, but you never came. Outin took me across the road, reaping what I have sowed. You wonder what's in sight. I can't read and you don't write." And he jumped off the balcony. Kyle caught my legs as I was halfway through the Window.

"No!" I screamed. It took all three to hold me back. "No, Dustin!" I kicked and cried, knowing it was too late to save him. I'd been too late to save him my whole life.

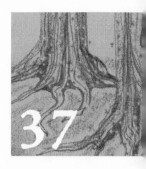

It took twenty minutes before I could tell them about the fifth lake. The whole time they gently coerced me away from the Window. The Outin time difference was working against us because we needed to get out while the soldier was still alone. We knew we should go to the lake, but with a soldier still at the entrance, it was too risky—everything was.

As soon as we exited Outin, I saw Crowd's body, and even before reaching him knew he was dead. Bloody bullet holes stained his chest. I read the scene with Vising. He'd been protecting the area, but even soul-powers couldn't save his human life from the weapons of man. Still numb from Dustin, death didn't affect me as it used to, but Crowd had twice saved me and was much more a friend to me than any of the other mystics.

"Oh, Crowd," Amber knelt next to me and touched his forehead. He had saved her too. His death was a sobering reminder that I was not invincible. Months earlier, Spencer had warned not to be seduced by my powers, but after surviving so many attacks and beating death a few times, my ego was inflated. "He's with Dustin now."

"Crowd and Dustin... What cost, this war?" I whispered to myself, pushing my palm into the blood on his chest. I heard him say, "It has only just begun, Nate."

"Look at this," Kyle hit my shoulder and pointed to broken twigs. "Nate, come on. The other soldier went this way. He can't be far."

I shivered, realizing for the first time how cold it was.

"What? Are we going to track him now?" Amber asked.

I could see a path wrecked through the underbrush. The soldier must have been injured to have disturbed the leaves and pine needles so much. Crowd did some damage before he died. "Let's get the bastard," I said, pushing past Amber.

"Nate, you can't avenge Dustin and Crowd. Let's just get back to Outin and go to the fifth lake," Amber said.

"We need to stop this guy. There's still a chance they don't know about Outin. Let's stick together. Let's finish this."

"How do you finish this?" Amber asked. "How in hell is this ever going to be finished?"

"One step at a time," I said, picking up my pace.

"One death at a time," Kyle said.

"Hey, if you guys don't want to come. I'll go alone, but I think protecting Outin is probably the best thing we can be doing now."

"You might think more clearly if you meditated more," Kyle said.

"I'm thinking plenty clear. If you have a better idea, let me know."

"I tried," Amber said.

"Nate," Linh whispered, stopping and crouching ahead of me. She pointed to our missing soldier, dragging himself behind a downed tree a hundred yards ahead.

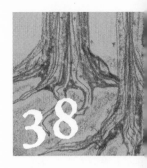

"What should we do?" Linh asked.

"Oh, you mean you're not going to run up there and execute him, Linh?" Amber asked.

"It's your turn, Amber," Linh shot back.

"Shhh. You two remember who we're fighting," I said. We were crouching behind a cluster of young cedars.

"He's armed," Linh said.

"He's injured, and he can't walk," Amber said.

"He knows we're back here," Kyle said.

"How do you know?"

"Because he stopped once he got around that fallen tree. He would have been out by now."

"Maybe he's resting," Amber said.

"A special ops soldier wouldn't stop moving unless he was dead. He's setting up a defense."

"I'll torch the tree."

"Nate," Amber said.

"Amber, we followed him to stop him. He's going to die. Do you think Crowd was trying to give him a hug when he did that to his legs?"

"Crowd wasn't just defending Outin. He was trying to protect us."

"So am I."

"Do it," Linh said.

"Wait," Kyle said. "What if the fire spreads and you can't put it out?"

"Maybe that's the best way to protect Outin."

"I doubt it," Amber said.

"Damn it, do you hear that?" I asked.

"What?"

"Choppers!" I looked at the white sky, Skyclimbed up through the trees, and landed unseen fifteen feet behind the soldier. I then quickly used Gogen to fling him high above the trees. I watched him plunge to his death much as Dustin had. The helicopters were getting closer, coming from the direction of the Outin veil. "Run!" I yelled to the others. For the next five minutes, we ran down hill with no idea where we were heading.

"Nate!" Linh called. I turned to see that Kyle had tripped and was still rolling through the leaves.

"I'm fine," Kyle got up.

"Let's wait a minute," Amber began. "Where are we running?"

"Away from them." I pointed back toward the helicopters. One was landing near the veil while the other hovered. "They don't seem to know we're here yet."

"How long do you think that'll last?" Linh asked, panting.

"They've got us cut off from Outin; we can't go to the car and we're not exactly dressed for the cold," Kyle said, dusting himself off. "We need some help." It started to snow. "This isn't the kind of help I meant." In minutes it went from flurries to heavy snowfall, like it does in the mountains.

"Let's go," I started jogging down hill.

"Go where?" Amber asked again.

I gave no answer because there wasn't one. It was urgent that we move away from the helicopters and at the same time try to get to a lower elevation below the snow line. Beyond that, if we were still alive, I'd figure out where to go. None of them had anything heavier than a fleece, and I was just in a long-sleeved shirt.

It was difficult to tell which way we were heading, even the sensation of moving downhill was lost in the whiteout. I was afraid we might run right off a cliff. At least the helicopters couldn't fly either.

"We need to build a shelter. We can use Gogen," Kyle said. "Keep warm with Lusans."

"No. They can track me."

"We'll die out here," Amber said.

I stopped. We huddled against each other, our faces inches apart. "You can keep Kellaring on. Do you really think they've got enough gifted people to track us all?" Kyle asked. Amber rubbed her hands briskly up and down on my back. I was shaking and finding it hard to think. Linh, although trembling too, handed me a Lusan. We all renewed a bit in its glow. Kyle moved branches with Gogen and was working on a decent lean-to. The pine forest of Mount Shasta in a snowstorm seemed like the quietest place. Night would come early if the blizzard kept up.

Amber stopped rubbing. I caught her glance. "Thanks." Her half-smile revealed she was still upset, but we were fine. Linh and Amber helped Kyle finish, while I got warm and resisted using any powers. Thanks to Gogen, we were inside in less than fifteen minutes, huddling around three Lusans, tossing out ideas on how best to get off the mountain and where to go once we did. I tried to reach Spencer on the astral, but as usual came up with nothing. It was Crowd who would have typically rescued us in a situation like this. And, ironically, the safety of Outin was all around and we couldn't get in. With Kyle's urging, we decided to meditate.

"A solution will come," he said.

Ten minutes later, the silence was broken by a rumbling growl, and at the same time powerful lights swept past.

Kyle peered between the logs and branches of the shelter. "Sno-Cat!" We pushed through the downside and were running again. Before the lights made another sweep we were safely behind a screen of spruce trees. Looking back, there were at least three Sno-Cats working a line, maybe another one in the distance. "What are we going to do?"

"Get out of the snow, keep running down," I yelled.

39

For twenty minutes we fought through blinding snow, dodging trees and stumbling over brush. The Sno-Cats moved much slower, and the distance between us increased. They now appeared more like sinister little toys.

"Wait!" Amber shouted. "I think this is a road."

Amber had spotted a narrow, snow-covered logging road sloping down to the left. The rest of us had run right across it. The road wound down the side of the mountain in a series of switchbacks. The Lusan cradled against my chest kept me from freezing to death. We each had one. They allowed us to avoid exhaustion and also helped with our breathing. Then, suddenly the snow changed to rain. My feet welcomed hard muddy ground. Now we really made time, knowing the snow level would follow us down as the temperatures dropped. The rain was constant. After jogging another hour with no sign of Lightyear, we slowed.

"Do any of you have a clue where we're headed?" I asked.

"Down," Kyle answered.

"Seriously. These old roads can crisscross the forests endlessly. We can't walk all night."

"Walk all night?" Linh said. "We won't be that lucky. There could be hundred soldiers over the next rise. And as soon as this storm passes, you can bet the choppers will be visiting."

"Maybe there's an old cabin around," Amber said.

"I've been asking my guides for help ever since we left Outin and nothing. I don't understand it."

"You'd think if the universe is so powerful, we could get some assistance," Kyle said.

"Listen to you all," Amber said. "Do you mind not wallowing in so much negativity? These Lusans are keeping us warm. Gogen built us a shelter and helped Nate kill that soldier. Even the snow grounded the choppers with their guns and infrared detectors. But I guess you children need someone to hold your hands before we cross the road. Geez."

Amber moved ahead of us.

"She's right," Linh said.

"As usual," Kyle added.

I tried to catch up with her.

"Just leave me alone," she said. "I'd rather walk alone for a while." I dropped back with the others. We strategized on what to do when we inevitably reached a house, town, or highway.

Amber was getting too far ahead and disappeared around a curve. I didn't want to call out, so I started jogging. Suddenly she came bolting back toward us, backlit by headlights.

Kyle and Linh ran into the trees. I waited until Amber reached me. The vehicle wasn't more than six feet behind her when I grabbed her and went tumbling over the edge of the road. Linh and Kyle were hiding somewhere unseen by my night vision.

"Nate," a female voice called from the road. I froze. Peeking around the tree I could see a figure standing in the front of the lights. "Nate, it's Gibi, I'm here to get you out."

"Is it?" Amber asked.

"It sounds like her," I whispered, then yelled, "Are you alone?"

"Of course I'm alone, but if we hang around too long, I have a feeling we won't be."

"Turn off the lights."

As she reached in and turned off the lights, Kyle and Linh found us. "Gibi is the mystic from the redwoods, right?" Linh asked.

"Yeah. Maybe our help has arrived." Without the headlights, my night vision could see well enough to recognize
Gibi. "Let's go, it's her." They followed me to what turned out
to be an old VW van and climbed in back while I got in front.
She turned the van around and drove back the way she came.

"You were just in time," I said, turning up the heat.

"That thing doesn't work. You're better off with your
Lusans," she said.

"Where are we going? Are there roadblocks?"

"The storm is getting worse. It'll help us get out."

"Did Spencer send you?"

"No, he doesn't know I'm here."

"How'd you find us?"

"That's a long story."

"I've got time."

"I'll be happy to tell it to you once we're out of harm's
way."

"You're not really Gibi, are you?"

"No."

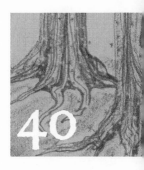

W e were traveling slow enough that leaping out of the car was an option. "How did you know?" she asked.

"Gibi doesn't know Spencer," I said.

"Ahh, yes. Well, let me assure you that you're all quite safe with me, assuming we avoid the soldiers and Lightyear agents. My name is Yangchen." She morphed out of the shape-shifted form of Gibi into a slender Asian woman with long black hair. "I am Tibetan."

"And a mystic?"

"Yes."

"Then why disguise yourself."

"We're extremely short of time. Wasn't I correct that you were not likely to trust a stranger on this day?"

I nodded, but she probably didn't see me. "Do you even know Gibi?"

"Of course. We're very close, and I knew Crowd as well." She took a hand from the wheel and patted the top of my head. "Crowd has crossed over. His life was for you, and he was ready to give it. This is not your fault. You still do not understand much."

"I'll miss him."

"Yes, you will."

Yangchen drove faster than the narrow, edgy roads allowed and was barely paying attention. "Maybe you should slow down," Kyle suggested.

"That would be a good idea if the state police weren't working to block all the roads."

"Are we going to make it?" Amber asked.

"Oh, Amber, let's hope. I've been so looking forward to all the conversations we're going to have," Yangchen said.

"You know me?"

"Many times, my friend."

The wipers couldn't keep up with the sheets of rain. It was impossible for her to see the road, which was fast becoming a muddy, rutted mess. Linh screamed as the van took a turn too wide and rocked over the edge for an instant.

"Are you using soul-powers to drive?"

"Foush." That was no surprise because it was one of the five great powers that controlled and enhanced the senses.

"How are we doing on time?"

"Don't ask."

I let her concentrate on Foush because she was also using Timbal, the power to view time and to read our place in the future, and probably Vising, to help keep us on the road. Yangchen was a powerful mystic.

We bounced along perilously for forty minutes, glad to be drying out and not be walking. For most of the trip, Amber held my shoulder from the seat behind. What I'd give to be back in her room that day she first talked to me about reincarnation and shapeshifting. We veered off onto an overgrown trail and, after a few minutes, pulled in next to a crumbling barn. Gogen opened two wide doors, and we dashed inside.

"A plane," Kyle said. The old dusty turbo prop hardly looked airworthy.

"But we can't fly in this storm," Linh said.

"Isn't there a portal nearby?" I asked.

"We'll be fine," Yangchen said. "But we must go.'"

Kyle, Linh, and Amber squeezed in behind me. Yangchen called me her copilot.

The engine started after a few sputters, and she taxied out.

"Is there even a runway?"

"Should be enough grass. Kyle, would you mind moving the van into the barn?"

As soon as he was back in the plane, the barn collapsed onto the van.

"Did you do that?" Linh was alarmed.

"Yes," Yangchen said, as we picked up speed. Night vision kicked in and I could see we were barely going to make it above the trees.

"Where are our lights?" Kyle asked.

"Too risky," was all she said.

We did get above the trees, but she kept us close to their tops.

"Now, Nate, I need to teach you something that will, hopefully, save us from getting blown out of the sky."

**41**

Heavy rain and snow pushed our plane down while we grazed the treetops. "Now, listen to me, Nate."

"Can you talk and fly this thing at the same time?" Kyle asked.

Instead of answering she tossed him a fresh pack of cigarettes. His had become soggy in the rain. They were even his brand.

"We're in danger," I said.

"No kidding," Yangchen agreed.

"No, I'm roasting hot, it happens when I'm in serious jeopardy."

"It's the heat. It's got two settings: hell-fire and off," Yangchen said, flipping a switch. I exhaled. "There's more to Kellaring than you know," she continued. "There is a way to use all your other powers while still being protected by Kellaring's shield."

"How?"

"It's complex, but by using the energy of DNA, you essentially transfer your human pattern to someone else."

"English?" Amber said.

"You can all do this. You simply use Kellaring, but you loop it around someone with a similar DNA sequence as yours. DNA is an energetic imprint for your physical form and has nothing to do with your soul. But this is how remote viewers find people."

"Wouldn't we need a close relative?" I asked

"Yes."

"My only living relative is my mother."

"She'll do."

"What happens to her?"

"When they look for you they find her instead."

"Forget it."

"Nate, don't you think they know where your mother is at all times any way? She is monitored in every way."

"I can use my sister Bridgette," Amber offered.

"What about us?" Linh asked.

"Anyone related to you will work, but two of you can't use the same person."

"Kyle could use my mom and—" The plane lurched forty-five degrees before Yangchen righted it. "I could use my dad, but are we sure nothing will happen to them?"

"They're already watching them. Maybe there'll be an extra search or two, but your families are Lightyear's best chance of finding you. That's why they've been basically left alone."

"It seems risky."

"Everything is risky. And don't you think, if you asked your parents, they would do anything they could to protect you?"

She had us get an image of our eyes surrounded by white light until they were no longer visible. Then we imagined hugging the person we were transferring our imprint to. It was pretty simple, as most soul-powers were. Yangchen confirmed that all four of us were successful.

"Now, let's see if we can pull up out of this storm." She fought the turbulence. It occurred to me that, although temporarily safe from Lightyear, we still might die in a crash. After a harrowing half-hour we punched through into blue skies and rode above the clouds.

"It's so peaceful up here," Amber said.

"Yes," Yangchen said. "Peace is the only way to our souls." No one spoke for a while.

"Where are we going?" I finally asked.

"There are some people you need to meet."

"Mystics?"

"No, extraordinary ordinary folks from IM, the Movement."

"Will Spencer be there?"

"No. Spencer and I aren't... well, let's just say we don't exactly agree on everything."

"What's that mean?"

"Spencer thinks you've been handling this all fairly well, making good decisions."

"And you don't?" Amber asked.

"No. We cannot reach our souls through violence."

"Wait a minute. These people have been trying to kill me for months. They've killed most of my family. Aren't I allowed to defend myself?" I erupted.

"Of course you can defend yourself. But this does not need to be done with violence or killing."

"They get to kill all they want, but I can't?"

"They are not trying to return to their souls."

"I'm not either. I'm just trying to stay alive."

"What is the point of living in a life preserved by carnage and hostility?"

"So you want me to just let them kill me?"

"If there is no other way."

"Incredible."

"Look Yangchen, I consider myself a pacifist, but sometimes defensive force is necessary," Kyle said.

"Then you're no pacifist."

"That's not fair," Linh began. "Nate didn't ask for any of this. He was just living a normal life six months ago. Then Lightyear started trying to kill him. How can you say he should let them? He'd be dead."

"Life isn't fair."

"And what about the Movement if he weren't around?"

"IM can handle another loss; there have been many."

"If IM is to defeat Lightyear without fighting back that could take a thousand years, maybe five thousand."

"Time's a funny thing."

"You're wrong," I said.

"Then love is wrong."

"Are you sure you're a mystic, or are you really a peace-and-love hippie?"

"Is there a difference? I didn't say you couldn't fight back. All I'm advocating is nonviolence. Adding to the hate, injustice, and violence does nothing but, well, add to it."

"But I'd be dead."

"Would you? How do you know?"

"It's hard to imagine how I could have survived all that."

"Then maybe you should try harder."

"Trust me, they would have killed him by now if he hadn't fought back," Kyle said.

"Okay, Kyle, I trust you. What if he had been? Would that be so bad? He's been dead many times before."

"Can you see the future?" Linh asked.

"I see the changing changes changing ahead."

Amber laughed.

"What about using violence to stop violence. What if killing one Lightyear agent would stop a mall full of innocent people from getting killed?" Linh asked.

"I'm sorry Linh. Killing one more person is making more violence, not less."

"But if it saves the kids?"

"Life's not fair."

"So, what if you could have killed Hitler in 1938 and saved millions of lives?"

"No."

"You're crazy," I said.

"Karma, the universe, God—whatever you want to call it—love, nature, the cosmos... these are all forces far more powerful than me, than my understanding. I trust love."

By the time the plane landed, a half-hour east of Las Vegas, I wasn't interested in talking to Yangchen about anything. A couple of guys got out of a big truck and refueled us. They must have been members of IM because we were in the middle of a desert and wanted fugitives. It was good to stretch and be back on solid ground. Fifteen minutes later we were back in the air.

"It's time to land," Yangchen said quietly, shaking me. It was daylight; the sun might have been up for an hour or so. A stark range of snow-covered mountains stretched ahead. I glanced back to see Linh waking; Amber and Kyle appeared to have been up for a while. We circled above an endless sea of sagebrush. A deep meandering gorge cut through the land. The plane found a narrow washboard road and came to a stop next to a battered old Range Rover. "Welcome to Taos."

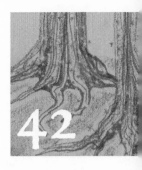

"**B**ut you've been here before, haven't you, Nate?" She smiled. "Not in this life, of course. But Taos was where everything changed for Clastier. It was the second most important incarnation you've known, and I was with you then too."

"Is that why we're here?"

"Perhaps." We climbed into the Range Rover. "Taos has maintained much of the energy that existed here during your time as Clastier. And attracted more. This area is called Greater World. All the houses are Earthships. Every one of them is constructed of tires, old bottles and cans, earth and slanted glass." We drove among structures that could only be described as primitive-futuristic post-apocalyptic. Solar panels sprang up among the dripping dirt towers and windmills.

"Are you sure we didn't time travel?" Kyle asked.

"There are probably seventy Earthships in Greater World and they're all completely off-grid. Each home does its own heating and cooling, catches water, grows food, even fish, and they process their sewage—completely self-sufficient. Makes you wonder why we aren't all living this way?"

"Northern New Mexico has an ideal climate for solar; this town even has a solar powered radio station, KTAO."

We stopped in front of a particularly beautiful one, sunlight filtering through colored wine bottle walls, rich woods, and copper. A man came out of an arched opening. "Nate, this is Tiller Hobson."

Tiller, in worn khakis and a faded sky-blue T-shirt, looked like he belonged in the desert: three days of stubble; curly, dusty hair the color of sundrenched dirt; and dark sunglasses. "Happy you're still alive Nate." He extended a hand.

"Likewise."

He laughed at my response.

"So, is this the headquarters of the Movement?" I asked, looking from him to Yangchen.

That made Tiller laugh again. "No, ha, maybe the headquarters of the peace faction of IM but not the whole thing. Not sure where that would be—an island somewhere probably."

"There are different groups within the Movement?" Kyle asked.

"Hell, get more than three people together for anything," Tiller said, taking off his glasses, "and there'll be disagreements, rivalries... wars." His blue eyes sparkled.

"You're another peace freak, huh? Gonna tell me I've been doing everything wrong."

"Peace freak?" He laughed. "I'm no mystic. I've seen the news reports about you but that doesn't mean I know what you've really done."

"What would you do if someone was trying to kill you?"

"Depends. Suspect I'd run."

"Pretend you were locked in a room and two guys were about to kill you but there was a loaded gun in your pocket."

"Think I'd avoid that kind of room in the first place."

"Tiller, it might help to answer," Yangchen said.

"I'd like to say I would lay down like Gandhi and offer no resistance, but it's hard to know until you're in such a situation."

"Exactly," I said.

"But, Nate, I do believe peace and nonviolence should be pursued at any price. The question is, am I strong enough to live... and die by my convictions?"

"Who's that?" Kyle pointed to a Jeep approaching, leaving a long dust cloud in its wake.

"My bet is it's your friend Spencer," Yangchen said, looking disappointed.

"How did he get here so fast?" Amber asked.

"Portal. They're all over Taos."

"If you two don't get along, then why is he coming?"

"For you."

"Spencer doesn't want you to influence Nate about using nonviolence in the Movement?" Amber asked Yangchen.

"Factions and disagreements," Tiller said.

"Yes, Amber. Spencer believes the ends justify the means. We are both committed to returning to our souls and enlightenment. This, of course, means that Lightyear and others must change; we agree on that, and on many, many things we share common beliefs. But how those goals are reached is where we differ."

"He wants to use violence and you don't?" Kyle asked.

"It's not that he wants to use violence—I think he prefers not to use it—but, he is willing to use it... and I am not."

The white Wrangler was closer now. Although a brisk morning, it was sunny and the Jeep's top was down. Spencer sat in the passenger seat, while a man I recognized from the photos of Booker's employees drove.

"Clastier is our only hope now, Tiller. Will you see to it?" Yangchen said.

"What about Clastier?" I asked.

"You need to know him better. Will you go with Tiller?"

"Where? Why?"

"Spencer will want you to go with him. Please, Nate, ask him to wait. Let Tiller first show you more of Clastier, more of who you are. There is time for this. Please."

I looked at Kyle. "Let's hear what Spencer has to say," he said.

"Remember what Wandus taught you," Amber said. "It's all connected. And all your lifetimes are one to your soul. Clastier is you; that time is part of this. Trust yourself."

Linh was about to speak, but the Jeep arrived.

Spencer climbed out, nodded at me, then walked straight to Yangchen.

"What were you thinking?" he said to her. "Do you realize the consequences?"

**43**

"I did what was necessary."

"For who? You or the Movement?" Spencer asked in a calm whispered tone that didn't match his obvious frustration.

"What's necessary for the Movement is the same for me."

"You believe that, don't you?"

"Hey, would someone like to explain what you're talking about?" I asked.

"When Yangchen decided to kidnap you—" Spencer began.

"I did not kidnap them; I saved them."

"They should have gone back to Outin."

"They were nowhere near the entrance when I found them."

"As if that matters. And what about the advanced Kellaring? What do you think will come of that?"

"Wait... are our families safe?" I asked Yangchen.

"That's not a fair question," she said.

"Seems simple enough to me," Kyle said.

"What do you think Lightyear is going to do when their remote viewers continually report that you're with your mother, Nate? They will keep searching, asking and arresting her. They won't believe she isn't hiding you or doesn't know where you are. These people use torture, and it doesn't even need to be secret; the government sanctions it."

"Is this true?" Linh asked.

"We can turn off Kellaring right now," Kyle said.

"No!" Spencer and Yangchen said in unison.

"Why not?" I asked.

"We'd be massacred in minutes," Yangchen said.

Spencer nodded.

"How can we help them?" Linh asked.

"Is love enough?" Yangchen asked.

"No. Why did you do this?" Linh asked.

"Listen to me Linh. Spencer doesn't know how Light-year is going to respond, but I can tell you this: if I hadn't picked you up, all of you would have died. That is the truth. And I'm sure your parents would rather give their lives so that you could live."

"That's a choice between us and them," Linh shot back. "And Spencer said we were supposed to go back to Outin, so we weren't going to die, right?"

Yangchen looked at Spencer, and he shook his head. She stared out across the sagebrush to the mountains.

"What?" I demanded.

"Linh—" she began.

"Yangchen, no," Spencer said.

"You were going to die at Outin, all of you. Only Nate survived."

Silence. Everyone let it sink in. Spencer and I stared at each other.

"You're unbelievable, Spencer. Is this a game? Are you placing bets on who dies when? On which future we wind up in?"

"Nate—"

"No Spencer, I'm not interested. You were supposed to be helping me save the girls, not letting them walk into a death trap. How do you sleep?" I scoffed. "Come to think of it, do you even sleep? Are you even human?" I walked to the Range Rover. "Tiller, let's go meet Clastier."

Tiller looked at Yangchen, she nodded. Linh followed me.

"Nate, I thought we were beyond this," Spencer said.

"So did I." I got in, slammed the door then rolled down the window as Linh opened the backdoor. "Amber, Kyle, let's go."

"Yangchen, can I stay here? Will they be long?" Amber asked.

"Of course. They'll be back soon."

"I'm staying too," Kyle said. "I want to talk to Spencer... someone has to."

"Why, what's the point? He only tells you what he thinks you need to know."

We drove across the mesa in silence until Tiller turned onto a paved road. "What do you think we should do about our parents?" Linh asked.

"Tiller, can you get a message to them?" I asked.

"Between Booker, Yangchen, and Spencer, I'm sure we can figure something out."

"No, I want you to do it. Do you know someone you trust who can reach our parents? Now that we're beyond Outin's reverse time, Linh's parents will be wondering where she and Kyle are, and Amber's mother too."

"I have a few friends up there. Might be able to do something, depending on the heat. There are probably more feds in Ashland than DC right now."

"I appreciate you trying. Once we get back, we'll sit with the others and come up with a message."

We crossed the gorge I'd seen from the air; it was even more dramatic up close. The Rio Grande washed through, 700 feet below, providing a stunning backdrop for a surprisingly large portal visible only to me. We were approaching town. Linh was tense, we stopped so I could go back and sit next to her. "I don't want anything to happen to my mom and dad."

"I know. We'll figure it out. I'm sure Kyle is pumping Spencer for every possible way to protect them right now."

"Amber is probably doing the same with Yangchen."

"Definitely," I said, while wondering the real reason Amber stayed behind.

Tiller parked in a dusty lot behind several small adobe buildings. We followed him around the corner and up the street until he stopped at a window to talk with a Native American woman. Another twenty-five feet and, quite unexpectedly, I was staring at a thousand-year-old Pueblo. It was the first time I'd visited the site of an Outview, and it was more than I could handle. I collapsed to the ground.

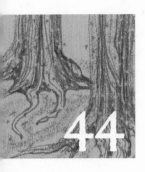

44

Tiller and Linh managed to get me to a bench. I was dizzy with Clastier's life and words. It came not as an Outview but as memory. The taste of elk and roasted chilies I'd never eaten, the fear and love of the Catholic Church, candlelit discussions, all came back as if I was thinking about the slide on my first-grade playground. Clastier's passions and beliefs were mine. Thomas Mercer and Tagu, who had done so much to assist me/Clastier, were familiar to me in their appearances and personalities, even the sound of their voices. They were friendships greater than those of Kyle, Linh, and Amber.

I recalled angry meetings with the bishop and fellow priests, pleading with me to recant, and the day a stranger approached me at El Santuario de Chimayo, saying the Catholic hierarchy would soon banish me and then order my imprisonment and death. The stranger was Spencer in another incarnation. It was our only meeting in that life. On the long journey back to Taos, I/Clastier had planned my escape. That evening a priest, who'd been a lifelong friend, hid me in San Francisco de Asis Mission Church, where I remained hidden for several days until it was safe for Tagu to arrange for my refuge at Taos Pueblo.

Linh and Tiller listened to me babble about my life, nearly two centuries earlier, before Tiller suggested we find the room I stayed in as Clastier. Remarkably, I knew just where it was, now a tiny shop selling Indian jewelry and pottery. An old woman nodded as we entered. The fire burned in the same place it did when I was there as Clastier, and the scent of cedar and piñon pushed me into that life, as mine as Nate dissipated with the wood-smoke. I sank to the floor and, to everyone's surprise, spoke to the woman in the native language of Tewa. She looked at me, concerned. I gulped the stale air, trying not to pass out, and told her I wasn't feeling well.

"The walls speak," she looked around, waving, grinning a toothless smile. "Remember things they tell you. For a thousand winters the smoke has carried a message to the sky."

I thanked her and asked if it would be okay to stay a while. She nodded. Linh and Tiller wanted to know what she said and if I was all right. Linh told me later they waited outside for over two hours, while I sat in contemplation, recalling Clastier and his/my writings from that lifetime. The philosophies so threatened and angered the church that, to this day, the destruction of any remaining Clastier papers, is still a priority of the Vatican.

When I emerged, I peered at Linh and Tiller, expecting Tagu and Thomas Mercer. I looked up at sacred Taos Mountain, recalling the Outview of me fleeing along the narrow river, miles up through pine forest before reaching Blue Lake. It was all so immediate: the leathery smoked scent from elk hide, the fear in Tagu's voice as he warned of the Bishop's posse, the ache in my calves. As I wondered how I'd been tangled into so many secrets and hidden knowledge, "it is all connected, the knowledge must see light," Wandus' words echoed.

Tiller interrupted, "Nate, do you understand why I brought you here?"

"Yes. And thank you."

"Why?" Linh asked.

"The core of Clastier's philosophy was peace."

"What would *he* have done against Lightyear? Could he have stuck to nonviolence?"

"In many ways the opposition I faced as Clastier was a stronger force than Lightyear. The Catholic Church had been the single greatest power on earth for hundreds of years, controlling kings and conquering lands, shaping the world we know today."

"What happened to Clastier?"

"You can see, he lived again as me and others. But the real question is what happened to his teachings, the writings?"

"Well?"

"Thomas Mercer got them out of New Mexico and hid the papers back east in North Carolina."

"Then what?"

"I don't know."

"But you could recreate those, couldn't you?"

"The authentic papers are needed, if they're to have an impact."

"Can we find them?"

"That doesn't appear to be my destiny," I said, crouching in the dust. "I have things far more important to risk my life for. My lifetime as Clastier has taught me much, but his teachings are on their own."

"What about Rose's journal?"

"I don't know if those pages were to lead me here, or if they have something to do with stopping Lightyear."

"So, is Yangchen right and Spencer wrong?"

"Clastier thought it best to avoid judgments like that. Peace *is* the path. Our soul cannot be reached through violence."

"So, we've been wrong?"

"No, we've been learning."

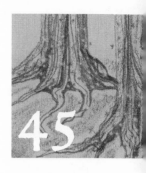

45

When we returned, Tiller gave us the key to his Earth-ship. Kyle and I would share one room, Linh and Amber another. Fresh clothes and jackets awaited on soft futon beds. We all wrote messages to our parents, careful not to say where we were. Tiller promised he would do his best to see them delivered.

"I asked Spencer why he was going to let us die at Outin when he had promised to help save Amber and Linh and stop the mall attack," Kyle said, once we all gathered again.

"I'll bet he had an interesting answer."

"He did, I wish I could explain it like he did but—"

I interrupted and in my best Spencer impersonation said, "I'm trying, but it's very challenging—juggling and weaving through dimensions..."

"How'd you know?"

"I can read minds, remember? But you don't need to be psychic. I've heard his excuses so many times." I walked over to the large built-in planters where vegetables were grow-ing and marveled at indoor trees, heavy with fruit. "And you know something, I do believe he's trying to help. He knows so much more than I'll ever understand about fate, destiny, time, and dimensions. It doesn't make sense that he's not the one supposed to be leading the Movement." I sat on a small stool next to a pond full of fish. "But he and I aren't always going to agree on the best approach, and I'm not going to leave our lives in his hands anymore."

"Then what are we going to do? Who are we going to trust?" Linh asked.

"Me. We're going to trust me."

"Okay," Kyle said.

"I think that's a great idea, Nate," Amber said. "You haven't met all these mystics by accident, including Spencer. They're here to help you, even die for you, like Crowd."

"I know. His death will always keep me humble."

Work occupied us for the next few weeks. December was mild in the high desert. We pounded dirt in tires for a new Earthship and tended indoor gardens, which grew a large amount of the food we were eating. I trained seventeen people in basic soul-powers. Even before the introductions, these people knew me. It wasn't just the media reports; I was a legend in the Movement, tracing the origins of stories about me became a hobby of Linh's.

The advanced Kellaring was working so well that I started to relax for the first time since Cervantes. Teaching the others was difficult, but Yangchen also taught me a few new tricks. Many were beyond her capabilities, but I could do them as one of the seven. They would take practice, but she reminded me how to strengthen or weaken the powers of others; the way to manipulate water, light, shadows, and darkness; and the technique to change objects temporarily, or even permanently. Each time I learned a new power, the next one came easier; that was the promise of the five great powers.

Kyle said Spencer wouldn't leave without me, but he didn't want to have "another unnecessary confrontation." Still, there were large periods of time no one seemed to know where he was. Kyle, the girls, and I meditated several times a day, and it helped find a calm center to rely on. Spencer and I had been through too much over many lifetimes, and it was complicated, filled with trust and mistrust, competition and collaboration. I needed to know more and was determined to

work with him in this life to help the Movement and defeat
Lightyear, both necessary to achieve goals of keeping the girls
alive, protecting the Jadeo, and getting Clastier's work out.

Yangchen said it was fortunate that no one had recognized me at the Pueblo, but from then on, when outside
Greater World, I'd shapeshift into a freckled face and curly
red hair. With practice I could hold the "shape" for hours
and it left me only mildly tired. Kyle and the girls were also
able to do short periods as long as they didn't deviate too far
from their true form. But the most important thing Yangchen
taught me was how to take Kyle's theory of using Vising to
read me and project my experience to others. In that way it
was possible for Kyle, Tiller, the girls, and Yangchen to see me
meeting with Storch. It was a major step because if enough
people could see the damaging meeting, Storch and Lightyear
could be brought down.

Yangchen agreed that if there were a way to somehow
record the scene so it could be shown online and televised,
IM's victory would be assured. "There's only one individual
who could possibly figure out how to do such a thing," she said.

"Who?"

"Spencer Copeland."

"Let's go talk to him."

"We can't. He's not here."

"What? I thought he wasn't leaving without me. When's
he coming back?"

"He didn't say when he'd return," Yangchen said, with a
grave look on her face. "But if Spencer is willing to leave you
here alone with me, then whatever took him away must be
critical."

46

Waiting for Spencer to come back was painful; his absence heightened our concerns about our families and the mall attack. But Tiller was monitoring the media and said nothing unusual was being reported. Thinking of doing any of this without Spencer left me anxious. He and I were interconnected, and as angry as he made me, there was no one more important in my life.

I took to meditating while levitating over the gorge at night when I couldn't be seen. The portal I'd spotted on my first day was one of several. Yangchen claimed not to know anything about them, but I wasn't sure she was being honest. It would be too dangerous to explore them without knowing more. I could wind up anywhere, in any time.

Thinking about Clastier also occupied my thoughts. It was liberating to recall a lifetime without an Outview, but something blocked my view of Clastier's later existence and I needed to know how he died.

The four of us often began our days at one of the several hot springs along the Rio Grande. We would meditate or talk about powers, occasionally bringing up our happy lives before Lightyear. That was tough for everyone, so we never dwelled on it.

Tension between the girls had reduced, and we all talked of our commitment to IM and following a nonviolent path.

How that resolve would be tested, if and when we were forced back into the "real world," was something that nagged at both Linh and me. Kyle would have been willing to avoid using force without question, so long as Linh wasn't in danger. Linh, on the other hand, would most likely resort to violence if any of us were threatened. One morning, she and I wound up at the hot springs alone. Kyle had worked late helping to engineer a solar system for one of the Earthships, and Amber was on one of her many walks with Yangchen.

"I have a feeling we're going to have to leave Taos soon," Linh said.

"Why?"

"Spencer's been gone for eight days. It must be something awful."

The spring was small, and we were alone. I put my arm around her, our naked bodies pressing in the velvet water. She turned, the delicate beauty of her face framed by rising steam. Her deep eyes penetrated mine as we tried to read each other through the emotional turmoil of our lives. Then a kiss, brought on by pent-up passion. We'd been running scared so long that in the starkness of our plight that moment was a blissful dream. It was tragic when it ended. We stared at each other.

"We should meditate," Linh said. The sun was rising over the Sangre de Cristo Mountains, but the gorge remained in dark shadow.

"I don't feel like meditating," I said and pulled her close, kissing again.

"Stop, it's not fair."

"To who?" I asked.

"To us. To you and Amber."

"What?"

"She loves you so much." I recalled Amber naked in San Francisco telling me how much Linh loved me. Girls were weird.

"Linh, you love me."

"We've had our time, in another life," she said softly. "Rose told me that day she did a reading for me."

"Just because we've been together in a past life doesn't mean we can't be together again. Ever hear of soul mates?"

"Ever hear of star-crossed lovers? I think this time you and Amber are meant to be."

"Oh great. Amber thinks you and I should be together, and you think Amber and I should be. Don't I get a say in the matter?"

Linh giggled. "What do you have to do with it?"

"Nate, Linh, are you guys down there?" Kyle yelled from the trail.

"Yeah," I answered reluctantly.

"Spencer's back."

We dried off and dressed. Just before we reached Kyle, a thought crossed my mind. "Linh, don't do anything crazy to try and protect Amber. She can take care of herself."

"We watch out for each other. Look at all you've been doing to try and stop Amber and me from getting killed by Lightyear."

"That's different. Promise me you'll save yourself first." She was quiet. I stopped and held her shoulders so she'd have to look at me. "Linh?"

"We each have a purpose."

"Promise me."

"Nate, come on. Spencer's waiting," Kyle's voice was stressed.

"We'll talk about this later," I said, as we Skyclimbed out of the gorge.

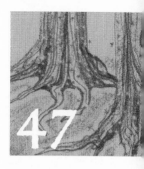

47

We gathered in Tiller's Earthship. Spencer looked tense. "I'm sorry to have to tell you that Linh's parents, Nate's mother and Amber's sister were arrested yesterday by the FBI."

"Are they okay?" Kyle asked.

"When?" I asked.

"What about Bà?" Linh was working hard not to cry. She was even closer to Bà, her and Kyle's Vietnamese grandmother, than to her parents. We all knew that the only ones targeted were our DNA matches we used for the advanced Kellaring.

"And my mother?" Amber asked.

"Bà and Amber's mother have not been picked up."

"Where have you been all this time?"

"Trying to stop it from happening, but there were too many intertwining destinies coming together."

I nodded, seeing the strain of his efforts on his face. He was expecting an explosion from me. "Thank you for trying. What can we do to get them out?"

"It won't be easy. Apparently their plan is to hold them until you surrender."

"There must be something we can do."

"Our best hope is to expose Lightyear. Anything else brings more risks."

"Aren't there portals? Or couldn't we use Outin's reverse time?" Kyle said.

"What about the Calyndra portal? Do you know where it is?" Amber asked.

"Outin's reverse time would just lead us into a loop in this case. That is to say we would keep winding up with them arrested and us pushing back time to stop it, and so on. Other portals might offer possible angles to change things or free them, but it's too complicated."

"And Calyndra?"

"Calyndra, assuming it still exists, presents so many opportunities to change the past, present, and future that it boggles my already boggled mind. But you should stop wasting time thinking about it. No one knows if the legends are true... there are mystics and seekers who have searched for lifetimes only to wind up lost or wasted."

"Then what's our quickest way to beat Lightyear?" I asked.

"Are you really willing to give up on Calyndra without even trying?" Amber asked.

"And trying other portals?" Linh asked.

"There are so many portals, and like Spencer says, we could spend a lifetime and still get nowhere. Exposing Lightyear achieves everything we want and is something we can do."

"Can we?" Linh asked.

"Tell Spencer about the Vising of the Storch meeting."

Before I could respond, the eureka-look on Spencer's face told me he understood, hadn't thought of it before, and that it might be possible. "Show me the meeting," he said.

I opened and allowed him to read me. He smiled. "It's hard to believe he said 'If you insist on fighting us, I'll blow up a mall, or an airplane... and I'll blame it on you.' and 'People are expendable—do you know how many are born every day? We're sure as hell not running out of them.' Incredible," Spencer said.

"Can we get it on television?"

"I believe there's a way."

"Let's do it."

"We need help."

"Who?"

"Gibi and Dustin."

"But Dustin's dead." I cried.

"That's not true," Spencer said. I was puzzled how he didn't know.

"I'm afraid it is. I saw him jump off a building."

"We all saw," Kyle said. "Through a Window at Outin."

"Things aren't always what they appear, especially in Outin."

"But we saw him," Linh said.

"I'll bet you didn't see him land."

"No," I said, remembering. "Is my brother still alive?"

"Yes."

"You've seen him?"

"I don't have to. Every life has a physical energy, and when it is gone the entire energy field of the planet changes. His change has not been made. Dustin is alive."

**48**

"We need to find Dustin," Linh said.

"Story of my life." I was almost giddy.

"Nate, if you go back to Outin—" Yangchen began.

"Leave this alone." Spencer interrupted.

"I will not." Yangchen was firm. "Nate, you will land in a battle the likes of which you have never known, and in that fight you'll face a choice of death or killing, and you cannot kill again."

My eyes met Spencer's. They answered my unasked question.

"Is there a way to find Dustin without going to Outin?"

"Nate can stay here, I'll go," Amber said.

"Me too," Linh added.

I was stunned.

"And me," Kyle said.

"No, not without me."

"You don't always have to be the hero, Nate," Kyle added.

"Won't they face the same dilemma?" I asked Yangchen.

"I would need time to see."

"Their journey would be different, but they would easily find trouble," Spencer said.

"And what would you do? " I asked Kyle.

"Thich Nhat Hanh says, 'At any moment, you have a choice, that either leads you closer to your spirit or further away from it.' Do you understand?" Kyle looked deeply at me. "We can no longer use violence against them."

"Nate was asking you what powers you would use," Linh said. "It's my parents, Kyle. We have to do whatever is necessary. Lightyear has no morals. Are you willing to sacrifice my father, the man who saved you... for a concept mankind can't even accomplish?"

Before Kyle could respond, Spencer interjected, "We cannot defeat Lightyear in this lifetime without using violence. It's a machine."

"At what cost?" Yangchen asked.

"A cost that is minuscule compared with the price exacted by our failure," Spencer said.

"We can convince ourselves of all kinds of things, even that doing terrible harm is okay," Yangchen said.

"Terrible harm? Shall I detail the crimes of those who support Lightyear?" Spencer raised his voice. "The horrific truth of Lightyear is more than these children can take, Yangchen, and you stand here while their remaining families are facing torture and execution because of your direction—*your* direction! And you ask them to sacrifice all that is dear to them in order to uphold your idealistic utopian vision. Can you at least ask them?"

"Ask us what?" Linh's voice quivered.

Yangchen was silent.

"Ask them what you want them to do," Spencer pressed again. "Tell them that your path can only lead to one unimaginable ending."

The four of us stared at her. She was breathing deep and slow, eyes closed, trying to find the right words. Spencer didn't give her the chance.

"Ask them, Yangchen. Are they willing to die along with their parents, siblings, and even Bà?" He paused to let it sink in and turned to us. "Nonviolence leads to death. No survivors, no second chances, just death. That's the price."

"No," Yangchen whispered. "Death is no price at all. Death is nothing." Her voice deepened. "Violence leads you away from your soul, far, far away. That is the price. And that price is too high!"

Spencer shook his head. "And what is the cost of letting this go on for centuries more?"

"I'm going to Outin," I said.

"Spencer is wrong," Yangchen said. "Crowd would still be alive if you had followed nonviolence."

"I'm sorry about that," I said.

"Don't be," Spencer said gently. "Crowd knew he would die for you. It was his destiny."

"Is it mine?" Amber asked.

Spencer studied her and nodded so subtly that only Amber and I noticed.

"It doesn't have to be," Yangchen said.

"I'm sorry, Yangchen," Linh began, "but I will use violence and whatever else to save my family and that includes Nate. I'm not Gandhi or Jesus. I wish turning the other cheek was in my nature. I may look like a sweet young girl, but there's a warrior inside."

"Linh, you're a beautiful soul, but you must know that love never kills. It cannot. If it does, it ceases to be love," Yangchen said.

"Let's get ready to go," Spencer ordered.

"I need a few hours," I said. "There is one more thing Clastier needs to show me."

"Clastier? Nate, don't get distracted."

"I'm trying not to. But Spencer, it's all connected." He stared at me.

"Okay, we'll leave at sunset." It was clear that, in spite of his earlier protests, he knew I was right. It was increasingly possible that Clastier learned of the existence of the Jadeo, Hibbs discovered the Clastier papers, and both of them got a glimpse into the future where Lightyear would be the greatest enemy of enlightenment. Among their papers, they left clues for me/their future self to finish the work commenced in their lifetimes. If there was any hope of beating Lightyear, I needed that information.

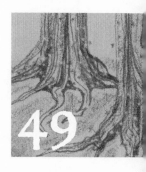

49

With the morning still brisk, I went alone to the gorge, the site of my last memory as Clastier, nearly two hundred years earlier. I/Clastier had convinced Thomas Mercer to take the papers in a final attempt to preserve my discoveries and philosophy. While the Church was pursuing me, he could escape through the Cimarron cliffs to the Great Plains and make his way east. Tagu and I were en route to Colorado when the posse spotted us on Hondo Mesa. We dove into a ravine leading to the gorge. Now, as Nate, I levitated in the same place, trying to recall what happened next.

"Come here, quickly," a familiar voice called. It was Yangchen. I soared over to her, but she didn't acknowledge me. I turned to see who she was yelling at and saw Clastier and Tagu running toward us. They had just jumped into the ravine. Since I'd never seen beyond that, I assumed Clastier was about to die.

"Clastier, you must follow me," Yangchen said, as they reached her. The area looked exactly as it did in my time, except the Gorge Bridge was missing.

"Who are you?" he asked.

"I am Yangchen, a friend you must trust," she said, taking his hands and staring deep into his eyes. The horses were storming across the mesa; the posse was more than thirty strong.

"Tell us what to do," Clastier said.

Tagu looked at him with only an instant of concern. He trusted Clastier and if Clastier trusted this woman, he would not question it.

They followed her along an edgy path, forty feet from the top of the gorge, still six hundred above the rushing Rio Grande and jagged rocks below. Even with my Skyclimbing and levitating skills, I was nervous trailing behind them. They reached a ledge with just enough room to stand. "Now where? We're trapped," Clastier said, searching for a way to climb out. "Surely the Church's men are in the ravine by now."

"Yes," Yangchen said. "Do you truly believe what you have written?"

"Of course. I've given up everything, risked all that I am. Is that not proof enough?"

"Then you should have no fear."

"I fear not for my life, only that my work continues, my discoveries shared."

"But Thomas Mercer has already reached the Cimarron Cliffs. Your writings are on their way to good hands in the east."

"How do you know this?"

"I am not from this time."

Tagu studied her.

"You have theorized about passages between times and worlds. You understand that the life of a man is not even a flickering to the soul."

"Yes."

"It's all true. All that you have dreamt, everything you've written... and more."

Clastier's eyes filled. "C'est vrai, je savais que ce," he whispered.

The hoofbeats of the gathering storm thundered as the posse rode along the edge of the gorge. At the same time, half a dozen men were just three hundred feet behind us. There was no escape. This is how Clastier was going to die. Yangchen must have been there to simply let him know he was right. But why didn't she help? Dying a martyr did nothing for his cause. History had forgotten Clastier. He could have been much more important living, advancing knowledge of the soul by two hundred years, possibly negating the need for much of the barbaric suffering of the twentieth century. Why wasn't he helped? The men continued toward us.

"You must jump," she said.

"What? I'd rather not take my life. If they want me dead, they must do it."

"I did not say anything about suicide."

He and Tagu looked at the approaching men, and then Clastier peered over the ledge. "No chance to survive that leap." His eyes burned.

"They will be upon us in less than a minute. As you have written, life is not always what we expect. The truth of life is in the unknown. You must leap to understand what you know." She looked at him one last time. Yangchen possessed a serenity that was as powerful as any force I'd encountered.

"You needn't come, Tagu," Clastier said, then quickly whispered a prayer in French, "The stars bring the truth." He jumped. Tagu followed immediately.

Yangchen turned to me. "You too, Nate. I can't see you, but you are here."

Surprised, I tried to respond, but she couldn't hear me. I slid past her and looked down into the gorge. "It all makes sense," I said, then somersaulted off the ledge.

50

The Milky Way embraced me as I picked my way through the sagebrush toward Greater World on a freezing winter night. It was impossible to know how much time had passed since I'd gone to the gorge. I was in no hurry to return to the pressure of the Movement versus Lightyear, but I knew my friends would be anxious, even Spencer. A few minutes later, as the light from Tiller's Earthship came into view, so did a silhouette, almost gliding, his arms flowing slowly back and forth. It could only be Spencer.

"Happy to see you," he said.

"How did you know I'd be returning tonight?"

"I didn't. I come out every night, hoping."

"How long was I gone?"

"Just over two weeks."

It was longer than I'd thought.

"We'll need to find another favorable time to leave Taos," Spencer said.

"Everything okay here?"

"Is that a trick question?" He laughed. "Lightyear hasn't done anything too bad, but all your folks are still being held. Kyle, Amber, and Linh have been pretty worried, not just about them, but you, too."

"I had no sense of time. Did you think I was dead?"

"The energy field remained strong; your change had not been made." He hesitated. "Yangchen was gone too."

"She should be along soon," I said, leaving him unsatisfied. Spencer was keeping his cool better than I would have guessed. He'd spent two weeks wondering where I was, knowing his rival was with me, imparting her influence and philosophy over his. He was right, she had.

"There are two sides, Nate, and the truth often lies in the middle."

"No more violence."

He stopped walking and stared at me, almost pleadingly. "I cannot see a victory. Do you understand? Into ten thousand futures I have gazed, looking for a way without using violence, and there isn't even a dream of it."

"The future changes every instant. You should keep looking," I replied.

"Nate, I'm against all forms of violence, but it's a matter of trade-offs."

"I know. And I'm not saying there won't be mistakes made. We can't control everyone in the Movement. But I can lead by example and renounce violence. I need your help Spencer, please."

He gazed long into the heavens. "Let's hope you're right."

"The truth is in the stars," I said, relieved.

"Yes, it is."

The hugs and kisses I expected when we went inside turned out to be angry questions. "I'm sorry. Yangchen took me on a strange journey. I was remembering my life as Clastier, and suddenly he appeared with her."

"You've been gone for weeks. How did we know you weren't dead?" Linh snapped.

"Didn't Spencer assure you I was alive?"

"Even if we believed him, it could change in an instant. Half the world is hunting you," Amber said.

"Welcome back, Nate. I wasn't worried about you at all." Kyle winked.

"There aren't any phones in portals. It didn't feel like more than a day to me. We wound up in this forest up in the mountains."

"Who?" Amber asked.

"Yangchen, Clastier, me, and Tagu, who's this really wise Indian that helped Clastier."

"Yangchen was in Clastier's time? How did she get there?" Linh asked.

"She went back in time... through Calyndra."

Spencer let out a deep audible sigh.

Amber looked straight at me. "I knew it. Where is she? When can she take us?"

"She said that once you return from Calyndra the entrance moves and is no longer visible to you. Like a one-time shot."

"And she used it to meet you and Clastier in the woods?" Spencer asked.

"It was more than that. She saved Clastier."

"And indoctrinated you," Spencer said quietly.

"How did you get back?" Kyle asked.

"It's hard to explain—"

Spencer interrupted. "He traveled through an Outview. We can all visit past lives, but to interact with them, to actually sit down and have a conversation with yourself in another life, you need to find a portal into that lifetime, and not just any portal will do. Did Yangchen show you one?"

"Yeah."

"It's a time-transcendence portal," Spencer said.

"Like Calyndra?" Amber asked.

"Not really," Spencer began. "Calyndra supposedly can take anyone back anywhere, and back again. I can't imagine a more powerful portal. A time-transcendence portal is more like a chat room. You can sit around and talk to yourself. Nate could tell Clastier about the future, and Clastier could explain all kinds of stuff to Nate from that life. It's new to both of them and only available to a shared soul."

"So, we still can't get to Calyndra?" Linh asked.

"I don't think so," I said.

"But we know for sure it's real. And we know someone who found it. Yangchen may not know just where it is now, but she knows how she found it and will help us," Amber said.

Spencer quietly left the building.

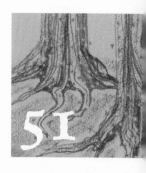

The next morning Yangchen returned. We pushed for details of Calyndra, but either she didn't know or wasn't willing to share much more than we already knew. The entrance to Calyndra was somewhere along the thirty-two mile Skyline-to-the-Sea Trail, which descends from the ridge of the Santa Cruz Mountains to the Pacific Ocean through two California state parks, Castle Rock and Big Basin Redwoods.

"I found it in Big Basin, but long ago it was in what is now Castle Rock State Park. Portals are not simply door-ways... they are alive." She emphasized the word "alive" as if it was filled with magic and adventure but stopped speaking when Spencer entered the Earthship. They made eye contact, definitely communicating, but I couldn't catch it. "You need to leave now," she said.

"Leave?" Linh asked.

Spencer nodded his agreement.

"Where are we going?" I asked.

"To find Calyndra," Amber said.

"That is up to you," Yangchen began. "We know you're concerned about your families, and the Movement may seem secondary, but on this Spencer and I agree: your interests in protecting your loved ones, and those of IM, are joined."

"It's not just our families. We still need to prevent Amber and Linh from getting killed and stop the mall attack," Kyle said.

The reminder that time was running out for the girls tensed my jaw as I spoke. "Where are they safest?" I focused on Spencer.

He hesitated too long then looked at Yangchen. "They're safest on the move. No single place is better than another. As you've seen, even Outin can be breached."

"Then, where can we go?"

"Nate, you cannot live in fear of death. As powerful as you are, no one can escape the end of the physical. Do not be attached to the body; it is not real in as much as it is not permanent. Your soul, their souls," Yangchen swept her arm toward the girls, "continue... always."

"But..." I began.

"No, there is nothing else to consider. Amber and Linh will always be. The experience of them in this physical form is a gift... every moment a precious gift."

I was ready to argue and about to cry, but I knew she was right.

"In order to project the Storch meeting online, you need to find Gibi... and Dustin," Spencer said.

"And searching for Calyndra is no easy task," Yangchen added.

Linh was still processing Yangchen's statement that seemed to mean we would probably not be able to keep them alive for much longer. Her voice, shaky, "You tell us how to get our families safe."

"It's not that simple," Spencer began.

"Damn it," her voice stronger, "make it simple."

"There is always a way," Kyle added, angrily.

"It may not be your priority, but it is ours," I said, looking from Linh and Kyle to Amber. They all nodded.

Spencer sighed, which made Yangchen giggle. "Trust the universe, Spencer," she said. "You can't just trust the universe when it's convenient."

"I want your families to be okay, but it's really all the same. In order to get the government to release them, you need to meet people, use the Movement, and prove you're all innocent. You can try to go back in time and flip things around, but that's tricky business. Or you can get what you want by destroying Lightyear," Spencer said.

"Go see Gibi, then find Dustin. When you return, we'll broadcast the Storch meeting and release your videos and Lee's documents. Lightyear will be finished, and your parents will be released," Yangchen said.

"And *all* of us will be able to resume our lives, right?"

"Nate, remember our deal? I can issue no guarantees about the future. A man, taking a wrong turn on some back street in Istanbul, just changed the future for all of us. And now a young woman in Montreal, who lost her house keys, changed it all again," Spencer said.

"Whatever. Let's go find Gibi and Dustin; they're both crazy, but they'll probably make more sense than you do." I shook my head.

I said goodbye to my students; they'd made considerable progress and would continue to work in my absence. Yangchen was staying behind with Tiller to work with them and another group expected soon. "Will I see you again?" I asked her while we walked alone on the mesa.

"I expect so. Taos has a way of bringing people back. And if not, I'll see you on the astral."

"What about saving Linh and Amber?"

"I thought we settled that?"

"No, you and Spencer may think you settled it, but I'm not accepting your answer."

"Nate, dear one, suffering comes from attachment. Let go."

"I can't. There must be a way to save them."

"Only by letting go can you find clarity. If there is a way, you will be unable to see it in your suffering." She hugged me. "Now, let go."

"What am I doing here?"

"Same thing you've been doing your whole life, preparing for a battle. It's just more intense right now."

"I feel like I'm heading off to war."

"You are, Nate, but remember it can be a peaceful war."

52

We were surprised when Spencer told us we were actually traveling to the redwoods by car, twenty-four hours of driving. "Isn't it risky?"

"Risk is impossible to avoid right now. We need to see some people along the way." Then he asked me telepathically if I had the Jadeo. I answered yes the same way and wondered why he wanted to know. His reply was strong and clear. *Nothing* is more important.

Kyle rode up front with Spencer for the first part of the trip. I sat between the girls in back. Amber was explaining more about Calyndra to Linh and me while Spencer and Kyle talked about the physics, or lack thereof, in portals. I could follow both conversations at once and knew Spencer could too. "Calyndra is different from typical portals, according to Yangchen. It will only open to you when you're ready. They're part of the collective consciousness, and they know everything that is happening at every moment," Amber said.

"We all do, but we're so messed up with fears and attachments that it gets buried," I said.

"We can find it, Nate," Amber said.

"Our best chance is Gibi and Dustin. We're going with that first," Linh said, looking out the window.

"It's sort of like a back door to parallel universes that are really just a millimeter away from us all the time," Spencer said to Kyle.

After six hours of driving, we reached Moab, Utah. Spencer took a series of turns to increasingly smaller roads. The red dirt and smooth rocks gave way to a forested area, then three security gates requiring key codes and security cameras. Eventually we came to an incredible home that we all assumed belonged to Booker.

"Booker's not IM's only wealthy supporter," Spencer said.

Instead of going into the house, he led us to a garden shed nestled in a stand of pines. Inside, he touched a button concealed in the ceiling and an old lawnmower raised and swiveled, revealing a ladder. One by one we descended into a lit tunnel approximately three feet wide by seven feet tall. At its end, some sixty feet away, there was a steel door. Spencer caught up and squeezed past us to enter a code. Through the door, a wide staircase was revealed which opened into a room the size of our high school gymnasium with a dozen hallways leading out at various points.

"What is this place?" Kyle asked.

"This is an IM center," Spencer said.

"IM's headquarters?" I asked.

"No, just a center. There are at least fifteen in this country, another thirty worldwide."

"All like this?" Linh asked. "It's beautiful."

"Some bigger, some smaller," Spencer replied. "Moab isn't exactly a major city, but most of the other centers are even more remote and far more transitory. This one was blasted out of the limestone cliffs and is like a fortress."

"What do they do at these centers?"

"Training, teaching, monitoring, all manner of things."

"Does Lightyear know about the centers?" I asked.

"Until recently we didn't think so, but in the past few months several of our less secure sites have been raided. We're still trying to figure out how they're locating them."

"Did the raids start after Lightyear discovered me?"

"Yes." Then he changed the subject. "It's not safe to travel any farther. We'll have to wait until something changes." As usual he was vague. I was about to push for more details when a group of twenty people entered from one of the halls. For the next three days I worked on training them while Spencer decided if it was safe to continue to the redwoods. The center was extensive; almost sixty people lived there at any given time, meditating, training in soul-powers, and studying. There was also a group who worked on computers and only spoke to Spencer while I was busy with the others.

On the fourth day, Spencer interrupted a session on Gogen with grave news. "The FBI has penetrated the first gate."

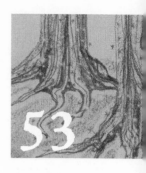

53

In the frantic minutes that followed, we learned that more than thirty FBI, ATF and DHS agents, plus local law enforcement, were taking part. Spencer believed the raid was unrelated to my presence simply because no helicopters or military seemed involved. The three routes out of the cave, including the garden shed, became filled with IMers. Once outside, groups scattered, but escape was going to be difficult because the only road was now blocked. By the time the feds made it through the third gate, we were scurrying down an old wash into a shallow canyon, about a quarter mile south of the cliff. Four students ran with us; the others mostly headed up the cliff trail or escaped into the trees. I thought we were in good shape until Spencer yelled, "We've got to get out of the wash, now. Skyclimb through the canyon. There's a portal in the hills on the other side."

"Amber can't Skyclimb," I yelled back, as we all ran faster.

Flashing red and blue lights broke through the dimming light of the setting sun. "Go Nate! Get out of here!"

"Amber," I shouted.

A stern voice crackled through a speaker, "Halt! Drop to the ground with your hands clasped behind your heads or we will fire."

"Nate, Skyclimb, now!" Amber screamed. Kyle and Linh pulled at me, and we flew up into the canyon, hitting different boulders and trees as we went. But by the time we reached the hills, Kyle wasn't with us. We stopped high in a ponderosa pine and saw him heading back toward the wash.

"What the hell is he doing?" I asked.

"We can't wait," Linh said.

"Splitting up is not a good idea," I said.

"We won't be able to help anyone if we get killed or captured, especially them," How much she'd matured in the past months. Linh was the toughest among us; no one would ever have predicted that. "Spencer will take care of them," she added.

"How? They're probably already in custody. Why did Kyle go back?"

We Skyclimbed a few hundred yards back, trying to follow him, but we had to retreat as more agents entered the canyon.

"The light will soon be gone. Let's find that portal," Linh said, taking my hand.

It ended up being a very obvious one. If not for its remoteness, and being twelve feet in the air next to an inaccessible rock outcropping, anyone could have seen it. We dove in, unsure where it would take us. Linh's first portal experience turned out to be a rough ride—spiraling light and extreme cold temperatures, combined with a rushing noise that made it impossible to hear each other. Linh clung to me. We were in the portal for maybe ten minutes, but when we found ourselves dumped into deep snow next to a frozen waterfall, it was night. Without speaking, we made Lusans to keep warm.

"Are you okay?" I asked, as we knelt huddled around several Lusans.

"No." She pushed her way into my arms and kissed me, reckless and wild. "No."

I held her tight. "Me neither."

"Where are we?"

"I'm not sure, but that sound in the portal was exactly the same thing I heard when we first got to Crater Lake."

"What on earth are you doing back here?" The Old Man of the Lake appeared from a curtain of pines. "Disturbing me at this crazy hour, and here you are all cuddled up like bunnies, bah."

"It's freezing. We're just trying to keep warm," Linh said.

"Course it's cold. It's January at seven thousand feet." Old Man coughed a laugh.

"We need to get to the redwoods."

"Gibi?"

"Yeah."

"Better get you over to Wizard Island portal before you freeze to death."

We followed silently through the woods. It took considerable effort to Skyclimb above the snow, while trying to avoid slamming into trees and losing sight of the Old Man. Once we reached the cliff and made it down to the shore, he offered to shapeshift into the floating log and carry Linh across. I was now able to run alongside him, over the water.

Ten very cold minutes later we looked down into the portal. "You've learned much, boy. And you're still alive. You make an Old Man very happy."

"Good to see you again, too," I said, surprising him with a hug.

"Still got that chip-stone I gave you?"

"Sure do. Why, what is it?"

"It might be useful some time, or it might just remind you of an Old Man."

Linh hugged him too.

"You two get out of here. All this affection is bothering me."

We jumped and almost instantly landed in snow again; this time it was only a couple of inches. Linh made Lusans while I tried to find Amber and Kyle on the astral. No connection with Amber, but Kyle came through quickly.

"What happened?" I asked. "Are you okay?"

"I had to go back. As we were Skyclimbing out of there, I remembered knew he only considers you and him important to the Movement. So I knew he'd disappear and Amber would be alone. When I got back there, all that remained were two burning police cars and swarming cops."

"No sign of Amber and Spencer?"

"Nothing. And it was too dangerous to look further, so I backtracked toward you guys, but the canyon was filling with agents. I Skyclimbed around the other end. I've been dodging patrols for hours. I guess they figured out how important this place was once the cave blew up."

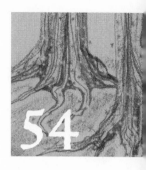

54

It seemed likely that IM had some kind of failsafe that would detonate explosives to destroy whatever evidence existed in the cave. But that also brought attention to the site, which was now probably the destination of hundreds of officials and representatives of the media. I gave Kyle specific directions to the portal and explained the detour to the lake. Then we lost contact.

I told everything to Linh. "Why didn't he tell us he was going back for Amber? We could have helped. I never should have left her."

"He didn't tell you because he didn't want your help. We're all trying to keep you alive. You must know that."

"Well, yeah, I guess I do, but we need to keep all of us alive."

She took my hands, her eyes inches from mine. "No, Nate. That's not the plan. You just never seem to get it. You're the one who has to survive, and you need to stop worrying about the rest of us. There's too much at stake and too many destinies involved. Stop trying to control everything."

"I won't let you guys die."

"You're not God." I looked away until she touched my chin to return my gaze. "We all believe in reincarnation and... that death isn't what people think. We've talked; we want the Movement to win. That's why we're alive, to be part of that."

"One doesn't preclude the other. We can help IM *and* keep us all alive."

"Maybe that's true. We're just not willing to let you march through fire to find out."

"Am I interrupting something?" Gibi's voice came through the darkness.

My night vision quickly found her. "How did you know we were here?"

"Whenever someone comes through a nearby portal it can be heard. You should be able to hear it too."

"That rushing sound?"

She nodded. "Quite wonderful to see you again." She hugged me. "Linh, my you're lovely, aren't you? Come, let's get out of this snow, shall we?"

Gibi led us through the forest for a few minutes until we reached a small sloping meadow surrounded by towering trees. It was close to dawn. She knelt and looked from the earth to the sky several times.

"Look Nate, it's incredible." Linh laughed.

Gibi created a dome of warm air, not much bigger than a two-car garage. It's part of Vising," she said. "Want me to show you how?"

"Yes," Linh and I uttered in unison.

During the sunrise, and for the next few hours, Gibi showed us how to manipulate weather, light, shadow, darkness, water, and temperature. Linh didn't get it all, but by the time we were ready to leave, I was able to surpass Gibi's abilities in many aspects.

"These powers are the difference," I said.

"To what?" Linh asked.

"To defeating Lightyear, without using violence."

"It will take many forms of the five great powers to do that, my friend. And you must remember all that your soul has ever known, if you're to have that chance," Gibi said. "Such a serious business is this."

"Yes. But we came for another reason," I said.

"Many reasons, indeed."

"I need to know how to use Vising to show the world a meeting I had with the head of Lightyear."

"Ah, I see. The meeting does not portray them well, I take it?"

I shook my head.

"Yes, that would be an effective and nonviolent strike at them. Hmm. It is not easy, and you will need someone else to show you parts of Solteer. I'm unpracticed in that power."

"Dustin?"

"Yes, this is a kind circle, too. He needs to be needed, poor boy."

"How does he know something you don't?" Linh asked.

"Mystics do not remember everything." She smiled. "We're mystics because after a certain amount of knowledge returns to us, there is enlightenment, but that is not to say we're enlightened." She giggled. "Anyhow, Dustin is a wise old soul, and thus he chose an incredibly difficult life for himself this time. Painful to watch without understanding the beauty of what his soul really is, who he really is."

"Sometimes his craziness scares me."

"Your love has to be even greater than your fear… in all things."

"In the future," Linh began, "Nate, Amber, and I meet here in the redwoods and Dustin comes, but you don't. Why?"

"Remember, the future is not another place far away. Time is not like that. The future is stacked up right here, right now. It gets sorted and shuffled a zillion different ways, every day. Say, do you play cards? Next time bring cards, and we'll play hearts."

"Okay," Linh nodded hesitantly.

"Gibi, you were saying," I said.

"Yes, yes. The future you saw or experienced, or maybe just heard about, may not be, but then again, it may be, over and over again… Don't worry so much about the future. It may never come."

Gibi showed us all the ways we could use Solteer and Vising to record and show events in our lives and how to retrieve past ones. Dustin's piece of the puzzle was the method used to project it in the three-dimensional world, so it could be filmed digitally as if it were happening right then.

"You must begin your journey back to Outin now."

"How will we find him?"

"You're not going only for Dustin. There is so much looking to do there." She smiled then with a dreamy look and continued. "You'll find many things in Outin. I suspect Dustin might be one of them."

"What else is waiting for us?" Linh asked.

"Outin holds so much. Sad and happy play together. Don't you love the colored birds and bubbles?"

"It's a pretty place," I said.

"It is everywhere and all time at once, laid open for all to see," Gibi said. "But you must look with different eyes to see the whole party. And when you witness life and death at Outin, remember, like this dimension, the deeper in nature, the farther from the hand of man, and therefore the more power you will have. That is…"

"Damn it! A helicopter!" I yelled.

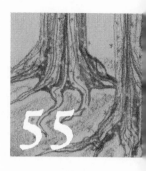

55

"Wait!" Gibi called, as Linh and I were running away. "Friends are flying in."

We stopped. I felt no heat warning and looked at Gibi.

"Spencer and Amber."

Our meadow wasn't large enough so they set down closer to the Smith River. Although the snow had let up, we waited in the warm dome for them.

I ran to Amber and only ended our embrace because I was self-conscious about Linh. "I thought it was over, wasn't sure we'd see each other again," she whispered.

"We were quickly overwhelmed," Spencer explained. "I fought back, but once the police shot down four IMers, I grabbed Amber and wrapped us both into a Timefold."

"Nice, nonviolent tactic," Gibi said.

"What's a Timefold?" I asked.

"The only thing trickier than doing one is explaining it," Spencer said.

"It is a simple manipulation of time," Gibi began. "By adjusting time, relative to the dimension you're in, you can become invisible for short periods."

"How?"

"It takes remarkable concentration." She nodded at Spencer with a smile. "And you cannot move more than eight or nine feet or it will collapse, but with practice, one can manipulate the time to dimension ratio so that you're there but those not in the fold may see the same area as it appeared ten minutes earlier or five minutes later, or some combination of before and after."

"I want to learn that."

"You already know it."

"We need to go," Spencer said.

"We need to wait for Kyle."

"There isn't time," Gibi said. "I'll help him find you."

"Kyle isn't even to Wizard Island yet. He can catch up to us from there," Spencer said.

"At Outin?"

"They're all over Shasta right now, so we can't get to Outin yet. But we'll stay close. Booker has a place not far from here."

I reviewed the list in my head and remembered the name Marble Mountain. "Gibi, will you come?"

"No." She hugged me fully. "Take care, my precious friend." In her embrace she imparted so much information that I pulled back and gasped. She smiled softly.

We raced back to the helicopter and were quickly airborne. I was asleep while still over the redwoods. When I awoke, the girls were still sleeping; Spencer was staring out the window.

"The Jadeo is safe," he said silently.

"Is that a question?" I asked with my mind, patting the artifact inside my pocket.

"No. It's safe. Nate, I know you're torn about whether using force is the right course but—"

"I'm not torn."

"It's one thing to let Lightyear be victorious in these times, or to sacrifice the Movement, friends, family, even your own life, but the Jadeo is something different."

"The Jadeo has survived a long time without me."

"No, don't you see. It has only survived all this time because of you. You and a band of the truest souls who have spent lifetimes doing nothing but protecting it."

"One of those protectors was not true, and yet it survives."

"The universe is strong."

"That person is part of the universe... who is it?"

"I do not know."

"Don't you?"

He stared intently. The helicopter banked and the girls woke, startled.

"Where are we?" Amber asked.

Spencer turned back to the window. "We're about to land at Marble Mountain, one of Booker's wilderness cabins," he answered.

A golf cart was waiting as we left the copter. I recognized the driver from Booker's roster of employees. We wound through woods, up and down hills, until a massive log mansion appeared through the trees. Flanked by two fortress-like stone chimneys, perched on the edge of a canyon with a view of limestone and black metamorphic rock peaks, Booker's spread bordered the Marble Mountain Wilderness Area, a rugged landscape of canyons, lakes, and rivers.

"Nate," Booker boomed, as we climbed the steps to the four-thousand-square-foot front porch.

I was surprised and happy to see him. "Spencer didn't say you'd be here," I said, holding out my hand.

"Hell, I don't even know where I'll be from day to day. Once I heard about the Moab raid, I thought we should talk." Booker pulled me into a hug. As we went inside, a grand room greeted us with a rugged loft on one end, a wall of windows, and a glorious stone fireplace with a mantel carved from a tree. The huge ceiling beams and chandelier dwarfed the giant leather sofas. The other fireplace anchored a master suite, complete with sauna, skylights, and automated everything.

The five of us gathered around the fire. Booker filled us in on how desperate Lightyear was to get us but admitted he was baffled as to how they found the secret limestone cave in Moab. "That doesn't matter," Linh said impatiently. "What about our families?"

"Our lawyers have seen them, but the administration has limited the amount of time we get. Your mother and father seem to be holding up. And Bridgette is fine. Nate, your mother also seems okay."

"But nothing has changed. The only way we can get them out is to expose Lightyear."

"We've committed crimes," I said. "Maybe they framed us, maybe they forced us to defend ourselves, but at the end of the day we're not going to be pardoned just because bad people were after us."

"Kyle, Amber, and possibly Linh might avoid prosecution if they were to vanish right now," Booker said.

"But Nate, you know, your life is something different. Already there are ordinary people who want to follow you as a leader, and others who will hunt you as a threat. From now on it will be a great challenge to convince people that you're the same as them." Spencer's face looked worn.

"But—" I began.

"Nate, you've walked on water on national TV," Amber said.

"But they can explain that." I looked at Spencer.

"I've never walked on water… but it's just energy. Water can be vaporous or hard as ice."

"No, I mean that thing about the Chinese military suit."

"People will believe what they want. You're a cross between a superhero and a villain… no one knows," Booker said. "Half the people are going to want you to succeed, half will love to see you fail, and some would like both!" Amber picked up an old leather-bound book from a shelf and admired it for a moment before replacing it. If there were time, I would use Vising to read his entire library.

"How can all of the government be involved?" Linh asked. "There must be someone who can help."

"The whole government isn't corrupt by any means." Booker smiled then caught himself. "Lightyear just plants suggestions, such as Nate killing federal Agent Fitts, and then gives that info to the FBI. Once the FBI is after you, everyone assumes you're guilty, and most people will run, fight, or lie to save themselves. And once the media has something to entertain and scare the public with… it just gets out of control."

"The same principal holds true for wars," I said. "Remember The Maine, Archduke Ferdinand, Pearl Harbor, 9/11, weapons of mass destruction—it's an old concept that always works."

"Nate's right," Booker said. "There weren't witches in Salem, nor were there dangerous Communists in McCarthy's 1950s America. Looking for terrorists is the latest witch hunt. It's all an excuse to gain control, give the people something to fear… something to hate." A server brought in fresh carrot/apple juice and incredible veggie wraps.

"Enough history. This time it isn't about just millions of people or even entire countries. This is the big one for all the marbles," Spencer said. "We have to win… by any means."

"But Spencer, history is a great teacher, and across thousands of years we have seen that nonviolence is the way to win," Amber said.

"It's not what defeated the Nazis."

"I'm not sure we really defeated them," I said. "We beat them back but their ideas still survive."

"We've had this discussion. It's a matter of trade-offs, how many die."

"How many die, when?" Amber asked. "Everyone dies. True change, enlightenment comes at a price."

"These kids have gotten wise," Booker said to Spencer. "Their souls are coming through. Spencer, you need to remember they're not a bunch of teenagers; they're as old and experienced as you. They just haven't spent as much time thinking about it as you have."

"I do remember. My frustration only comes from *them* not always remembering that fact."

We were all silent for a minute, until Linh asked, "Why isn't Kyle here yet?"

56

"He's making his way here," Spencer said.

"He should have been here by now," Linh exclaimed.

"Where is he?" I asked, giving Spencer a hard look.

"Kyle is fine. Contrary to what you may think, I don't control time and space. Go on the astral and see for yourself." Spencer walked over to the windows.

And I did. The astral was warm like a Southern summer night. Kyle was in a holding cell in a facility outside Washington, DC. The Wizard Island portal had taken him there and was still holding his legs. His uncle, Linh's father, was whispering to Kyle. I interrupted. Kyle had already been to see his aunt and was on edge about being discovered. There wasn't much risk because he was standing in a portal, but my distraction wasn't welcome. He hadn't been able to contact them on the astral, so he went to them. Kyle waved me off.

Previously I'd tried my mother several times with no luck, but now, knowing where they were being held, I made another attempt. It was successful. She came in and out, and cried, hearing my voice. Her cell seemed a little nicer than the sterile space Kyle's uncle was in.

"We're working on a plan to get you out," I said.

"Oh, sweetie, don't. Don't do anything more."

"Are you okay?"

"I'm fine but you—" she was gone.

"What?" I repeated.

"Turn yourself in, Nate. Surrender before anyone else gets hurt."

"Mom, if I turn myself in they'll execute me."

"No one is going to execute a child. Once you're safe in custody every—"

"Mom, can you hear me? I keep losing you."

"I'm here. Please think about it. You'll be able to use your abilities for good, instead of all this trouble."

"You don't understand what's really going on."

I couldn't hear anything for almost thirty seconds.

"How's Dustin?"

"He's okay. Mom, I have to go. We'll get you out of there."

"Please surrender. Walk into the *New York Times* and tell them your story, then ask them to call the police. This is too big for them to just make you disappear, but if you keep running they will kill you for sure."

Next, I checked in on Bridgette. Amber was still mad at her, but they were sisters. She was distraught and was trying to tell me something, but, probably because of her high emotions, nothing was coherent.

Coming off the astral sometimes left me weak and dizzy for a few minutes, but just as often it could leave me feeling energized and strengthened. This time I collapsed. It took almost an hour to recover and required a healing from Spencer. He couldn't explain what caused such an adverse reaction, but he theorized it might have to do with encountering the person I was using (my mom) for the advanced Kellaring, along with crossing a portal's energy with astral energy.

Once I felt better, the girls had more questions about their relatives than I could answer. Linh was relieved to know Kyle was with her parents. We assumed he'd be back with us any moment. I repeated my mother's urging to turn myself in.

"Don't worry about it, Nate," Booker said, walking back to where we were. "The feds have people whose only job is to brainwash and scare people. They've convinced her that if you don't surrender you'll be killed, probably told her that they'll go easy on you if she can get you to come in. Routine stuff."

I looked at Spencer for confirmation, but he was staring toward the mountains. "One thing is for sure," I said, "if the mall attack happens, not only will hundreds of innocent people die, but my chance at proving my innocence will evaporate."

"Do you really think you'll ever be able to prove that?" Amber asked.

"It's not for the government," Booker began, "that's a lost cause. It's for public opinion. Speaking of PR, when can I see the Storch meeting I've heard so much about?" I used the methods Gibi taught me to let him view it. "This sure helps things." Booker laughed. "Are we going to be able to get this out to the world?"

"Once we find Dustin, we'll be ready. It's just deciding the best time and place," Spencer answered.

"The sooner the better. This alone could stop them from resorting to the mall attack," Booker said.

"What about it, Spencer? How's it looking to stop the attack? And what about saving the girls?"

"It's not a good time for such questions. In fact, we will need to be on our way very soon, and you still have people to see here."

"A simple yes or no?" I asked.

"Nothing about the future is simple."

"Then I guess I know your answer."

"I'm glad one of us does."

"Nate." Linh shook her head, seeing my anger building. "Deep breath."

"Who does Nate need to see?" Amber asked, joining in on the diversion.

"There are a number of IMers waiting to meet you. You're already revered in the Movement. They're inspired by you, by the possibilities."

"I don't want to be worshiped."

"Good. Then you'll be happy about the other person waiting to talk with you."

"Who?"

"Wandus."

"He's here? Let's go." Wandus was the most mystical of the mystics. His words stayed with me while my mind continually wrung more and more meaning from them. So much had happened since we met. I was desperate for his guidance.

## 57

We found Wandus meditating next to a small lake. The evergreens and high canyon walls were reflected in the still water. Spencer left us there. I added some sticks to a fading campfire. The girls and I waited silently for almost ten minutes before Wandus smiled and came out of his deep state.

"So good to see you again." His face was bright and warm. "Sit, sit."

"There's so much I want to tell you," I said.

"Yes, for me too, so much I want to tell you. Time has been kind to allow this visit, but terrible too for giving such a short dance."

I looked at him puzzled.

"Let's talk of important things now before the anger of the world takes you away again."

"Is something bad about to happen?" Amber asked.

"Within the world of humans something bad is always about to happen. This is not the natural way. In all of the cosmos and on earth, something beautiful is always about to happen. That must be remembered; man has forgotten."

"Can you tell if Amber and I will be alive in a year?" Linh asked. "It seems like every time we see into the future, one or both of us are dying."

"They're all just versions of the same future... Linh and Amber, you're meant to die, but every time something is changed in the present, the future will be rearranged, and how or when you die becomes different."

"Then let's keep rearranging because I want them in this life," I said.

"But yet, they still die. We all die. Life is short even if you live very long because time is like that. Do not fear this thing called death. What it teaches is to live for every moment. This life is a rare gift you were given by the universe. Most waste it. Do not live like most; show them what it is to truly live."

I read the girls' faces. They were brave but sad. I didn't care what Spencer saw, or even Wandus. The future could be changed, and I was powerful enough to do it. The key was stopping Lightyear. As long as they existed, Linh and Amber were under a death sentence. "How do I stop Lightyear?"

He smiled then looked down at his clasped hands. My eyes followed as he opened and turned them—empty. But when he flipped them back over, a large butterfly fluttered. The girls gasped at his magic. He placed his fingertips softly under my hand so that the butterfly moved into my palm. "The butterfly is a magnificent creature with many teachings."

"The symbol for reincarnation," Amber said.

"Yes," he said with a smiled at her, "but also symbolic of great mystery. The caterpillar takes wonderful secrets into the cocoon then with incredible magic emerges in a fantastic transformation—the butterfly."

I stared at the gentle beauty, well out of its season, and for the first time felt the power of what it is: change personified, forceful, yet peaceful change, a result more beautiful than its origin.

Wandus saw my understanding. "You have gathered much. Rose's journal, the rest of the Clastier papers, the pages from your father's desk," his fingers moved constantly as if typing in slow motion. "Lee's hidden evidence from the mausoleum, the documents rolled in Hibbs' safe, the Jadeo... You see, they are all connected, these secrets from the past, all revolve around the same thing... bringing knowledge forward."

He smiled, his hands now flowing in circular patterns. "These secrets can change the world... although it is not a certainty this will happen."

"Because of Lightyear?"

His eyes squinted, head tilted in a nonanswer. "They could remain secrets or just become ignored truths." He raised a finger and looked up into the trees. "Ah, there are many of those already. But if you do what you came to do then, like a butterfly, the world will be changed to something unrecognizable from what it was."

"How do I do this?"

"Illuminate... teach."

"I'm not good at that."

"Outviews hold the key to teaching. But the Outview of this life is more critical than all the others. You must choose wisely in how you wage this change, where you look. What you *do* is more important than what you say."

"Peace," Amber said. A hawk soared overhead, catching the thermals in the canyon.

Wandus nodded.

I've been thinking a lot about peace and nonviolence. Clastier was adamant about the subject."

"You are Clastier," Wandus said.

"I know."

"This is all the same battle. It does not end with one lifetime. The same trouble follows, but also wisdom and goodness follow. You are Clastier, Hibbs, Nate, and many, many more. It has been a very long time. Do you understand?"

"I think so. It has felt like this was all happening to me out of the blue, but actually this life is like just another year in an eternal war."

His smile stretched, pulling his twinkling eyes tight as he nodded and looked as though he might burst into laughter.

"But if it's a battle, doesn't that mean there will be violence?" Linh asked.

"Yes, there has been much violence in this war, but battles can be won in many ways. Violence is not one of them; it only fools the victor into thinking they've won but it cannot be. No victory can come from violence."

"But Spencer says that without violence, this may go on another thousand years or more."

"Dear Spencer is sometimes confused. With violence it will most certainly last more than a thousand years, as it already has. The only way to stop this is to stop the violence."

"Peace," Amber said again.

"Yes. Love and peace. Not hatred and violence." His smile receded. "Please go now. There are difficulties close at hand, and you must keep moving." For the first time I saw concern in his face.

"When can we talk again?"

"Another time," he lifted my hands slowly until they were over my head and the butterfly flew off. "But think about what has been said. This will give you an answer to the question you should be asking... 'If it is not the first time I've fought Luther Storch, then who is he?' The answer may save you."

58

A group of IMers stopped us on the way back to the cabin. Right away I could tell the difference. The Taos students were influenced by Yangchen and clearly supported her non-violence doctrine. The Moab ones, guided by Spencer, seemed unsure, like I was. Their questions all centered around how to use powers to destroy Lightyear and stop raids. They had also been trained better. And, even though Spencer was like a general to them, and Booker their president, I was revered as a savior. Instead of fighting the label, I decided to use it to help them understand.

"There is an abundance of energy in the world. All that is necessary to do anything is to reroute it to your senses or your consciousness." I looked at each of them, then whispered, *"anything."* I created a dome around us with blowing spirals of snow and immediately changed it to near tropical heat and rainbows. I shapeshifted into Spencer and told them, "Soul-powers are enough, and violence does not need to dilute them. We will defeat Lightyear because we're connected to our soul's true power... love."

"Remember, Wandus said we need to go. We don't have time for this right now," Linh whispered.

"We don't have time *not* to do this right now. These are Spencer's handpicked. They need to see another point of view," I shot back.

"Excuse me, my name is Ren, and I was wondering how Lightyear gets around using soul-powers negatively?" a Japanese man with a long ponytail in his late twenties asked. I stared into his eyes and gasped. It was Sanford Fitts—or at least his soul. I couldn't get an answer out. Did Spencer know? Was he infiltrating the Movement? Or could it be possible this man was unaware of his Fitts incarnation? Amber and Linh both sensed my change.

Amber answered the question. "While it's true that soul-powers are not effective when used for evil purposes, the line between good and evil is more complex than you would imagine." I looked at Ren while she was speaking, trying to decide what to do.

"What's wrong?" Linh mouthed.

"Ren has Fitts' soul," I told her over the astral.

She looked as if I'd slapped her but regained composure and glanced casually at him. Amber was fielding another question, "We're fairly sure that the majority of the psychics employed by Lightyear have been misled and think, as most of the world does, that Nate and us," she indicated herself and Linh, "are true terrorists. So those psychics believe they're doing good by helping to apprehend us."

"Hug him," Linh said quietly.

Right away, I knew what she meant. Vising would allow me to read Ren's whole life and would show me which side he was really on. I nodded back to Linh and told her silently what to do. A couple of minutes later, there was a lull in the Q&A session and Linh grabbed the opportunity.

"Nate would like some one-on-one time with each of you before we go. There may not be time to get to everyone but we'll see how far we get." They were all excited. Linh arranged it so that Ren would be fourth, as we didn't want to tip him off. I spent about three minutes each with the first two. Number three was just approaching me when Spencer suddenly pulled up in a golf cart.

Two of Booker's people got out with him. One filmed us all, while the other took photos. "What's going on?" I asked Spencer.

He pulled me aside and started to whisper something but then stopped. "I have some horrible news," he addressed everyone. "I'm sorry to have to ask you this in the face of such a tragedy, but each of you need to sign this affidavit stating that you were here with Nathan Ryder during the past few hours."

"What's all this about?" one of them asked. "What you're asking us to do puts us at tremendous risk. Swearing we were with Nathan Ryder while he is the most wanted person on the planet is, at the very least, aiding and abetting a known fugitive and, at the very worst could be deemed accessories after the fact." The woman was probably an attorney.

"And what's with the cameras?" someone else asked, while shielding his face.

"I understand your apprehension," Spencer began. "But Lightyear has escalated things to a whole new level, and the future of IM and Nate's life may depend on your willingness to jeopardize your own liberty."

"Damn it, Spencer, tell us," I said.

"The Mall of America was just attacked, hundreds are dead."

59

The girls looked at me terrified. We had failed to stop it. All those innocent people dead, and they were next.

Out of the stunned silence, someone asked, "What does this have to do with Nate?" They didn't know about the future like we did. And if they did, would they count us as partially responsible because we couldn't stop it, didn't report it, or at least warn people somehow?

"The attack happened less than an hour ago. They don't even know how many are dead, but they already are blaming Nate and his brother." Everyone turned from Spencer to me. He continued, "The FBI director reported that two fuel tanker trucks intentionally crashed into mall entrances and detonated."

"God, no!" someone cried.

"DHS claims Nate and Dustin hid on the edge of the parking lot and shot at people trying to escape the flames with AK-47 assault rifles."

I shook my head.

"Most of the victims are teenagers. They expect the death toll to be six to eight hundred, possibly more. It's the second worst terrorist attack ever."

Everyone started talking at once. "Who would do such a thing?"

"How can they blame Nate, when he's here?"

"Would Lightyear really do something so gruesome?"

"Where is Dustin Ryder?"

It was that question, which raised my own. "I thought you said they wouldn't risk doing the mall attack unless they knew my location?" I asked Spencer, telepathically.

"It seems Storch is so desperate to stop you that he's willing to take wild chances."

"Or," I said, looking at Ren, "Do they know where I am?"

Spencer followed my thoughts. It only took a minute for him to complete the picture. His face registered the same shock I'd felt. He hadn't known.

"I thought these were your handpicked people," I said silently, "some of the best in the Movement, and now we find out Fitts is among them—Fitts!"

"He can't be aiding Lightyear."

I stared at Spencer, asking more.

"Just because he shares the same soul as Fitts, doesn't mean he shares the same ideas."

I thought of the slave trader, and the betrayals of Amparo. What secrets are concealed in the innocence of our souls? Is each of us both Caesar and Brutus? In the depth of the dark night, are we paying for crimes we've committed and long forgotten?

"We must prepare to leave," Spencer proclaimed loudly. His voice shattered my thoughts, leaving them unfinished and filled with angst and regret.

Booker's men had collected signatures from more than half the IMers. Linh suggested I thank them individually as they were heading back to their rooms to gather their belongings. I communicated with Spencer and told him about trying to read Ren. At the same time, I asked what the evacuation plan was for the IMers and where we were going.

"They'll be flown to Cervantes, if we can get them out of here in time. You and the girls will be going to Outin. Finding Dustin is more important now than ever."

I thought of my mom and wondered if she would see the news. Surely a guard would tell her. I made sure to make connections with several of the IMers and hugged them so it wouldn't seem suspicious to Ren.

When Ren finally stepped before me, I was nervous. Here was the soul of a man who murdered my dad and Aunt Rose, pretended to be my friend before hunting me, and even in his final gasps of life had tried to kill me.

"I admire you greatly," he said, with a clipped but warm Japanese accent, while shaking my hand.

"Thank you, Ren, right?"

"Yes," he nodded, bowing slightly.

"How did you come to be with the Movement?"

"Same as you."

I looked at him puzzled, eager to hug him and end the small talk that couldn't give me any answers. "How do you mean?"

"Sanford Fitts killed my father, too."

60

It was hard to breathe for a moment. "I'd like to talk with you, but with the awful events today, my time is no longer my own," my voice strained.

"Yes, I understand," he bowed again, preparing to walk away, "Thank you."

"Ren, I'd like to read you."

"I don't understand."

"Would you please open your arms?" I demonstrated with mine. He didn't hesitate. His life was noneventful until seventeen years of age. His father was a spiritual man, a practicing Zen Buddhist who, through deep meditation, had discovered a few soul-powers, mostly related to healing. Locals began seeking him out for help with ailments, but soon people from around the world were coming with life and death issues. A powerful American businessman was among his frequent visitors. This eventually led to a recruitment effort by Lightyear. He resisted and confided the story to Ren, who by then was twenty. As his powers grew, Ren's father learned too much about Lightyear. Fitts arrived with a final offer, which he again refused. His healthy father suffered a massive heart attack while Fitts was still in the room; Ren found him minutes later. Ren was unaware that he shared a soul with Fitts.

"I'm so sorry for your loss," I said, hugging him, tears welling in my eyes.

"Thank you," he bowed.

"We'll meet again, I promise you," I said, as he walked away.

Even with hurrying the remaining people, it was almost half an hour before Amber, Linh, and I got back to the main cabin. Booker and Spencer were in the middle of a disagreement. The girls were pulled in by the horrific images on TV that I didn't want to see.

"Did you talk to Ren?" Spencer asked.

I nodded. "Fitts killed his father."

"Incredible!" Even Spencer could be surprised. "Does he know?"

"He knows Fitts killed his dad but has no clue he shares a soul with Fitts." I'd told the girls on the way back to the cabin. We all agreed Ren could benefit from some time with Wandus when they got to Cervantes.

"Should we take him there? I mean, he was one of Lightyear's top people," Booker asked.

"They only share a soul. Two very different personalities, not the same people," Spencer corrected.

"What about souls being corrupted by a lifetime with a very strong personality? I've read about that happening." Booker asked. "I mean would you want to have Hitler's next incarnation babysit your kids?"

"Is that possible?" I asked.

"Not in my experience. People have theories, but nothing has ever been documented," Spencer replied.

"So you don't know for sure?"

"I know Fitts is no Hitler."

"Tell that to my family."

The sound of a helicopter unnerved me. Linh and Amber started toward the door. "It's just Tiller Hobson and three of the IMers from Taos. Once Moab got hit we decided to take some of the key people from Taos and bring them here. Now they'll all go on to Cervantes."

"Nate, I'll be taking this copter out of here," Booker said. "I can't take any chances of being affiliated with the Movement. I'm its bank you know."

"How many people are in the Movement?" I asked.

He looked at Spencer.

"A few hundred thousand in varying degrees," Spencer's answer surprised me.

"What does that mean?" Linh asked, joining the conversation.

"There are hundreds of thousands of people who share the same core beliefs and philosophies as IM."

"How many actually know it exists?"

"Maybe five thousand."

"And at the centers?" I asked, deflated.

"Fewer than a thousand."

"How are we ever going to change things with numbers like that?" I asked.

"Every significant change in human history has begun with an idea from a single individual," Booker said. "We can do this. My fortune is at our disposal, and a chain of events, which began long before any of us were born, is already under way. There are cracks at Lightyear, and their opposition to all that we believe in will be the drive that propels us forward."

"I appreciate the pep talk, Booker, but there is so far to go. How can we get there?"

"You need to stay alive," he said, tapping my chest. He looked over at Spencer. "We're asking a lot of you, Nate. The truth is, going to Outin to find Dustin is not going to be easy. Assuming—"

"Booker, let me explain," Spencer interrupted.

"If you don't mind, I'd rather hear it from Booker," I said.

Spencer tipped his extended hand to Booker and nodded.

"Just getting back to Outin will be challenging enough," Booker continued. "But if you survive that, finding Dustin and escaping Outin again will prove almost impossible. It will require every power you've learned and a few you've yet to remember."

"What do you mean, *escaping* Outin?" Amber asked.

Booker looked again at Spencer and walked over to the stone fireplace.

"Outin is not the same place you left," Spencer said. "As far as we know, there had never been a killing there... until Nate and Linh killed the soldiers."

"Not the same place, how?" I asked.

"We don't know exactly. It's a whole other dimension, and I don't fully understand this yet," Spencer said.

"And Lightyear may be there," Booker said. "It's impossible to know if they've already found a way through. Even if they haven't yet, you can be damn sure they're looking for it. Finding Outin is likely more important to them than finding you, Nate."

"It's too risky to go," Amber said, pausing to look at me. "But we have to, don't we?"

"Without finding Dustin and securing Outin, there is no way the Movement will succeed, and there's no way the girls live much longer," Spencer said.

"When do I leave?" I asked.

"You mean when do we leave?" Linh corrected.

Amber nodded.

"It'll be dark soon. You'll go then."

**61**

We left the cabin and were immediately swept into the confusion of an evacuating refugee camp. I'd learned in Taos that IMers were all on the run from something. Often it was as benign as knowing the "normal" world wasn't right for them, but as I was learning fast, mine wasn't the only life Lightyear had touched personally. Others were called by visions or synchronistic events, or encounters with Spencer or other mystics. They all had nowhere "safe" to go, and feared Lightyear—not just because of the punishments they would suffer because of their acquaintance with me but also terrified of what the world would become should Lightyear win.

Tiller Hobson stopped us. "Yangchen sends her love."

"Where is she?"

"Hard to say, but she'll be fine."

"Amber, she said to remind you of the floating flower."

I looked at her for an explanation. She just smiled and turned away.

"It's begun; things are getting crazy. I've heard that ten centers are evacuating."

"What's begun?" Linh asked.

"The next stage… We're at the beginning of the great shift. Don't you feel it? Or maybe you guys are so much in the forefront that you sense it differently."

"We're just trying to stay alive, Tiller," I said.

"Amen, brother."

It started to snow. Spencer called us from the porch. He had a large duffle bag with fantastic clothes, all black. It started with one-piece swimsuits for the girls and trunks for me. The next layer had light cargo pants, T-shirt, and safari shirt, but instead of being solid black they were speckled with tiny points of white. He also had mountain boots, snow pants, warm jackets, and wool hats.

"Looks like combat fatigues for Outin," Linh said, half smiling.

Spencer nodded gravely. "You should dress now; put it all on." We scooped everything up and were heading inside when he added, "Nate, wait." I motioned the girls to go on in. "There's more. Here's a small pack for each of you. It includes all kinds of survival gear."

"Okay," I said, anticipating what was next.

"I want you to consider taking weapons."

"No."

"Nate, listen, please. I have to tell you, even with guns, your chances of getting away from Outin alive are slim..." He looked at me hard. "A million to one that you make it."

"And without them?"

"I've not seen it happen."

"That doesn't mean it won't."

"No it doesn't, but the odds are astronomical. This isn't a new power to me. I've spent decades watching the future, and then seeing it evolve and—"

"Then why are you letting me go?"

"There is no other way."

"Then let me do it my way," I replied.

"Is it your way, or is it Yangchen's way?"

"You've known me enough lifetimes, Spencer. You tell me."

Our eyes locked, pleading with each other. He grabbed me in a hug. "Damn it, you better survive this."

"I plan on it. If for no other reason than just to prove you wrong."

He surprised us both with a half laugh, and as we pulled apart, his eyes brimmed with tears. For the first time, I believed he might care more for me than what I was to the Movement. And I realized he *and* the Movement were enormously important to me.

The girls came out a few minutes later looking like ski bunnies. I left them to get dressed myself and ran into Booker inside.

"I've got a bus coming. Should be here in the next twenty minutes to take everyone out. You and the girls can ride with me. I'll take you as far as is safe. Somewhere near the base of Shasta, I suspect. From there you will have to find your way to Outin. The snow will help give you some cover, but they've got patrols and Sno-Cats out searching... for you and for Outin."

"Does the military really know how to look for a portal to another dimension?"

"You'd be surprised. But in this case, Lightyear has some psychic spooks on Shasta advising and sifting the data."

"Do you think we'll survive this?"

"Hell yes, I..." He stopped himself. "Nate, I'm no mystic. I'm a helluva lot closer to my personality than to my soul, in spite of all my efforts. I've just never found a way to reconcile business to spirituality. I don't believe they're mutually exclusive; I'm just better at making money than anything else," he paused. "Always remember that power clouds things." Some of his employees rushed through carrying boxes. "Anyway, that's not what I mean to be telling you right now. If I was to set this whole thing up as a business, I'd send you in there with a mercenary army and enough modern weaponry to give you a chance against the deadliest military the world has ever known. We'd have maps of Outin, spies, and surveillance equipment, bribes would be issued, the whole works. But this ain't like that. We're dealing with different forces. So, knowing what I know, if you're looking for an honest answer..." he paused.

I nodded.

"No, I don't think I'll ever see you again after today, at least in this lifetime. I think you're crazy not to take weapons with you, and I think Spencer is a fool to let you go."

"He says there's no other way."

"Damn, Nate, there's always another way."

"I have to try."

"I know. But Nate, make things right before you do. Get ahold of your mother. Tell her you love her and forgive her and all that stuff."

"Okay. Thanks for being straight with me."

He nodded. "And, Nate, I hope I'm wrong. There's plenty I don't know, about you, your powers, and Outin. So there's a fair chance I don't know what the hell I'm talking about." He went outside, and I finished dressing.

My mother was in the same cell when I reached her. "Nate, please tell me it's not true."

"What?"

"That you had something to do with this mall attack."

"Mom, are you serious? I'm a thousand miles away from that mall. Lightyear set me up. They're trying to discredit me."

"Nate, I'm sorry, but you're doing a pretty good job of discrediting yourself. I just don't believe they would kill hundreds of innocent kids to make you look bad. Of course I don't think you did either, but that's why you have to stop running, so we can get this sorted out. Our government wouldn't kill its own citizens."

"That's what they do. All the Montgomery Ryders... you should know better."

"Please, let's get you the best lawyer in the country and fight this thing the right way. No more running, no more killing. It's out of control. You're going to get yourself killed."

We lost contact for five or ten seconds, which gave me a chance to compose myself. "Mom, I love you. I know you don't understand most of this and can't believe the other half. But I'm your son. Trust me."

"I'm trying, but think about the lawyer. Not like Sam's sister. With all this publicity, the best attorneys will just line up to take this case."

"I'll consider it. There's something else I want you to know."

Silence.

"I forgive you, Mom."

"For what?"

"For everything, all of it."

"Oh, Nate, I just want you and Dustin out of harm's way. I don't know what to do anymore." Tears. "I'm just a mom who wants her babies safe. If I could hide you I would, but where do you hide from something like this?"

We lost contact. I was alone for only a minute trying to collect my thoughts when the girls came in. Booker had told them the plans.

"Does it really make sense taking everyone to Cervantes? Isn't it risky teaching powers to all these people?" Linh asked. The question of Ren's loyalty had made us doubtful about everyone we'd met at the centers.

"Spencer said that the more who connect with their souls, the better. Powers help bring us closer to that. Without understanding and embracing our true selves, we can't develop and perfect the powers. He really wanted us to take weapons. They don't think we have a chance without them."

"Do we?" Linh asked.

"Yes."

They both smiled.

"If going back to Outin is our best chance to keep you two alive, then we're going to do it. If we don't make it, then we'll all die together."

"Kyle better show up," Linh said.

"Where else is he going to go? He'll be there."

"And Dustin?" Amber asked.

"What time is Dustin in, what dimension?" Linh asked.

"Wandus told me that understanding my Outviews should help guide everything I do. They are my soul's experience on this plane."

"How are we going to get to Outin if they've got the mountain locked down? I still can't even Skyclimb," Amber said, sadly. "Sorry. I don't know why I can't—"

"Don't worry about it," I said. "Wandus also said that the connections of our past, present, and future incarnations can answer any question. Ren was Fitts. I was Clastier and Hibbs. Spencer was Hibbs' mistress. My father was my friend in many lives, protecting the Jadeo. Kyle is also Curry, the writer and Mayan scholar. Who were you Amber? Not just my sister—there were more lifetimes. And you Linh?"

Linh's expression suddenly softened to reveal depths of love I was unprepared for. I turned back to Amber and kept talking. "It's hard to know where it ends and where it begins. My mother, Dustin, Josh, Bà, Bridgette, Amparo, who were they? The more we understand about the relations in this life, the more we can find out about past connections, and then the answers will come and secrets will be revealed. And remember what Wandus said. The question I should be asking is, who was Storch?"

"How do we find those connections?" Amber asked.

"You could read us," Linh said.

"I'd rather explore Outviews."

"Can you do that now? I mean, control them?"

I nodded.

"You already have all the secrets Wandus talked about, and the rest of Clastier papers can't be hard to locate since you have his memories," Amber said.

"And you know what the Jadeo is, right?" Linh asked. "Are you going to ever tell us?"

"Believe me, it's better if you don't know yet. But one day you'll understand."

Spencer was at the doorway, making a helicopter signal with his hands.

"We're coming."

The girls waited next to the chopper, refusing to get in until I did.

The snow was worsening.

"What about Kyle?" Linh asked.

"He'll catch up with you at Outin," Spencer said. "One more thing."

"Let's go," Booker yelled from inside.

"Go ahead," I told the girls. "I'm right behind you."

"If you're going back there intent on avoiding violence, then I think you should give me the Jadeo," Spencer said.

"Will that really make a difference?"

"I don't know." He was exhausted and exasperated. I embraced my old friend.

"Here," I handed it to him. "I don't know either. If things go badly, you'll make sure it's safe?"

"Or destroyed."

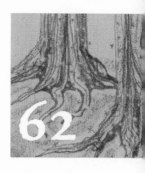

From the air I caught a glimpse of the charter bus turning off the main road onto the long drive to the cabins. Another small helicopter landed where we had just been. I tapped Booker on the shoulder and pointed.

"It's for Spencer, he's not going straight to Cervantes."

I stared out at the forest and mountains below, their calm majesty seemed strange considering the turmoil of the mall attack and our lives. Linh handed me a poem.

> They came like flies, or sweets, or rain
> down my throat, searing my veins
> convincing sounds, my head turns
> and eyes behold, unwarranted burns—
> that smell, that tear my skin into folds—
> breaks made. We never win. I hide,
> dear friend, like those around
> whose hands reach out, my tears fall to the
> ground. I beat, with body, curled and distant
> aching shame, to go where bidden
> notwithstanding, nor image rest
> upon this shore, where no man's test
> is here. Yes, here. Here! Look at vestige
> like a shipwreck, confound this absent brutal
> vex and shun, the soft skin of a sun-ripened

peach in your hold, your precious world,
teach its sweetness, that distinct taste of us
fresh, and silent, and sure… we are.
Oh, the magnificence of youth,
tis age is wasted on the dying,
and blood, is smeared with a reckoning
as honest as a baby,
the breath of innocence,
the kiss, the stunning clarity
of who you are,
be it, damn it. Be the power in your heart
and awaken my renewal.
I am crumbling
in the wake of my ancestors,
and this resurgence is
deafening.

We are here.
Here. Yes, here!
Now look in our eyes and spell
it out so they will come like sweets,
and not flies,
on our bloodied bodies,
our thoughts of ne'er.
Our flowers smelling soft
like rain.

How could Luther Storch have ordered such a massacre? After twenty minutes Booker's voice came across our headsets. "Nate, we're going to have to put it down here. I'm sorry we can't get you closer. They've got restricted airspace."

"This is fine."

"We'll add the film of you at the center and the affidavit to the propaganda videos," Booker said. "They'll be released when the time is right."

"Propaganda makes it sound made up."

"You're right. How about we call it 'the truth' instead? We'll get the truth out."

"When is the time going to be right?"

"Soon… when you finish up this Outin business," he said, with a wink, then hugged us all quickly and boarded the chopper. Half a minute later they were gone.

We ran to the trees for cover. I put the three of us in a warm dome and found, with a little effort, I could keep it moving with us. A particularly large sugar pine caught my attention.

"Let's meditate here," I said.

"Are you kidding?" Amber asked. "Soldiers could be anywhere. The snow is getting worse, and we have no idea how to get back to Outin."

"Exactly," I said, sitting beneath the lower branches.

"Nate," Amber said, "it's not safe."

"With the dome and our snowsuits, it's easy to ignore the cold, and if we hope to avoid soldiers and find an entrance, we need to be as in tune as possible."

"Remember, we need to meet Kyle, too," Linh said.

"I'm hoping he can just pick a spot at Outin to go from the Crater Lake portal."

"Then why didn't they just take us to Crater Lake, and we could have done the same?" Linh asked.

"Because it probably won't work. Outin is another dimension," Amber said.

"Come on, let's meditate. Then I'll go on the astral and see if I can find Kyle."

Time was tough to track. We might have been there half an hour or more. I silently thanked Kyle for teaching me the importance of meditation and Wandus for explaining that any answer I needed could be found.

"There are entrances all over Shasta," I began. "That means we should be able to find one easily, but that also means Lightyear could stumble upon one too."

"How did you find that?" Amber asked.

"I meditated on that question."

"If it's that simple, maybe you should meditate more. Where's Dustin? How do we defeat Lightyear? What's the best way to free our families? Stay alive?"

"I get your point, but it doesn't always work like that. This was a basic question. I might have to spend years in contemplation for those others."

"By then it'll be too late," Linh said.

"Can we go find Dustin, now?" Amber asked.

"We're going back for more than just Dustin." They both looked at me. "This is a battle for Outin."

"Nate, there are three of us, five at most if we're lucky enough to find Kyle and Dustin. If you're certain we're going to be in a battle, then we better get some help," Amber said, clearly shaken.

"We already have the advantage," I said. "Outin is a foreign country to them. They have no idea what they're going to encounter. The ground is a starry sky, the sky an ocean; it's all upside down. The soldiers will be disoriented. I mean there's never been a killing in there before us. Outin is the safest place we can be right now.

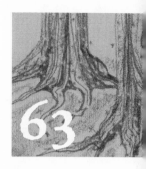

63

Once we were moving again within the air dome, Linh asked why Spencer didn't come with us. "They think we're going to die," I answered.

They were both silent for the next few minutes before Amber said, "Because of the nonviolence?"

"I think they believe that if we use our powers to kill all the bad guys, we would win."

"We would," Linh said.

"The battle but not the war," I said.

"I know," she said quietly.

"We're eventually going to have to face a choice," Amber said. "It might come down to us dying rather than taking lethal action. Yangchen said that was the danger point. If we can avoid getting ourselves into that kind of a position, we could succeed."

"What did she mean by her message about a floating flower?" I asked.

"Yangchen said that a flower is more than something beautiful to look at. The fragrance of a flower floats in the breeze, spreading beauty and the awareness of beauty. All who encounter it take it with them, and therefore the flower is everywhere. The flower is more than beautiful, it is powerful. She said we need to be like that."

"I don't really know what she means," I said.

"Not sure I do either," Amber said softly. "But she said that while we're at Outin, it would make sense."

"You two spent a lot of time together," Linh said.

"We've known each other over many lifetimes."

"She told me, too, that I cannot kill again or my fate will be forever changed. The Movement will be lost for millennia."

"But Spencer says the opposite," Linh said. "Who's right?"

The question was unanswerable. It was too hot as we trudged up hill through the snow so I lifted the dome. A few minutes later Amber pointed.

"What is it?" I whispered.

"Isn't that an entrance?" She ran over and reached her hands above her head. Linh and I looked at each other. We couldn't see it.

"Amber, what are you talking about? That's just blowing snow," I said.

She stepped inside and vanished. Linh and I ran over but couldn't find anything. A second later, Amber crashed into us.

"Now do you believe me?" Amber asked, as we untangled ourselves and got to our feet. "I was gone almost ten minutes. It's a part of Outin we've never been to before. Come on!"

Linh and I still couldn't see it so we both held on to Amber while she parted the veil. "Oh!" Linh screamed, as we went through. At the same time, I found I couldn't breathe. Suddenly we tumbled onto Outin's beautiful ground of infinite stars.

While still gasping for air, I crawled to Linh. Amber was already kneeling over her. "She's not breathing!" I pushed Amber out of the way.

"Make a Lusan." I laid my hands on Linh's face and began healing. It took enormous concentration as my limbs burned and ribs felt crushed around my lungs.

"When I came through before, I looked around and nothing seemed familiar. Outin is huge, we could be anywhere." Amber's tear-filled eyes were desperate. Her fear stole my confidence and the healing energy stopped.

She finished a Lusan and held it to Linh's chest. I Sky-climbed above a group of bright-white trees, hoping for a view of the lakes, but only miles of black and white forest were visible. I couldn't believe it; we'd come back to Outin only to have Linh die in the damn entrance. Maybe Wandus and Yangchen were right: the girls were going to die one way or another, and I was powerless to stop it.

"Nate, let's get her back to our dimension. The reverse time—we can save her."

"God, you're right," I scooped Linh up and crashed back through the veil, skidding in the leaves and snow of our world an instant later, but actually it was an instant earlier. Linh pulled herself up.

"Why can't we get in?" she asked.

Amber smiled. I hugged Linh, thinking I almost let her die and gave Amber a grateful glance. She nodded slightly. I could read her face; next time it could be her. We were sure to be in for more crises and challenges, and I needed to remain calm or one of us would die. Before I could explain to Linh what happened, my temperature rocketed. "Get down," I whispered, pulling Linh to the ground. As I scanned the forest, something moved about four hundred yards away. "Damn it, soldiers."

"We've got to get through," Linh said.

"No!" I barked back.

Linh looked at Amber.

"You may die."

Linh's face told me she didn't understand. There was no way we could do anything without the soldiers seeing us. There were only seconds.

"We're going to die if we stay here," Linh said.

I closed my eyes and asked my guides to show me. Nothing came for a painfully long moment. Then I saw the veil to Outin open, with Amber and Linh going through, and smiled.

"Amber, take her back through and then come back and get me."

"We go together," Linh said.

"If we do, you or I, or both, will die. Go, now!"

Linh threw me an angry glance, but her trust was absolute. Amber grabbed Linh's hand. As soon as they were on their feet, the soldiers spotted them. Just as they punched through the veil, shots whistled above me. I was almost sure they made it without getting hit. Vising allowed me to slam a wall of fog and heavy rain up against the Special Forces unit. Because of reverse time, Amber was back in seconds. She locked her hand around my arm and pulled me through.

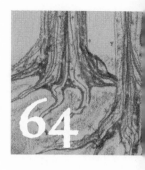

64

Linh appeared to be floating through space, lying on Outin's stunning ground curled up clutching a Lusan. Her eyes were open, and they brightened with a brief smile when she saw me. I added my healing energies to the Lusan and cradled her face in my lap.

"We may not have much time. Those soldiers could get through," Amber said.

"I know, let's just give her a few minutes. She'll be fine."

"What was different this time, and why didn't you or I get hurt?"

"It's because Linh and I killed people last time we were here. Remember, Spencer said no one has ever killed in Outin. And the portals are alive, part of the consciousness. It was trying to keep us out. As far as Outin is concerned, you're pure, so you could go through. As long as we held onto you, we could get in but when we all joined hands, it increased the negative energy too much. We could get through but also had to endure whatever powerful energy was blocking us. I felt pain but not as much as Linh."

"I'm ready to go," Linh said. I knew she didn't like to think about the killings. "Let's not wait around for the soldiers."

"Yeah, we led them here," Amber said, as we moved into the denser part of the shimmering forest.

"They may have their own issues getting through," I said. "And remember, they know about the other entrance."

"Where's 'here' anyway?" Linh asked, pointing to the trees. They weren't like the trees from our last visit. Their trunks and limbs, although massive, seemed to move altogether like a huge stand of seaweed flowing with an underwater current. I touched one and my hand slipped inside six or seven inches before hitting anything solid.

"There are no rules here," Amber said.

"At least no rules we understand," I said.

"Yeah, it's a different dimension, and we don't have a clue. There's no guarantee anything will even be like it was when we were here before. We may not ever see the lakes again."

A breeze blew the familiar pastel powder flakes and dust, but soon the gentleness was gone and heavy winds swayed whole sections of the forest. The sparkly powder storm nearly blinded us. I Skyclimbed to the treetops in search of shelter or a clearing anywhere, but visibility was worse at those heights. I could see that the ocean-sky, which was typically some exotic shade of blue, had changed to bright red while producing inverted white-caps. It made me nervous.

I returned to the girls. There was very little underbrush and nothing available for a shelter. The blowing powder and sparkles were eerily silent and brutal. Gogen kept us from being tossed around. After a few exhausting minutes, we found refuge in a group of trees growing close enough to block some of the monsoon. We quickly devised a plan to use Gogen to hold Amber on my back so Linh and I could Skyclimb. Battling our way through the storm kept me on the edge of panic. I knew it could consume us at any time, but I had to remain calm or I'd lose my concentration and Amber would fall off.

"Linh, look at the colors," I yelled.

"What?" She was ten feet away running-leaping-flying parallel to me on the treetops.

"Do you see the way the colors swirl? Even in these hurricane conditions, the pinks stay with pinks, blues with blues. Do you see it?"

Her face radiated with the glow. It was the presence of love completely extinguishing fear. We'd be all right. The overwhelming magnificence made us all laugh. We sailed through until it eased on the fringe of the forest. There, like a desperate beggar, the fear returned, and this time it was not alone.

## 65

We arrived at the place where Linh had shot the soldier, but the body was gone. Any chance our memories were wrong faded when we found the scene of my battle. All the bodies had been removed.

"Who moved them?" Linh asked.

"Lightyear must have found the entrance. They must be here." I'd been edgy since we discovered the first body gone, now I was struggling to remember the lesson I'd just learned, remembering what Wandus had said so many times, that we keep repeating until we learn, until we finally remember.

"What if the bodies just fell into space?" Amber asked. "I mean, we don't understand this dimension. Maybe if you stay in one place long enough you just fall into the ground and end up floating through space. Maybe if we had telescopes powerful enough, we could see them floating above our world."

"We have to assume Lightyear is here," I said.

"What about Kyle?" Linh asked.

"He'll find us. But let's go check out the lodge. If he's waiting, that's where he'd be."

"Yeah and if Lightyear's waiting, that's probably where they are too," Linh said.

"She's right," Amber said quickly. "Nate, can you do a Timefold, like Spencer did with me at Moab?"

"I tried a few times at Marble Mountain and wasn't successful."

"You know what happened up in the storm? We all felt it," Amber said.

"Yeah, the fear left," Linh said.

"We've got to hold on to that feeling," Amber said. "It was so empowering."

"The fear is already back," I said, looking around as we got back into the trees.

"I know, but we need to push it out."

Wandus had said conquering fear is one of life's longest battles but also one of the most rewarding. Now that I'd seen the reward I understood.

Along the way, we were nervous, knowing Lightyear agents or soldiers could be anywhere. The trees protected us from view, but our enemy had the same advantage and they had been here longer. "The mystics warned of a battle the likes of which I couldn't imagine," I said. "Yangchen was firm when she told me I'd face a choice of death or killing."

"She said you cannot kill again, Nate," Amber said. "Or you will forever change your fate, and everyone's."

"I remember."

"So let's make a pact. There are other ways. We saw it in the storm. Let's do this without any more violence on our part. No killing."

"It's not fair. They can do whatever they want," Linh began. "They have every weapon and kill so easily. And we're supposed to what, turn the other cheek? Smile while they cut our throats?" Linh was talking in a yelling-whisper. "Amber, are you saying you wouldn't kill someone to prevent Nate from being killed?"

"That's not a fair question," I said.

"Isn't it? We're all going to face that question about each other sooner or later. Probably much sooner than we'd like to think."

"I think me killing someone would do more harm to the Movement than if I let Nate die," Amber answered.

Linh scoffed. "How can you say letting Nate die is better for the Movement than letting some Lightyear assassin live?"

"Because. Love. Does. Not. Kill," Amber said.

"I don't understand a kind of love that *lets* someone you love die," Linh wasn't whispering anymore.

"Hold on." I stopped walking and turned to face them. "I agree with Amber."

Linh gasped and turned around.

"I want to beat Lightyear, but without the awakening, the victory would be pointless. I can't deny who I am. My lifetime as Clastier is part of me. As are my countless incarnations spent protecting the Jadeo and sacrificing everything else to preserve it. If I use violence now, after knowing what I know, it will all have been for nothing, and this will start yet again. I cannot allow that."

"Then do you get a free ride for the killing you've already done just because you didn't understand," Linh asked, then added, "because *we* didn't understand?"

"No, unfortunately, that karma will still have to be dealt with. And taking a life is not an easy debt to repay karmically. You know that from your Buddhist studies. Kyle will be able to help us understand that, too."

"So, we agree? No more violence," Amber stated.

"Yes," I said.

Linh closed her eyes, inhaled deeply, and, after a long pause, said, "Okay."

There were no Windows along the way, no trace of Dustin nor Kyle. As we neared the lodge, we stayed hidden in the woods, watching. The place seemed deserted. I surveyed the area from high up in a coal-black, silver-flecked tree. My black outfit camouflaged me well as I peered from behind luminescent-colored bubble-leaves. Finally, by unanimous decision, we cautiously approached the lodge.

It was probably ten tense minutes of complete exposure before we reached Outin's only structure. As we entered, I knew something was horribly wrong, even before we saw the bloodied body.

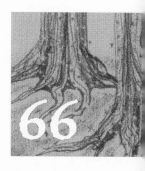

66

Linh screamed. I yelled for Amber to take her outside. Linh shoved Amber against the stone wall hard enough to knock her down. I used Gogen and all my physical strength to restrain her then forced her to sleep with Solteer. Then I had to come to grips with my own shock. Amber cried softly. I approached the body of my best friend. Amber looked away as I lifted Kyle's bullet-riddled body onto my shoulder.

"Wait here," I managed to say.

By the time I reached Floral Lake, Kyle's blood had saturated my clothes. I walked into the water and floated him among the healing flowers. As the water cleansed him, dozens of bullet holes became visible, confirming what I already feared—Kyle was not coming back to life.

When Linh and Amber had saved me in the same lake after the theater massacre, I was still alive. But Kyle appeared to have been dead for a while. And with the time differences, it could have been a day, or even longer. Still, I held his body for hours. Finally, I laid him half on the bank, so that his legs were still floating. Both girls were asleep when I returned to the lodge. I woke Amber quietly, and we talked about the best way to get Linh through this. Before we had a plan, Linh woke.

"Still think nonviolence is the answer?" She stared hard at me.

"We don't even know if this is real," Amber said. "It could be like Dustin."

Surprised, I looked at Amber. It hadn't occurred to me. Thinking of Kyle's mutilated body back at the lake, it didn't seem possible, but then again this was Outin. Anything was possible.

"We need to find Dustin. He'll know if there's a chance. He's been living here."

"He may be dead, too," Linh said. "And Kyle is dead for sure." She suddenly broke into tears, wailing. I was positive he was dead, not just from holding his lifeless body but because of what Spencer had said about every person having a physical energy that when gone leaves a void and changes the entire energy field of the planet. Once I tuned in, I felt Kyle's change had been made. He was dead.

At least now I knew death was nothing but a transition, and I would see the true Kyle again and again. His soul was forever. It was, in fact, still on earth in any number of incarnations, such as Travis Curry, the Mayan book guy. He was one of the entrusted nine. He and I were on a collision course to meet again—destiny would see to that. But even with all that knowledge, the understanding of soul-powers, and the overriding importance of the Movement, I ached. If it weren't for the need to keep the girls alive and find my brother, I would have been in the woods, crying and pounding the earth, like I did so often after my dad died.

Linh insisted on seeing Kyle. As my senses returned, I realized every minute we stayed in the open was too risky, but Linh could not be dissuaded. He was where I'd left him. He looked small and alone— a crippled, beaten orphan, dumped in the dirt. Our tears tore at us.

"We can't stay," I choked.

"We can't leave him here." Linh's voice was strained.

"What about moving him to the middle of the lake, it's beautiful. The flowers. He loved flowers." Amber looked at Linh.

She nodded.

I had already changed into one of the extra set of clothes Spencer had sent for Kyle and Dustin, and left the blood-soaked ones at the lodge. The girls quietly undressed and walked into the water. I stood watch on shore. Soon I lost sight of them as they blended in with the millions of flowers floating in the massive lake. After half an hour, my body began to burn. Then I saw soldiers coming from the lodge. No doubt finding wet clothes and a missing corpse had created a stir. There were ten of them; they'd seen me.

67

The mystics had taught me well. Combining the knowledge of my soul-powers with the experience in the storm of removing fear, I forged an energy within me that was enough to overcome my anger about Kyle. There is strength in nonviolence that many have known before me. Still, I wasn't interested in being a martyr and had to act fast to avoid being slaughtered.

I hoped my ability to manipulate elements worked in this dimension. Rain might not be the same, but I did have access to an endless supply of water. I surged a wave from the lake twenty feet high and then froze it. Instant barrier. I heard their shots behind the ice wall. Next, I took shadows from the closest trees and expanded them so that we were in total darkness. That's when I sent the wall of fire. It burned bright purple and black. I kept it at a safe distance, as a deterrent, not a weapon.

The fire gave me more time to gather more water. After a few minutes, they were enclosed by a rainbow maze of fire and ice. Twenty more soldiers approached from the other direction, still in full light. Using the same tactics, I quickly hemmed them in. There was still no sign of the girls. I couldn't wait much longer and had to decide whether to drop my guard and try to contact them on the astral, to swim into the lake, or to just keep waiting. There was no way to know how many soldiers there were. It would be foolish to lead them into the lake. Instead, I manipulated the light to cause a blinding ring of glare and flash, just inside the other barriers. I sat on the starry ground facing the water, quieted myself and concentrated on finding the girls over the astral.

They were on an island, miles in. I explained the attack and told them to stay where they were.

"No, we're coming to help you," Amber said.

"It's too dangerous. I'm not staying here. I'm going to the fifth lake."

"Damn it, Nate."

"How's Linh?"

"She's in pieces, but the lake is helping. We can be—"

"Amber, please don't follow me. I promise I'll be back soon. Stay with Linh. I can go faster alone."

"But why?"

"I need to get to the fifth lake. I think Dustin might be there, and something occurred to me... if we're supposed to save Outin from these invaders, how are we ever going to make them leave without killing them?"

"What if we just find Dustin and leave?"

"Amber, I can't stay. The soldiers will get to me. Will you do what I ask?"

"Yes, but—"

The bullets hit my legs in three places. My eyes flashed on the soldier crouched at the shore and the two others, still in the lake, who swam around the frozen wall. Another spray of bullets missed me as I was levitating and had us all in total darkness. It took almost half a minute for the soldier to toss a flare, but I was already behind a new wall of ice. The injuries to my legs were weakening me fast. I needed to get to the healing waters of the lake, but my own barriers were preventing me from reaching it. I managed to get two Lusans made, but it took almost all my remaining energy. It was inevitable that the soldiers would eventually get over the barriers and I'd be killed. The Lusans would take too long. I needed to get to the lake.

Kyle's voice came through, clear and calm. "Breathe. Slow-ly. Re-lax." I looked around, but of course he wasn't there. "Breathe." On the fifth deep breath I realized the walls of ice surrounding me were frozen healing water from Floral Lake. I used Gogen and fire to create a pool, took off my clothes, and slipped into the warm, healing water.

Through the wonderful combination of soaking in Floral's water, multiple Lusans, and my own healing soul-powers, I was moving again. My legs were still very sore, but I didn't dare risk slowing. There was no sign of choppers in the air, so I chose that as my route. I created a pastel windstorm, which included shadowy darkness with alternating bursts of blinding light, to render their night vision goggles ineffective. I floated and Skyclimbed above the disturbance until I was a safe distance away. My only chance for survival rested within the knowledge of my insane brother and resistance to the urge to use destructively the awakening powers of my soul.

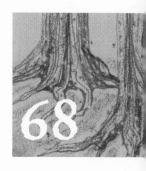

## 68

The fifth lake of Outin, hardly a lake compared to the other four, was right where Dustin said it would be, but Dustin wasn't there. It was the size of a tennis court, with crystal clear water, surrounded by rocks, and, according to Dustin, miles deep. He'd said you didn't need air—something about the water being so pure your body just absorbed the oxygen. It seemed incredible, but we didn't need food here. Looking down into the waters, I wondered if it might be a portal.

The lake was concealed in a thick grove of glass-like trees, and that grove was within a larger section of white trees. Their globe-leaves were unusual for Outin because they were also white and clear. It was like being within a natural sanctuary. Lightyear was far away from this place. Before entering the lake, I wanted to check on the girls and reached Amber on the astral.

"I'm at the fifth lake."

"Did you see many soldiers?" Amber was really asking if I'd killed anyone.

"No real trouble. How's Linh?"

"We're both okay. When can we join you?"

"There are too many soldiers around Floral Lake right now. You're safe. I'll be back soon."

"How do you know we're safe? Kyle's dead, yet *we* were the ones who were supposed to die."

"That's what I keep trying to tell you. The future is not for sure. We're changing it. Be calm, be strong."

"In spite of what they did to Kyle, Linh and I still believe nonviolence is the right path. Kyle would agree, don't you think?"

"Yes. It's the only way."

"I, we miss you."

"Don't worry. I'll see you soon. Trust the universe."

I hid my clothes and pack in the rocks, glad not to have the Jadeo with me. The water was hot, but as I kicked deeper, it cooled a bit. Dustin was right, breathing was easy and I wondered if babies inside the womb felt like this. Gradually I felt different, as if all the pressure and weight of my earthly existence were vanishing. Even my legs were pain-free. Suddenly a flood of information and images filtered through my mind. Dustin had said that the lake clarifies what you already know and brings new awareness to your perception of things in which you lack certainty. I decided to call the fifth lake of Outin "Clarity Lake."

The temperature of the crystal-clear water made me feel like I was floating in a strangely lit cave... I wasn't sure the water was even there. But my thoughts were commanded elsewhere, as the revelations and understandings came, one after another. Baca, Kirby, and Amparo were all in custody. How were they finding and capturing mystics? We'd known Baca, the Mexican farmer who saved us on I-5, was arrested but not identified by Lightyear as a mystic. Kirby, who taught us shapeshifting and Kellaring, should have been impossible to catch. And poor Amparo... they were all in custody—maximum-security isolation cells somewhere in Nevada. It was a real jolt discovering they were rounding up mystics. Then I remembered not all mystics could vanish at will, and although some might be ancient or possibly not even human, others were like me. I'd been a mystic for a few months, and I'd come close to death or capture many times.

Information continued to infiltrate my mind. Dustin was alive in Outin as Spencer had promised. But Kyle was truly dead, my lingering hope shattered. His aunt and uncle, Linh's parents, did not know yet. They, along with Mom and Bridgette, were still in custody in Virginia. At least the facility seemed modern, and they appeared in good health. How long before Kyle and Linh's grandmother, Bà, and my parents' business partner, Josh, got picked up? What about my history teacher, Mr. Anderson? Was anyone who knew or helped me safe?

The water of Clarity Lake was different than that of Floral Lake. Rather than healing, it seemed incredibly energizing—like toppling Lightyear could be a breeze. My feelings for Linh and Amber were deep and spanned many lifetimes. I loved them both. But, in this lifetime, I could only be with one of them, and that time might be short. Kyle's death was a brutal reminder of how close we all were to being taken away from one another. Even in the radiant magical waters of Clarity Lake, thoughts of Kyle's mutilated dead body filled me with despair. How had it come to this? The answer came instantly— the Jadeo. Although I thought this was all about Lightyear and the Movement, it originated and revolved around the Jadeo. It was the answer to everything and could save mankind, but if it appeared too soon or was recovered by Lightyear, then the human race would continue toward destruction. The Movement wasn't about protecting the Jadeo; that was the job of the nine original entrusted ones. IM was actually about preparing the world for the Jadeo.

I swirled through the waters, thinking about Hibbs and Clastier, topics that had occupied me during the prior weeks. Those earlier lifetimes were also just part of my education and preparation for this incarnation as Nathan Ryder. To my relief, I wasn't to be the leader of the Movement but rather an inspiration.

Another stunning revelation showed that I wasn't the "you" on the list of the entrusted nine from Dad's desk; "you" was actually Dustin. My dad had left the paper and the Jadeo for Dustin. What were the ramifications of that? Could either of us have carried it to safety?

Mom's decision to lock Dustin up could have been more than a tragic mistake; she unknowingly put us all at risk and jeopardized the Jadeo. It seems even Clarity Lake had limits of what it could answer. Still, Dustin being Dad's choice to take the Jadeo changed my thinking about everything and left me questioning even more about what wrong decisions or assumptions might have led to Kyle's death. It was somehow my fault, destined or not, regardless of the definition of death. How many others? Rose, Crowd? Who was next? Could I stop it? Would I cause more?

I saw that, unbeknownst to my dad, my soul was incarnated as one of the three remaining names on the list. But before I could discover which one, more information came, and it was so shocking it sent me swimming frantically for the surface in a flailing need for a taste of real air.

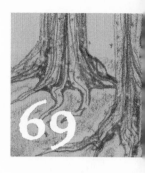

## 69

Aunt Rose was still alive. Hyperventilating, coughing, and crying, I clawed at the rocks as they scratched my naked, shivering body. She wasn't just alive. Rose was freely and willingly working with Lightyear to apprehend the Ryder brothers. Her death had been a ruse—no wonder I could never communicate with her. She had planted the dream in Linh's head that had confirmed her death. Did Spencer know? Of course he knew. He knew everything and had chosen, yet again, to withhold another piece of critical information from me. Why? Wouldn't it have been safer if I'd known? More importantly, why was Rose doing this? Perhaps she was the traitor from the original entrusted nine.

Somehow I dragged myself to my clothes. I managed to make a tiny Lusan while my teeth were chattering. Once I was dressed and meditating, my temperature returned to normal.

I found my mother on the astral. "Nate, my God. Are you alive?"

"Yes, I'm fine."

"There have been reports that you were dead."

I actually had to stop and think about it. How would I know if I were dead, especially in Outin? There was a possibility I'd been dead for a while and didn't know it. Going insane was easier than it looked—once everything you thought turns out to be different, and every day the lines between the past, present, and future, the living and dead, the possible and impossible blur or become erased entirely... there's no sense of reality left.

"Nate are you still there?"

"Yes, I am. Don't believe what you see in the media and definitely don't believe what the government tells you."

"Oh, Nate. Please turn yourself in before you're killed. There will be a fair trial, and you can explain how all this happened."

"Mom, Rose is alive."

"What? Rose, how did you find out? I mean..."

"Wait, did you know?"

"Well, I... yes, yes. Rose has visited me here."

"Jesus, why didn't you tell me?"

"Rose asked me not to. She said that she couldn't help you if you knew."

"That doesn't make sense. Why would me knowing she was alive stop her from helping me? Mom, she's working with Lightyear to arrest Dustin and me."

"Maybe she thinks that's the best way to help you."

"No, Lightyear isn't trying to bring me in. Why the hell don't you get this? They want me dead. Lightyear is trying to kill me, and Rose is helping them."

"Okay, what if she is? I never did trust that woman. But if it's true that they want to kill you, then you need to—" Mom was gone. It took almost three minutes to find her again.

"Are you back? It's funny how I can feel your presence. You have these powers to do good, not to run and hide."

"Mom, people fear what they don't understand. And the man who runs Lightyear is greedy and corrupt. He wants me out of his way."

"Turn yourself in. Once you're in custody, they can't hurt you. They've been treating me fine, and Linh's parents and Amber's sister—her mother's a movie star for goodness sakes. They have to keep you safe and have a fair trial."

"If I believed that, I would do it. But Mom, it's so much bigger than this lifetime, than these personalities."

"Just think—" I tried for five minutes to reach her again before giving up.

Linh came through fairly easily. I considered not telling her about Rose because they'd had a connection, and this betrayal, following so closely behind Kyle's death, seemed extra cruel. But I didn't want to be like Spencer, choosing what and when to tell such important facts.

"So my dream about her death wasn't real?"

"She must have used some form of Solteer to make you have the dream. *It* was real, but the information wasn't. She's alive. My Mom has seen and talked to her."

"I didn't know her that long, but working with Lightyear?"

"One thing I've learned through all this is everything is deeper than it appears. We aren't just acting in this lifetime. We get all mixed up about the events and drama of a few years, or even decades, when it's really about centuries, millennia. So I don't want to judge it, if that's the role she is playing."

"You sound like Yangchen. How can you let it go like that?"

"I can't. I'm just trying to."

"Will you come get us now?"

"Yeah. Let me get myself together. I may go into the lake one more time, and then I'll make my way back to you guys. I'll come tonight."

Alone in the strangeness of Outin, I tried to make sense of it all. My legs needed attention, and while doing healings on them, my thoughts bounced from Rose's betrayal to my mother's confinement, from finding Dustin to how to safely get back to the girls. But mostly my mind was consumed with failing my best friend. I'd been so concerned about saving the girls and stopping the mall attack that I missed the danger to Kyle. He did everything I asked and trusted me more than I do myself. "I'm so sorry, Kyle," I whispered.

Three fantastic butterflies flew above the lake, colors that Crayola couldn't invent. They danced around my head for a moment before disappearing into the crystal trees. "Thanks, Kyle."

The skywaves began to change from aquamarine to orange meaning it would be dark in less than an hour. I was almost ready to go. There had been no Windows along the way from Floral Lake, and finding Dustin seemed impossible. He had not been available on the astral since he left Cervantes. But I couldn't leave the girls alone any longer and figured the three of us would spend the night on their island then map out the best way to proceed. We couldn't leave Outin without Dustin, and we couldn't leave Outin in the hands of Lightyear.

"You may not leave Outin alive," a familiar voice startled me.

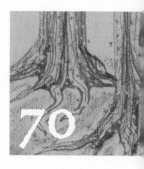

I turned to see Dustin emerging from the crystal trees.
"Been looking for me?" He smiled.

"For most of the last few years," I replied.

His hug was filled with my childhood, our dad, and the straining extremes of brotherhood that only brothers understand.

"Don't hold that stuff in, brother." He let me go. "Suppressed feelings lead to neurosis. Next thing you know, Mom will be taking you to Mountain View."

I choked a laugh. "You seem better than when I last saw you. Maybe better than I've seen you in years."

"Yeah, well. Outin is my kind of dimension."

"I thought you died."

"I know you did. Sorry about that. Were you kind of relieved?" He stared at me but didn't wait for a response. "I was in a bad place that week, or was it a year? Time's a funny thing, you know? Especially Outin time." He sat on one of the large black boulders bordering the lake. "But it worked out okay. I needed to be alone for a while, and you needed to go back to wherever it is you went."

"Do you go in often?" I pointed to Clarity's water.

"Are you kidding? It's a drug, man. I drink the stuff."

"Really?"

He laughed. "Not really. I did try, but it tastes a little weird, like dish soap. But I do swim in it as often as possible."

"Do you know about Rose?"

"Nothing in that water is perfect, it's all based on your perception. But is Kyle dead and Rose alive?"

"I held Kyle's body."

"I know, I'm sorry. I think he landed right in the middle of them. I mean he came through a portal, and it dropped him at the lodge when some soldiers were gathered there. I'd been watching them, but there was nothing I could do. It happened so fast. Outin really freaked them out and they got spooked, just started firing like they were under attack." He shook his head. "What I meant was, because it happened here in another dimension, is it possible he is still alive back home somewhere?"

"I've thought the same thing," I answered.

"Yeah. And I don't know for sure, but I've been in and out of so many Windows, been to so many parallel times, stark pasts, bloody futures, and twisted presents, that I'm fairly certain Kyle's actual personality is over."

"I feel it. Like Spencer says, there's that change."

Dustin nodded.

"But Rose is really alive. Mom has seen her."

"Okay, I saw it in the lake too, but did you see that Rose is working with Lightyear? I have a hard time with that one."

"Lightyear is powerful, and who knows what karma we have with Rose. How well did we know her, anyway?"

"I don't know, Nate, but at the worst time in my life, Rose was the only one who was there." His voice cracked. "She helped me; she kept me from going insane."

"Maybe she did it just to get to me."

"Why did Dad trust her then?" Dustin asked.

"I don't know. Maybe she fooled him, too. Dad didn't even know I was one of the seven."

"How do you know?"

"Because he was giving the Jadeo to you," I said.

He looked at me with narrow eyes.

"Do you know what the Jadeo is?" I asked.

"Yeah, little brother, I know what it is. I may have been a little impaired the last few years, but I've been catching up

here at Outin University. I know I'm also one of the nine entrusted. And I know what the Jadeo is. But I didn't know Dad
wanted me to safeguard it," his voice was shaky. "Dad wanted
me to have it," he said to himself. "And why is that so hard
to believe? Just because you're the golden boy, doesn't mean
other people can't do anything."

"Maybe he knew I'd be a target, so it would be safer if
someone else was protecting it."

"Well, we don't know what he was thinking. But we
know he wanted me to have it, so where is it?" Dustin asked.

"Spencer."

"Of course. He's not just running the Movement, he's
running your life."

"It feels that way sometimes." I walked around the side
of the lake and peered in. Neither of us spoke for a couple of
minutes. Dustin walked over and put his arm around me.

"I'm sorry, Nate. I don't want to fight with you. Our
fight is with Lightyear."

"We can't use violence," I said, turning to face him.

"Oh no, Spencer got you to go all Gandhi on me. What
good are all these powers if we can't use them?"

"It's not Spencer. He's fine with doing whatever it takes."

"I knew I liked something about him."

"But this is about our souls. You know what I'm talking
about."

"Yeah I know, but do you? These bastards killed Dad.
They killed Dad, Nate."

"I know."

"No you don't. 'Cause that's not enough. They killed
Crowd and Kyle and those kids in the mall. Hundreds!"

"But where does it end?"

"You tell me. Mom's in jail, although that's kind of po-
etic justice…" He smiled, but then his eyes saddened. "I'm sure
they'll let her out. And Bridgette's locked up, too. Hell, they may
start picking up all my ex-girlfriends. They're pure darkness."

"Darkness can't drive out darkness: only light can do
that. Hate can't drive out hate: only love can do that."

"Now you're getting all Martin Luther King, Jr."

"I'm making a point."

"You think we can stop Lightyear with love and flowers? They have access to the most lethal weapons in existence, and they have psychics. Without soul-powers, what do we have? A few hundred hippies and new-age housewives looking for the next workshop or retreat?"

"No one is saying we can't use soul-powers. We just can't use them for killing."

"Oh. Why didn't you say so? I'll use Gogen to bake a nice cake, and then I'll Vising up some pretty balloons," he waved his hands around. "And we'll invite those Special Forces guys to a tea party."

I couldn't help but laugh. He laughed, too.

"The guys running Lightyear use thugs to do their dirty work. We need to win this differently. We're smarter than them. And don't make fun of me, but nothing is more powerful than love."

Dustin made kissing noises, started tickling me, and in a falsetto whine said, "I love you, I love you, I love you."

"Get off me, you weirdo!" I laughed.

"Okay, tell me your plan."

"I was hoping you had one."

He looked at me, waiting patiently.

"Okay, I have the start of a plan. I met with Storch."

"How'd that go? Why didn't you kill him?"

"Haven't you been listening?"

"Brain damage." He winked, pointing to his head.

"I want to show the meeting to the world. He doesn't come across too favorably. Tell me how to project my meeting with Storch."

"Oh, I see. Dusty knows a trick that baby brother can't do. And I thought you came back to Outin 'cause you were worried about me."

"Shut up," I said.

"Okay. Here's the thing. It isn't that you can't do it. You just need two people connected to one another in the physical world to pull it off."

It was similar to advanced Kellaring, but he didn't know about that because Lightyear's remote viewers couldn't track across dimensions, and he'd been safely tucked away at Outin all this time. I explained it and he told me what we needed to do to be able to film it. Spencer had included a digital recorder in our pack so we could do it here. He must have known Dustin wasn't interested in leaving Outin, even to strike a blow at Lightyear.

"Once you've been in an asylum, if you're lucky enough to get out, you spend the rest of your life in fear of being returned to cruel confinement. Mom will feel the same way once she gets out of prison. It's not as bad, but close enough."

"You think you're safer here? Who knows how many troops they've got at Outin."

"They have 104 personnel in this dimension and all entered through the original veil we came through. Fourteen are psychics, and the remaining ninety are divided among three squads of highly trained 'black ops.' As of now, no Lightyear agents have yet gone into a Window or any of the four lakes, and they still don't know about the fifth lake.

"Wow."

"We can beat them, Nate. At least in the battle for Outin."

71

We filmed the Storch meeting. It was incredible. It looked just like it had been shot on Roosevelt Island where the actual meeting had been. Because it was an uninterrupted video of the event, it would stand up to all authentication techniques. I carefully sealed the flash-drive back into the waterproof pouch it came from, and zipped it into my pants pocket. I wanted to take one more plunge into Clarity Lake, but Dustin said we better go.

Along the way, he explained that the Windows, which moved by themselves anyway, could be moved manually. Every time he saw one, he dragged it to a remote region of Outin he called "the Vines."

"It's a wild impenetrable area. They haven't even been close to it yet. Outin is like forever big. But anyway, these twisty vines grow out of the starry ground. They start off black and white, but as they get taller, they turn into every imaginable psychedelic color and tangle together like the blackberry bushes back home, only these are like forty feet tall. It's intense to look at but almost impossible to get through, and some of the blue ones have razor-sharp thorns."

"How did you get the Windows in?"

"Skyclimbed." He smiled.

"You can do it now?"

"Oh yeah. Just call me Rocket Man." He did a high backflip.

"That's great, Dustin." I patted his shoulder when he landed. "Outin's been good for you."

"I never want to leave."

"You'll get lonely. This vast dimension and nobody living here..."

"Outin is full of beings."

"The birds and bugs probably aren't the best conversationalists."

"Not them. The trees."

"Trees?" I gazed around at the thin white ones we were weaving through. "What do you mean? Can they talk?" It would have been a silly question anywhere other than Outin.

"Not like us with voices, but they communicate and... they move."

"How?"

"You'll see."

It was dark now. Dustin's night vision wasn't great, but the starlight from the ground was so bright and the trees shimmered, so it wasn't really needed. I let the girls know we were on our way.

"How is he?" Amber asked.

"Better than he's been in years."

"So can we leave Outin now?"

"No."

"I was afraid of that."

"Push the fear away."

"It's just an expression. So you want to somehow make the soldiers leave?"

"We'll talk about it when we're together. Gotta keep moving."

"Let's go," I said to Dustin.

"So, have you done her yet?"

"None of your business."

"That means no."

"That means none of your business."

"Well, if she's anything like her sister—"

"She's not. Okay, can we talk about something else?"

"Sure. Have you done Linh yet?"

"Shut up, will you." I gave him a playful shove, then Sky-climbed. He followed. We soared through the trees of multiple trunks with holly-berry-sized round leaves of Sunkist-orange color. We made good time; it wasn't long before we reached the trees closest to the lodge and beyond that, Floral Lake.

"Check that out." He pointed to a group of ten soldiers near the lodge. We were on the top of some high trees and would be impossible to spot. "There should be twenty more somewhere nearby," Dustin said. "We need a diversion to get passed them. What new fun do you have in your bag of tricks?"

"How about a fire?" I said.

"Will you be able to put it out?"

"I can use lake water. I'll keep it away from the trees. Just around the lodge."

"What if one of them gets killed? What's that do to your nonviolence pledge?"

"I don't know. I guess that could happen." Though that thought made my stomach hurt.

"Yeah, it would be a real shame," Dustin said sarcastically, before seeing my concern. "Don't worry little brother, it has to be based on intent or something. I mean accidents happen. What if I accidently crash my car into someone? Does that mean I'm stripped of all my soul-powers. Who decided this stuff anyway?"

"There's a collective consciousness. I don't know exactly how it works."

"Don't let this nonviolence stuff get you all tied up. If you're afraid to move because you might squash an ant or something, where does it end? But if you aren't bold, you will catch a bullet in your head. These guys are trained to kill, and you're their target this week. Try to do no harm, but *do* something."

He was right. It was one thing to attack people, another to use force to defend myself, and something entirely different to try to avoid trouble. That's all we were trying to do. I sent fire and ignited two different areas on the other side of the soldiers, well away from us. We Skyclimbed in bounding leaps across the dark landscape. Unfortunately these elite fighters were trained in military tactics, unlike me, and recognized a diversion when they saw one. Four of them dropped to cover the fire. The remaining six sent flares to light up the area. The other twenty joined them. They had us surrounded and hadn't even spotted us yet. The water was still five hundred yards away. Another flare whizzed by me. I manipulated the particles and turned it into strobing stadium lights, aimed back at the troops. It gave us enough time to make it to the lake.

We undressed and waded in, holding our clothes and my pack above our heads. It was impossible to sink in Floral Lake, but by using a relaxed form of Skyclimbing, we moved through the water easily. I could have run across the lake but Dustin couldn't, and the idea of letting him out of my sight again didn't appeal to me. Once we were a safe distance, I sent water to quench the fires. The lights dissipated on their own. It took longer than I expected to reach the island.

"Linh, I'm sorry," Dustin said. "He was a good guy." She nodded but didn't look up. "And Amber, I'm uh… last time I saw you, I wasn't myself. What I'm trying to say is, I behaved horribly. I'm sorry." He meant it and was ashamed of himself.

72

Amber and Linh wanted to leave Outin and return to
Yangchen and Spencer. "We need help. At least when
we're with them, we have Booker and the Movement behind
us," Amber said.

"How are we supposed to get these hit men to leave
Outin without killing them first?" Linh asked.

"I've been thinking about that," Dustin said. "We're going to have to capture them."

"That sounds easy," Linh said sarcastically. "How many
are there?"

"A hundred and four."

"So, you can count," Linh said. "Then you've probably
noticed there are only four of us. And we're not allowed to
use violence."

"Ah, but we know Outin better, and we have an arsenal
of the most powerful tools at our disposal."

"Nate, let's leave," Amber said, "before another one of us
gets killed."

"Why does it matter what happens to Outin?" Linh
asked. "Why is it our job to protect it?"

"We led them here." I stood and paced. "This isn't just a
special place; it's important."

"And more than that," Dustin interrupted, "if we're going to defeat Lightyear, they cannot be allowed the advantages
of Outin's secrets."

"Some day you must tell me what those secrets are and why they're worth Kyle's life," Linh said, getting up and walking away. The island was about the size of a couple of soccer fields, so she wasn't going far. I was about to follow her, but Amber said she'd go. I didn't know if it was because she didn't want to be left alone with Dustin or didn't want me to be alone with Linh.

"They don't understand Outin. And you haven't told them what the Jadeo is, have you?" Dustin asked.

"No, I haven't told anyone. It's safer if they don't know."

"Are you sure? Maybe if they knew, they wouldn't be so quick to dismiss Outin."

"Kyle is dead, Dustin. His body is floating out there somewhere. Give them a day to get used to that."

"Did you mourn for me?"

"That's a complicated question."

"No, the question was simple and so was your answer."

"Shut up, man. You're my brother. I love you."

"No need to apologize. You got me out of Mountain View, that was enough, forever. Then you saved my life when Fitts tried to kill me, that was enough for another forever." He looked at me with his deepest, most serious expression. "There are more than one forever, you know?"

"Tell me about it."

"I will. In the meantime, you and your girlfriends are overestimating death—it's really a little thing. Kyle still exists."

"I know," I said.

"Then act like it. Be an example. It's one thing to be called one of the seven; it's another to *be* one of the seven. This great shift doesn't have to take decades. Hell, it should have already happened. But everyone is so attached to their human world, their human ideas, their pitiful human lives!" His voice was loud enough to bring the girls back into the conversation.

"Where were you, Dustin?" Linh ran toward us, screaming. "We only came back here to find you. What were you doing? Kyle never would... we only... where were you when

Kyle was getting filled with bullets?" She fell to the ground in tears. Amber knelt and put an arm around her. "No!" she screamed flailing her arms. "Leave me alone."

"She needs Bà," Dustin said.

That brought her to her feet. "No, Dustin. You know what I really need? I need you to stop being all woozy, all 'I got messed up in a mental institution, the voices were too much for me,'" she mimicked. "And grow up. Be a man. It's hard for all of us. Try being less self-involved." The anger calmed her. Dustin stood speechless. She walked off and I followed.

"Let's get out of here, Nate." Her voice was pleading. "I'm afraid another one of us is going to die."

"We can't just let them have Outin."

"Then let's use our powers to wipe them out. We've killed before. What difference does it make now? Just one last time. I want to kill them, Nate. I want to watch them all die." The anger lost to the tears. "Kyle was so good. He was so—" She fell into my arms, crying.

I held her a minute before speaking. "We're going to do better than kill them, Linh. We're going to beat them. We're going to win."

The missile's whistling provided just seconds of warning. My body temperature spiked, as I threw my body against Linh and we crashed to the ground.

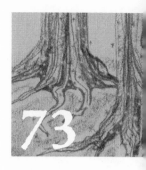

73

The island was half gone. We were lucky. It hit the other side and the four of us survived.

"Must have been a SAM," Dustin said.

"What?" My ears rang. I helped Linh up.

"You know a surface-to-air-missile, a SAM."

"Otherwise knows as a Fitts," Amber joked. We huddled together, dusting off. Amber had a bad gash on her arm, and Dustin's face was cut. Linh's hand hurt from where we landed on it, and a rock got my shoulder hard. But other than that, we were okay.

"They can only carry stuff in. No vehicles, helicopters, tanks or planes can make it in. So it must be a SAM. They're shoulder-mounted."

"How do you know they can't bring in tanks?" Amber asked.

"You hang around long enough, and you learn all kinds of stuff. Anything too heavy will fall into the stars. And nothing can fly in that sky." He pointed to the churning waves above us, dimly lit from the reflecting starlight.

"Let's go. They obviously know exactly where we are. I don't want to give them another chance." My temperature got hotter. "Now!" We dove into the lake as another missile finished off the island, where we had just been. "Swim, follow me."

"To where?" Dustin asked. "It's a big lake."

"You tell me."

I couldn't see his face but felt his confusion. "This way," he finally said.

Twenty minutes later we crawled from the flower-filled waters up a craggy black hill while another missile hit near the island. As we reached the top of the hill, two rubber rafts sped toward what was left of the island. Their bright searchlights scanned the landscape.

"Where to now?" I asked.

"Depends. Do you want to run or fight?" Dustin said. "We can see so much from up here, and they can't see us."

"How come?" I asked.

"This hill is only visible from a few feet away."

"Seriously? But what about us?"

"Not sure about that. I've never been on it and looking for myself at the same time, but if we stay near the top and keep down, we should be all right."

At that moment I heard Kyle's voice, "meditate." I couldn't be sure if it was real or imagined, but I decided, either way, it was a good idea.

"I'm going to meditate."

"Here? Now?" Amber asked.

"I'll keep watch," Linh said, allowing the slightest smile, the first since we'd found Kyle.

I moved into a small nook just below the crest of the hill. After a short time, the meditation took an unusual turn. I was invisibly in the midst of thirty black-ops soldiers. They had a small camp on the edge of what we called the First Woods and the clearing around the lakes. I stood in the camp as they were readying to move out. A hard-looking guy, who couldn't have been more than three or four years older than me, was checking his weapon. "I wish they weren't armed," I said to myself. At the same time, he threw his gun to the ground. He looked around confused.

"Can you hear me?" I asked. The question made him look. "You shouldn't be fighting and trying to kill me." That statement moved his expression closer to fear. He started moving away. "Wait, stay here." He stopped. "I'm not going to hurt you, but if I asked you to pick up your machine gun and shoot yourself, you'd do it." He leaned down and reached for it. "No, leave it on the ground. Stand at attention, soldier," I said firmly. He did. I looked around; no one else had noticed us. "Wait here."

Two soldiers passing nearby reacted just as the first one had. Within a short time, there were eleven, all held captive by my commands. Then I grew bolder and silently announced to the entire camp that they should place their weapons on the ground and assemble in front of the main tent. Astonishingly, they did as they were told. I guess when Yangchen said the battle for Outin would be huge, she didn't account for the incredible power of the mind.

I instructed them to sit on the ground in three rows of ten and calmly explained to them the truth about Luther Storch and Lightyear, and explained my innocence. They may or may not have believed me—it was impossible to know—but they were mesmerized. In the same state, I asked Dustin to guard them. Whether their obedience would last was very much in question, especially when I took my attention away. Dustin could collect and destroy all of their weapons. Things were looking up, if this was really happening.

74

Amber and Linh were pulling me down the hill. I was uncertain of my whereabouts, but the explosion brought me back right as a SAM blew off the top of our hill. I managed to get to my feet. The force of the blast sent Linh tumbling, but I caught her. Another missile seared by. In one motion, I pulled Linh into a Skyclimb and pushed Amber down with my feet. The SAM whizzed past. As we came back down, with Gogen, I scooped Amber onto my back, and carrying her, returned to the air with great leaps toward the trees. We flew through a hurricane of missiles and laser-machine gunfire and crashed into the forest. I somehow managed to get us all far enough into the trees to be out of range. All of us had gun burns. These advanced laser-machine guns didn't use bullets; instead they burned extremely painful holes or streaks into their targets. A headshot would certainly be fatal, even with soul-powers. Lusans worked on our wounds, but it wasn't until Amber made one four times the normal size that we learned one huge one had a thousand times the power of a few small ones.

"Where's Dustin?" I asked frantically.

"Don't you know?" Linh asked.

I looked from her to Amber and shook my head.

"He said you wanted him to go and supervise the prisoners."

"What prisoners? Oh my God, was that real? I couldn't—"

"What?"

"He didn't give us time to stop him," Amber said.

"How long was I meditating?"

"Maybe forty-five minutes."

I told them what happened and tried to recall how to get there. We raced through the black woods. Even with night vision it was difficult because of the uneven ground, low branches, and closeness of trees. Since I broke meditation, the soldiers may have picked up their weapons again, if they really ever dropped them.

As we ran, I attempted to reach Dustin on the astral, but there was only a void. Linh yelled, "Maybe we should stop so you can meditate again." The same thought occurred to me, but there was no time to waste. Once we reached the far side of the forest, there was still a vast open area to cover.

"You two stay in the trees. I can go faster alone."

"We're not splitting up," Amber said. Linh nodded.

"Okay." There was no way to win that argument. Amber protested for a moment, but we had to Skyclimb. This time she used Gogen to hold on, which allowed me to move at full speed.

Suddenly the heat hit me. "Look out!" I shouted to Linh. There was nowhere to hide; we were flying and leaping over open ground. The first SAM came whirling toward us.

"How are they tracking us?" Amber shouted from my back.

"It must be the psychics they brought."

On our next touch down, it seemed as if we hit a landmine. An explosion of black and stardust chunks of "glass" erupted, and something in the sky punctured as swirls of pastel-powder and sky-fluid enveloped us in some kind of tornado. The girls were both thrown toward the trees; I dove behind a cratered ridge. The incoming rockets appeared small compared to the raging storm. Something resembling bright purple fire swept out from a second impact. I didn't know whether it was a weapon of the soldiers or an Outin reaction. Thinking lost context.

"Get to the trees!" I yelled. But it was like one of those nightmares where you scream as loud as you can and you can't hear your own voice. In another twist of horror, I also couldn't run. There was a glimpse of Linh Skyclimbing toward the woods through the smoke. In the other direction was Rainbow Lake. I struggled to raise the water onto the troops but something blocked me. My temperature was hotter than ever—unbearable. Where was Amber? There was too much smoke, sky-fluid, flames, and debris to see much of anything. "To the trees," I repeated verbally, and to Amber over the astral. The heat from my own body was going to kill me. I couldn't move. The SAM propelled out of the hellish haze and pastel fog milliseconds before it exploded next to me.

Time's a funny thing. It felt like hours later, but it could only have been a few minutes. I watched soldiers approach my body and after an inspection, search for vitals. A young soldier looked up to his commander and said without emotion, "He's dead."

The commander motioned to someone. Another soldier ran up and began taking photos.

"Let it be noted in the record that Nathan C. Ryder was pronounced dead at 8:12 a.m. on 29 January. Not sure what the hell to say about location. Mount Shasta, California, will have to do—GPS doesn't work here in this... this alien land." My hearing was perfect, but I was dead. I scanned the scene for the girls, but there was still too much smoke and powder swirling.

I was dead; it was not a shock, and not even unusual for me to actively experience my own death. I'd been here hundreds of times, watching Outviews of every conceivable type of death. This one actually wasn't too bad compared with many of my torturous ends. It was surprising not to feel sadness though. The soldiers were busy looking for the girls. I tried to reach them on the astral, but that frequency was off; there was nothing. I turned around and began moving through a dense cloud. Intense gold light surrounded me, but it didn't hurt my eyes. It was very much like a portal. The air was perfectly pure and I felt free, relaxed, and on the verge of laughter—as if I was part of the laughter, playful and happy, like first love.

Kyle glowed in the light. As soon as I recognized him from a distance, we were instantly together. "Now I know I'm dead," I said to him.

"It's not your time, Nate," Kyle said.

"What? But I'm dead." Nothing seemed to matter—the girls, IM, Mom, Dustin, stopping Lightyear—everything was obscured by the absolute peace I felt.

"You can stay if you want. There are others who will try, but you have the best chance,. You know this."

"What do you mean, stay? I am dead, right?"

"Yes, you are clinically dead, but you can go back and live."

"Seriously, that's possible?"

He nodded, smiling. "*Everything* is possible."

"But how? Kyle, you look great. I feel incredible, so different, so light. Why would I want to go back to all that darkness and heaviness?"

"It's really a radiant place, Nate. It's extraordinarily beautiful. People have just cloaked the beauty with fear. You can help change that. Show them what they're capable of, what they really are."

"Do you want me to go back?"

"I want you to do what you think you should."

"Come with me."

"I cannot."

"Why? Was it your time?"

"Time's a funny thing." His smile made me feel extraordinary. Kyle's face was bright with love.

"I'm not sure what to do. I'd like to explore this."

"You'll be here soon enough, and it'll be waiting. You won't miss a thing. I promise. All the action is back there."

75

Again on Outin's starry ground, I was longing for Kyle and the light. Why did I come back? Amber. She was screaming, "No! No! No!" Her hands were manipulating a Lusan, which grew rapidly. When she noticed my open eyes, the screaming stopped with a gasp. The Lusan suddenly filled the space around me to a diameter of six feet.

I rose up in a translucent Lusan. Sixty stunned troops scrambled and took up positions. Without an order, several fired. Their bullets were ineffective against the shimmering orb. I levitated, and with the full force of Gogen, drove them into Rainbow Lake. I froze the colored water around them then heated their weapons to such a temperature that they flung them onto the ice. Their guns remained only moments before melting through and disappearing into the lake. The men who weren't screaming in fear were awed.

I collapsed into Amber's arms. Linh ran from the trees. "Is he okay?" Linh panted. "Look at him! My God. How is he still alive?"

"I'll be okay," I whispered.

They were inspecting my wounds, which the Lusan had improved but still were substantial. "One of these days you're going to get injured beyond healing. They thought you were dead," Amber said.

"When there's time, I'll tell you an interesting story." My voice was strained. "Can you make some Lusans for my legs and chest?" I pointed to some painful places. The giant Lusan still blocked us from the soldiers.

"What are we going to do with them?"

"Let them chill out for a little while." I forced a laugh. "We still have to get to Dustin."

"Not until you're better," Amber said.

"How did I die?" I asked, unable to argue.

"After the explosion, it took me a few minutes to find you. Five soldiers surrounded your lifeless body. They said you were dead. I screamed and two guys grabbed me, but I broke free and threw myself on you, crying and making a Lusan at the same time. About a second later your eyes opened, and the Lusan was suddenly gigantic."

"You saved me. Thank you, Amber." She kissed my forehead.

"Seems you have survived against all odds," Dustin said, across the astral.

"Are you all right?" I asked.

"Yeah, I've got the place secure, but I could use a little help over here."

"We'll be there soon."

"Amber, you spent more time in that lake than anyone," Linh said. "What are the soldiers seeing?"

"It keeps changing. Rainbow Lake is like a drug." Amber's words trailed off. "We control it. Every thought, every word changes it. And not just ours but everyone's. Each time I left Rainbow Lake, I wanted to go back in and see what changes there were."

I walked to the shore and addressed the soldiers. "You've killed me today. That was your mission, and it has been completed." I looked directly at the man who pronounced me dead. "This was not the first time I've died." The highly trained soldiers cowered amid pleas for mercy. My supernatural demonstration and whatever Rainbow Lake had shown them combined to dramatically change these men, and I stunned them further by asking for their help. Once a mental or verbal yes was received from all sixty, I thawed the lake. The commander I'd seen from the "other side" offered complete assistance and led us to the camp where Dustin was waiting.

"Don't you think it's risky to trust them?" Amber asked.

"We're walking with the enemy," Linh said, before I could answer. "They murdered Kyle. His killer is among us!" She hissed.

"It's about forgiveness. Before we left Gibi, she embraced me and imparted a vision that we're now a part of. I had no idea how it would happen, but it showed us walking in this field and the soldiers willingly following me. I'm their leader now." I stopped. The commander, who was just ahead of me, paused and turned because all the troops behind us stopped when I had. "I think we should jog now," I said. Everyone, including the commander, took it as an order.

Linh was not convinced. "I don't trust them."

"I'm not asking you to. Just trust me."

A few minutes later, we arrived to find Dustin patrolling the outside of a mess tent containing thirty unarmed soldiers and fourteen psychics. He was holding a machine gun. I used Gogen to pull it from his hands and added it to the pile he had collected.

"Hey, all you had to do was ask," Dustin said, annoyed.

"Sorry, didn't want to debate. Commander, please ask the others to join us out here."

He barked an order and quickly the entire force was lined up in formation. I spoke with the psychics telepathically and used Solteer to weaken their powers.

Amber ran up to me. "Nate, you can't just leave that pile of weapons there."

"Trust me." Amber looked at Linh. Dustin's stare moved from the girls to me to the troops. I tried to calm Dustin and the girls telepathically, but there was such tension that the entire camp seemed to buzz. The soldiers believed I could strike them down at any moment and had agreed, under duress, to commit treason. Even if they thought this was the best choice, it directly contradicted their basic nature and training. Dustin and the girls were another matter. For months they had been running from, and targeted by, these very men, and now we were on the same side?

The commander quickly brought everyone to order. "For those of you who were not witness to the events at the colored lake, please bear with us. And by the looks of what occurred here, with thirty soldiers and fourteen skilled advisers surrendering to one teenager, there was an extraordinary happening here as well."

"Thank you, Commander. I'll keep this brief. None of you are being held, and your weapons will be returned to you shortly." I didn't need to look at Dustin and the girls to know what they thought. "Many of you saw in Rainbow Lake what the future holds... unless we make change." Using Gogen, I floated the guns into a pile in front of them. "Please take them. We lost quite a few in the lake, but there should still be plenty to go around."

They looked unsure for a moment. Linh shot me a what-the-hell-are-you-doing glare. One by one they picked them up. "Now if any of you would like to shoot me, it's up to you. But my death wouldn't be real, and it wouldn't last." I looked around and stood silently. Every single person remained in place. No weapon was pointed. They never took their eyes off me. "There is a different future out there, waiting... it's a place where we're no longer motivated by fear and greed. Instead we help one another and improve not just one another but all of humanity."

The psychics led the applause, followed by those who had been in the lake. But everyone had been affected by my soul-powers and Outin's magic. I was dead and now stood before them speaking of the future, of peace, to those who killed me. The impact was undeniable.

"I don't know how we could ever trust them," Linh said.

"You sounded like a politician offering 'change we can believe in.' I think I'm gonna go puke now," Dustin said.

The commander joined us, "We're behind you, Nathan. What do you have in mind?"

"We'll escort you to the entrance. Go back and tell Washington that some unknown force pushed you out. You won't be able to get back in once we seal the entrances. You won't tell them anything about—"

"We thought you wanted us to travel with you as a kind of security force, but you're asking us to be spies?" The commander appeared genuinely dismayed.

I asked for everyone's attention again and addressed them while standing a couple of feet off the ground. "Let me be clear, I am requesting your help. It is not an easy thing I'm asking. You'll need to act as if you're still agents of Lightyear and not talk about what occurred here. You will keep this oath and be known to me, to the four of us, in the future when you'll help us. You will always help us. We will count on that... remember what you've seen here."

I moved back to the commander. "I have to tell you, Nathan, that once these soldiers get back to the real world and the memory of this place, and your magic tricks fade, some of them, not all of them, but certainly some, will honor their first oath rather than yours. Separating yourself from us is not the most advisable course."

"I'm sure you're correct, Commander. But that is what must be done."

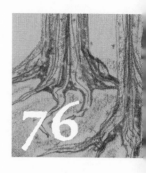

I purposely kept things hurried for the next hour. While the original sixty soldiers packed up every trace of their presence, the other thirty soldiers and fourteen psychics followed us back to Rainbow Lake. Amber was the one who suggested we get them in to see the future, believing it might ensure more loyalty once they were gone. When that was done, we ushered the entire group to the first entrance, the one Dustin and I came to months earlier and where Lightyear had entered. Before they left, their cover story was rehearsed among the group and I memorized every face, name, and home address; I knew their life stories.

They went through, and the veil closed. "How long before they come back here with ten thousand troops?" Linh asked.

"And that'll just be to protect the timber, mining, and oil companies who will start stripping Outin of its unique and valuable natural resources," Dustin added with cynicism.

"No one is coming back here," I said, Skyclimbing to the top of the veil. Just as Dustin had moved the Windows, I was able to move the entrance. Invoking Solteer, communication opened between my mind and the entrance. Like everything else, it was energy; it was alive. I asked the entrance to tune to a different frequency and to move frequently. It would relay these requests to all other entrances, and Outin was sealed.

"Then how are we going to get out?" Linh asked.

"I believe I can help with that," Dustin said. "There's this Window that opens into Cuba, about three months into the future."

"Seriously?" It was perfect. I'd been planning to go out the same place we came in. I'd still be able to locate the entrance for a few hours, but Dustin's idea was much better. "That's the best idea you've ever had. It saves us from having to travel during this intense manhunt, plus gets us safely three months away from the mall attack. And besides, Booker has a place there."

"Of course he does." Dustin laughed.

We stopped at Floral Lake to soak in the healing waters for a while and were getting dressed when Amber asked to see the fifth lake.

"I've named it Clarity. It's a little out of the way, but you two should experience it and I'd love to go back in."

"Uh, that's not a... the Window we need to go through is in the Vines, and they shift around. There are hundreds of them in there. So we need to get there before it moves too far."

"You really think a couple of hours more will make a difference?" I asked.

"Yeah, I've been worried about it the whole time we were soaking, but I knew you needed the healing, so it was worth the risk." Dustin was agitated. "But a sightseeing tour is another thing. We need to get to the Window."

Amber looked at me concerned, then shrugged. "I have a feeling we'll be back to Outin some day. We can see it then."

"Yeah, we're probably safer getting back to Booker and Spencer as soon as possible," Linh added.

"Give me a minute to try to reach them." It was a bit garbled and I was only able to get to Booker. He seemed to understand that we'd be at his Cuba house in eighty to a hundred days, but I lost him before I could be sure.

"Amparo, Baca, and Kirby are all in custody," I said as we hurried on.

"You didn't tell us that before," Linh said.

"There hasn't been time. The question is how are they finding mystics?"

"Rose?" Amber asked.

"Just because Rose was arrested doesn't mean she's helping Lightyear," Dustin said.

"She faked her death, she has never once contacted me on the astral, she's visited Mom, and in Clarity Lake I felt it."

"Anyone could have sent that dream into Linh's head, and maybe something has blocked her from getting to you on the astral. And so what, maybe they let family members visit each other. None of them have done anything illegal other than helping you."

"What about what I saw in Clarity Lake?"

"Outin is an amazing place, but we don't understand it. I mean, look behind us right now." Dustin said, stopping. We all turned around. It took a second to notice, but the trees were moving—very slowly—actually closing the trail.

"Why are they doing that?" I asked.

"The trees can move!" Amber exclaimed.

"Who knows why they do it," Dustin said. "But the very definition of a tree is a woody perennial plant rooted in the ground... well, not so at Outin. So whatever you felt in the lake could just be an illusion."

"Fine. But let's just act on the assumption that Rose may be helping Lightyear."

"You do that, but I'm not abandoning Rose," Dustin said. "And we shouldn't leave any of them in the hands of Lightyear—Mom, Linh's parents, Bridgette. And what about Baca? He saved us. Kirby did too by teaching us Kellaring and shapeshifting."

"And if you truly forgive, then even Amparo should be rescued," Linh said.

"Wait, hold on. Are you guys suggesting we try to rescue them? Break them out of a maximum security, top-secret government detention center?" I was stunned.

"You once asked Kyle and me to break the law and help free your brother from where he was being held," Linh said.

"That would be suicide," Amber said.

"Not with our 104 new friends," Dustin said.

"Like we can trust them," Amber snapped back.

"They think Nate is the second coming. They'll do whatever he says," Dustin said.

"First thing we're going to do is meet Booker and Spencer in Cuba and give them the Storch meeting film," I said, patting the flash-drive still in its waterproof bag in my pocket.

"That means my parents will remain in jail for at least three more months," Linh huffed.

"I'm sorry, but I'm going to Cuba. We'll find a way to get them out from there."

Linh walked alone for the rest of the time. Dustin was resigned to let me make the decisions, at least for now.

"The longer you stay here, the more you connect with the knowledge of your soul," Dustin told us. "Outin is free from the distractions of a personality-created world. This is a spiritual realm."

"What about the legends of Shasta?" Amber asked. "Have you seen any beings?"

"Shasta seems to be the main entrance to Outin, but it's not the only way. There are entry points all over the planet. Outin is a dimension, not just some place like Patagonia."

"It's that big? There must be someone living here other than trees, birds, and bugs." I said.

"We've all heard stories about little people living somewhere around Shasta, descendants of survivors from the lost continent of Lemuria, starships landing here, even a higher-dimensional city of Telos inside the mountain, Ascended Masters, subterranean tunnels whatever. I think it's all true. They pass through Outin like a gigantic galactic Grand Central Station. Outin's Windows are entrances into other dimensions, and if you do it right, they can be exits from those worlds too," Dustin said.

"Oh my God," Linh said, pointing a few hundred yards ahead.

"The Vines?" I asked.

"Obviously," Dustin said.

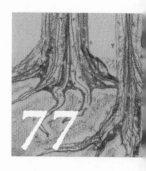

B efore us, actually growing as we watched, were towering vines as thick as my leg and taller than most trees. They twisted and braided as their black roots rose from the planetarium below our feet.

"Those thorns are guillotine sharp," Dustin said, pointing to some three feet long.

"How are we supposed to get through this?" Amber asked.

"Skyclimb!" Dustin took off. "There are lots of clearings inside."

Amber looked doubtful. "Come on," I said. "Let me carry you."

"Are you strong enough?" Linh asked.

"Sufficiently recovered, doctor." I smiled, happy she was at least talking to us again.

Amber climbed on, and I followed Dustin. Even with us both using Gogen, her fingers dug into my shoulders. "If I fall into that wicked spaghetti, it's certain death," Amber said.

"Don't worry, I won't let you fall. But can you press against me a little tighter?"

I looked back to see Linh in a graceful up-flight. Dustin went down into an open area and immediately jogged to a collection of Windows. We counted twenty-two. They were eerily addicting and challenged our perceptions. This many in one place was like flipping channels on some inner-dimensional TV.

"It's not here," Dustin said. "Probably in the next clearing. I don't always come in the same way, and they move so..."

"How many have you collected?"

"Close to a hundred."

We all looked at him. The images in those Windows weren't from a Hollywood studio. They were real places and times we could walk right into and live another existence, possibly affecting our own time in ways we would never be able to fathom. If Lightyear could get control of Outin and exploit the Windows, human history would be forever changed. I stood staring at only a portion of Dustin's collection and wondered what was more important, the Windows or the Jadeo? I couldn't decide.

"Are you sure the entrances are secure?" Linh asked.

"No."

"Come on," Dustin said. "Let's go." He was up again.

This trip was a little longer and the next clearing, smaller. It also had more than twice as many Windows. Dustin sorted through them, and after more than forty extraordinary worlds, he exclaimed, "Cuba!"

We all peered into a postcard scene. Pastel buildings and brightly colored vintage-1950s American automobiles contrasted with white sandy beaches and blue waters.

"How do you know we're not going into a different dimension?" I asked.

"When you come back through a Window from another dimension, your memory is split. It's like being brain damaged. Only half of your life remains; the other half is from the dimension you visited. It's a mental nightmare, and believe me, I'm an expert on that subject."

"How do you get normal again?"

"Floral Lake."

I nodded.

"And when you come back through Windows that stay in our dimension, it's normal. As far as I can tell, it's just the time difference. It was almost three months ahead when I was there. Of course that might change. I only went once."

"I still don't understand what happens with that lost or extra time."

"Beats me, brother."

"Since you've been there before, why don't you lead the way?" I suggested.

"Oh, Nate. I'm not going."

"What?"

"Look, you got what you came for. The Storch film is ready to show to the world. I'm delivering you safely to Booker and Spencer..."

"No. We need you, Dustin. You have to come."

"You're right, you do need me. Someone has to stay and make sure Outin remains free. I know this place. It feels part of me. It's part of my destiny."

"How do you know?"

"You told me."

"What? When?"

"You, or who we called Future Self, came back from the future again and told me."

I wasn't sure I believed him, but it was true: Outin needed to be protected, and who knew if those entrances were really safe. I could have used my powers to force him to come, but that would be ugly and end badly. I hugged him instead.

"Love you, brother," he said, holding me surprisingly tight.

"I love you, too." I stood back to look at him. "Are you sure?"

He nodded, sniffling, closing his lips tightly.

"I'll be back."

"I know, dummy. I just told you that."

I laughed. "Stay out of trouble."

He cocked his head and gave me his best devilish smile.

We changed clothes quickly. Spencer always seemed to anticipate what I would need and had thought of the swimsuits, cargo pants and T-shirts. I made sure to snap the film in a small pocket then gave a last wave to Dustin as we stepped through the Window onto a cement sidewalk.

78

The warm, humid air of Cuba and immediate hunger pains brought me slamming back to reality. Knowing we were international fugitives, I was ready to shapeshift, but the few people who were around didn't appear to notice our entrance.

As expected, there wasn't a Window opening back to Outin, but Dustin had told me the way to get back. When he explored his first Window, returning was a problem. After trying for hours to make the Window reopen, he just sat there and watched the spot. Finally, the next day, after a complete rotation of the earth, he saw a glint. When he got close enough he could see a translucent version of Outin's sky, but it only stayed for as long as it had taken him to come through originally. Then the following day, when it opened again, he returned to Outin. Later, in Clarity Lake he discovered that once someone goes back through the Window, it closes again, even if it wasn't the original traveler. If no one goes back, it will be available indefinitely.

A busy road kept us from the beach. We walked to a nearby café where the aromas awakened a craving for Million-Layer cake from the Station, my parents' restaurant. A man wearing a white linen suit approached and eyed us suspiciously. "Americanos?"

"Si," I answered. I gave him the address, memorized from Booker's list.

"Si, Si! Señor Lipton." He smiled, pleased that he had met some of Booker's friends. Then he offered to take us to him.

The girls both shrugged. There were no heat warnings, so I accepted and thanked him. He led us to his 1956 shamrock and white Pontiac and acted as a friendly tour guide for the forty-five minute drive into the country. We reached a gate but still couldn't see the house. The guard spoke to our driver in Spanish and then asked our names. "Spencer Copeland." I answered, adding that these were my sisters. A few minutes later, Booker and an employee rolled up to the other side of the gate in one of his deluxe golf carts. His face lit in relief at the sight of us. He paid our driver two hundred dollars and shuffled us into the cart.

"I have to admit, I wasn't sure I'd ever see you again. It's the last time I'll ever underestimate you, Nate." He laughed.

"I'm happy about it, too." I patted his shoulder from the backseat. "Dustin said to say hello."

"Is he okay?"

"That's always a loaded question concerning Dustin. He's alive and wanted to stay."

"I see. Well, I'm sure Spencer will have something to say about that."

"Is he here?"

"Oh yes. I can't trust that son of gun to be off by himself."

"I guess not."

"Seriously, Nate, this has been hard on him. It's taking a toll. Go easy on him."

"Spencer and I are fine," I said, surprised. "We're not arguing about anything."

"Yeah, but that doesn't seem to last between you guys."

The house was a small mansion flanked by matching miniature casitas. Palms and flowers, manicured to Booker's natural tastes, allowed glimpses of the ocean and an empty, white beach.

"Beautiful," Amber said.

"Well, thank you, Amber. Wish I could take the credit. A Coca-Cola executive had it built in the early '50s. Castro scooped it up during the revolution and paid favors with it until fifteen or sixteen years ago. When I assisted the Cuban government in some business transactions, they let me borrow this lovely property."

Booker gave us a brief tour of the first floor before having to take a phone call. He pointed us toward the oceanfront. We found Spencer sitting on the back veranda, and not surprisingly, staring out into the turquoise waters. When he turned to look at us, I couldn't hide my shock. "Man, Spencer, what happened? You look dead!"

"You should have seen me a few weeks ago." He hugged me. "You got through, Nate. You're really here." I'd never seen him this emotional. He wiped a tear. "Dustin stayed at Outin?"

"Yeah."

"Okay. How was his state of mind?"

"A little reserved but otherwise the same ol' Dustin."

He nodded.

"Spencer, why do you look so awful?" Linh asked. "Has something terrible happened? Are our families okay?"

"Yes. They're still in custody but in good health."

"It's because Nate died, isn't it?" Amber asked.

Spencer turned back to the sea.

"Is that true, Spencer? Was my death somehow felt by you?"

"Soul-powers aren't just about flying around and battling Lightyear agents. That's really just a small part. Once we open to the universe, we can experience everything, and it is often difficult on our physical body."

"But those same powers can heal our physical body."

"While we're encumbered by the physical, there are things that require so much concentration that we must neglect our human forms completely."

"But you've had three months since I died. Why do you still look so sick?"

Spencer smiled. "As I said, you should have seen me before. The cells can be controlled and manipulated by energy work, but the results take time, depending on the extent of damage."

Booker returned, "Sarasota has been raided."

Spencer nodded.

"They're still raiding centers?" I asked.

"Averaging two a week since the mall attack."

"How are they finding them?"

A woman brought out a large tray of fruits then returned with additional ones full of veggies.

"Nate, it's like a psychic arms race now. Ever since the mall attack, and you were dubbed America's most-wanted terrorist, he has people volunteering."

"He, meaning Storch?" Linh asked.

"Yes."

"His troops killed Kyle." Linh's voice was bitter.

"I'm sorry, Linh. He will pay," Booker said.

"And I have the video that will show the world the truth about this bastard!" I handed the drive to Booker. He took it to a nearby table and pushed it into a laptop computer. "I'm copying it onto this hard drive, and simultaneously encrypting and sending it to dozens of my servers around the world. Now, let's have a look."

"How can he survive that?" Amber asked, after we watched the film.

"He can't," Booker said. "He's a slippery snake for sure, but this, combined with the other information we've put together, should be enough to indict him even in the current corrupt system."

"When?"

"We'll release it to news outlets and Internet leak sites, as well as the FBI, first thing in the morning. In the meantime, try to catch your breath, relax, and enjoy the beach."

We showered and changed. Amber and Linh both fell asleep in cushy lounge chairs on the beach. Spencer and I went for a walk.

"Spencer, we have to find the rest of the Clastier papers." I stopped to look at him. "Are you going to be all right?"

He nodded. "I'm fine."

"Can I do some healing on you? I do you owe you a few."

He smiled. "Really, I'll be okay. Thank you." He wasn't quite frail but wasn't his old self either. "I'm glad you came back."

"It was tempting to stay dead."

"I'm certain of that. And it may seem, because you survived death at Outin, that your nonviolence stance has been validated as a way to get through this. But the release of the Storch film and surrounding evidence will not end your trouble, and it will not spell instant victory for the Movement."

"Nonviolence did work. The battle for Outin was no small matter, and it can be used as a template for the Movement going forward."

"Not everyone will agree."

"Clastier's papers and the ideas they put forward will help inspire the Movement and any who disagree. His wisdom and understanding are a guide."

"Look, you can worry about Clastier later. There are urgent matters here *now*. The dreams and musings of a defrocked priest who has been dead for two hundred years can wait."

"But IM is supposed to be about getting soul-knowledge out to everyone, and that's just what Clastier was doing, way ahead of the Movement."

"Is that what you think? Do you imagine that you, as Clastier, were the grandfather of IM? Nate, the Movement has been around for millennia. Why do you think the Jadeo exists?"

"It's all connected."

"Why do you keep saying that? Of course it's all connected. That's not the point. It's a matter of priorities. It's about timing." Spencer coughed.

"Time's a funny thing." I didn't say it to be flip—it suddenly felt like the answer to all the most difficult questions.

"The final page from your dad's desk... it's a key to the missing Clastier papers, the ones that didn't make it east with the others."

"Why didn't you tell me this before?"

"It's timing, Nate. I'm telling you now so you will keep focused and stop chasing ghosts."

"And Hibbs?"

"Hibbs knew about the Clastier papers, though he never found them."

"But I have now."

"And that may explain part of your excessive distraction with them. Author and seeker come together."

"So you admit they're important."

"Yes, vital, but they're not for this moment. We're dealing with a human world, and things must be done in a certain order—steps taken. We can't just carry the entire human race through a portal and show them where we've been."

"Why not?" I asked.

He gave me an exasperated look.

"Did Hibbs see this far into the future?"

"Is this necessary?"

"I want to know everything. I've earned that."

He was quiet for a moment, watching the incoming tide. Finally he spoke, "Yes, I suppose you have. Hibbs had the documents to prove Omnia existed and that they were manipulating world events."

"So Omnia is real?"

"Yes."

"My dad mentioned Omnia once but didn't want to talk about it, so I researched online and found out about Omnia on some of those conspiracy theory websites."

"What do you think you know about Omnia?"

"They're a secret group of extremely wealthy families who manipulate the public through the media and even world leaders. They set most government policies. They've been behind wars and revolutions. Everything they do is to further consolidate wealth and power into their hands. But many claim they don't exist, that they're another Internet myth."

Spencer squinted against the sun as he looked into my eyes. "No. I'm sorry to say Omnia is very real and far worse than you describe. The worst events of human history over many, many centuries have been perpetrated by them… genocide, assassinations, wars, coups, and plagues… the list is long and disgusting."

"I had no idea they were that bad. I thought they were just a bunch of greedy bankers."

"They've taken greed to planetary proportions. They want everything... including the Jadeo."

"The Jadeo? They know of it?" I was shocked.

"Who do you think we've been protecting it from all this time?"

"I thought... I mean, that the world wasn't ready for it yet."

"Omnia is the reason we aren't ready for the Jadeo," he said.

I needed to let that sink in and sat down on the warm powdery sand, digging my bare feet into the cooler grains beneath. Spencer seemed relieved to sit as well.

"Why are there so many enemies?" I asked.

He considered the question briefly. "Wandus would say there is only one enemy."

"Fear."

He nodded.

"Did Clastier know about the Jadeo?"

"You tell me. You were him."

"Our conversation didn't get that far."

"He must have known. Whether he believed it was legend or real, I couldn't say."

"Then if Hibbs and Clastier both knew what humans, through their souls, were capable of and that the Jadeo existed and what it was, they also knew this future might come where Lightyear and Omnia would be the greatest enemies of enlightenment. I don't understand why they didn't fight and win this battle a hundred years ago, two hundred years ago?"

"True, it would have been a smaller battle, but it was also a much more difficult time to get the word out. No twenty-four hour satellite news, Internet, social networks, or smartphones in every pocket. There has never been a time in human history in which all global inhabitants could receive and share messages on such a scale."

"Then Clastier's papers are even more important than I thought."

"Yes, just not quite yet."

"But—"

"Hibbs and Clastier knew they would return as you and left clues for you to finish the work begun in their lifetimes."

"And the papers were part of that."

"Please, Nate." He turned to stare at me and spoke silently, "First Lightyear must fall. While Lightyear exists, we cannot win. There is no uncertainty in my prophecy on this matter. It is absolute. You may try it peacefully if you must, but they have to be destroyed or the Movement, the Jadeo and even the great Nathan Ryder will be buried, forgotten, and not have mattered at all."

**79**

"May I have the Jadeo back?" I asked.

"No."

"It belongs to me." My fists clenched.

He raised an eyebrow.

"It's been entrusted to me," I corrected.

"By who?"

"My dad."

"Are you sure?"

"You know he meant it for Dustin?" I looked at him and answered my own question. "Of course you do. So, what? Are you going to save it for Dustin?"

"No, your father was mistaken. Dustin is in no condition to handle the Jadeo in this lifetime. His soul-wisdom is astonishingly deep, but his personality is desperately damaged. No, it is yours to carry and protect. I will return it to you after you return from Washington."

"Washington?" I choked.

"You need to speak with Storch one more time, once the tape is released."

"That's way too dangerous."

"You'll be in a portal."

"Who is Storch? This isn't my first lifetime dealing with this monster. But for some reason, I can't figure it out."

"Maybe you'll remember tomorrow. You'll go late in the day. There's a portal in the mountains that will take you to

Crater Lake. From there you'll use the Wizard Island portal to reach his office."

"A regular subway system, these portals."

He smiled.

"I'll go if you say I must, but tell me why."

He didn't answer.

"Spencer, where'd you go?"

"The truth is Nate, I don't know why you have to go, just that it's important."

"Really? I'm in Cuba right now. You want me to jump into a portal that will wormhole me to Oregon, where I'll get into another portal to my archenemy's private office, in a building filled with thousands of trained agents who have orders to kill me... and you don't know why?"

He shook his head.

"Come on, Spencer. Where does this stuff come from? Is someone giving you these orders?"

"Wouldn't that be nice? Someone I could scream at and blame. You have me, Nate, but I don't get a face. I'm floating out there in the universe, trying to collect all the bits of light and fragments of energy and stitch the whole mess into something that makes sense."

"I thought the universe was perfection."

"It is, Nate. It is... but we humans aren't, and it's so bloody big. It's everything, and I ache trying to grasp even a corner of it. Try putting the ocean into one of your Coke bottles, now imagine the water is boiling, and the bottle has holes, and a thousand people are chasing you with guns! That will give you a hint of the enormity of it."

"Thank you for finally understanding how *I* feel."

He looked at me and started to laugh. "Yeah, you do, don't you?"

"On the good days." I laughed, too.

"Will you go?"

"I really need to?"

"Yes."

"Do we really need something more incriminating on this guy?"

"I don't think it's about that."

"All right, we'll find out." I ran my hands through my hair and let out a long, exaggerated moan. But in truth, the prospect kind of excited me. I was tired of running and more interested in connecting the pieces. It was the only way it was ever going to end. And, after seeing Kyle in the light, dying just didn't worry me anymore. "You have more explaining to do," I said.

"Let's not discuss Rose right now," he said, reading my mind. Spencer had lost weight and his normally sparkling turquoise eyes were faded.

"Did you know she was alive? Helping Lightyear? Is she the betrayer from the original nine?" I asked.

"I don't even know who all the original nine are."

"How can you not know, after all these centuries?"

"That was your dad's thing. He wanted to know who they all were, but his list doesn't matter because one name can represent the soul of many multiple incarnations—Kyle is Curry, you as another name, etc. You're obviously one of the nine, and yet your name doesn't appear on the list. Your dad didn't know."

"My dad knows now. Why isn't he helping?"

"He helps. You're not able to see that yet, but you will. But forget about the list and forget about Rose."

"The list is an urgent matter because the betrayer likely knew of this future and left ways to help himself, or herself, too. And if Rose was one of the original nine, then her power is even greater than we think, and her betrayal even more dangerous."

"Anything is possible, Nate."

"I don't understand how you can let this go so easily. How can you still be surprised by the future?"

"There is no limit to what a soul can see, but there is a limit as to how close a personality can get to its soul… and I don't know where that point is. But, damn it, Nate, I don't know everything and neither do you."

"My soul does."

He took a deep breath, put his forehead in his hand and then spoke quietly. "There are good people dying and good people such as Baca, Kirby, Amparo, and many others you haven't met who are subject to interrogation, imprisonment, and torture. I understand you've died and been beaten up pretty bad, but I sure wish you'd finish growing up." He stood, gave me a weary, loving look and then walked away.

On the way back to the house, I ran into Amber and explained what happened. It was hot; we moved to the grassy shade of some palms and sat soaking up the view. I felt isolated in Cuba, safe.

"Going to see Storch is crazy." She broke the silence. "Spencer is just trying to put you into a position to use violence. What if Storch has a gun in his desk or a button that summons armed security? You'll be all alone... I'll come with you."

"No."

Amber climbed on top of me and suddenly we were kissing, rolling in the grass. Lightyear and Storch were gone. The Jadeo meant nothing. Everything that mattered was inside of Amber, and that's where I wanted to be. The balmy sea air played with her perfumed hair as I surrendered to the velvet feel of her perfect skin. The bikini top gave no resistance while my other hand explored an area of which, before that moment, I'd only dreamt. Amber's mouth was like swimming in the smooth water of Clarity Lake; wonders swirled in my mind. Suddenly a shadow passed my closed eyes. It took a second to focus on the figure standing there.

Linh was already running away when I pushed Amber off. She forgot to Skyclimb or I never would have caught up, or maybe she wanted me to catch her. "Linh, I'm sorry."

"Why are you sorry? Because you want her? Who wouldn't? She's a Barbie doll, a new age princess."

"No. I mean..."

"It's okay, Nate. You never promised me anything more than friendship."

"Linh." I hugged her. She shoved me away hard. Tears ran angry across her glaring look.

"Leave me alone." This time I didn't follow.

I ran back to find Amber and met her at the steps to the veranda. Before I could say anything, she asked. "Is Linh okay?"

"She's mad."

"A couple of lessons for you because I know all this girl stuff is new to you." Her tone and look were surprisingly stern. "One, Linh is not mad, she's hurt. Two, when you're making out with a girl, never, *ever* toss her off like she's a used piece of gum." Amber turned and walked deliberately up the stairs, then disappeared into the house. I needed lesson number three: do I follow her or not? I sat on the bottom step and let the sun heat the cold out of me. Then I stared at the ocean, searching for the answers Spencer saw out there, looking for anything at all that made sense.

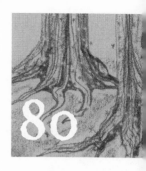

80

Booker joined me a few minutes later. "Rough afternoon?"

"Yeah, how'd you know?"

"I've been sitting on the veranda, watching. Well, trying to work, but your antics have distracted me."

"Can I ask your advice?"

"About Spencer?"

"No, about girls?"

He roared with laughter. "I was afraid of that. I've conquered the world of business, and I've bettered governments across the globe, but probably only because they're dominated by men. We're a simple lot, us guys. The female side of our species, on the other hand, is much more complicated, deeper, smarter, and..." He patted my back, winking. "And more desirable, too."

"Okay, so how do I fix it?"

"The best thing you can do is choose one. Who do you like better?"

"What if I don't know?"

"Hmmm, that makes it trickier. I'd suggest keeping things friendly, nothing more, until you figure that part out."

"That doesn't sound easy either."

"These things have a way of working themselves out. You're a little too busy with saving the world to be trying to figure out your prom date anyway." He laughed again, then turned serious. "But, Nate, Spencer really is your biggest fan and your strongest ally. You'd find life easier if you started treating him as such."

"You should tell him the same thing."

"I have. You two have a lot to work through. Maybe you'll get to that in this lifetime, maybe you won't. But the two of you do want the same things; you just differ in how and when to get them."

Amber came down the steps.

"If you'll excuse me," Booker said, "I've got some calls to make."

"He's tactful," Amber said, when Booker was gone.

"Amber, I'm sorry."

"Forget it, Nate, I know you well enough to understand what happened. I'm not here for that. Tomorrow is a big day, and I don't want to waste any of the time we have left."

"You make it sound like we may not see each other again."

"Don't you know that's possible? Every day, we're stealing from somewhere. Time's a funny thing. It always takes back."

"What are you talking about?"

"While in Taos, Spencer told me a lot of things. He was trying to convince me that we had to use violence. He knew Yangchen and I were growing close, and he believes I have influence over you."

"You do." Just looking at her made my legs feel rubbery.

Amber took my hand in both of hers, pulled it to her lips, and left the softest kiss. "He told me Kyle was going to die."

"What? He knew?" I pulled my hand away. "You knew?"

"It wasn't like he said Kyle will die returning to Outin. I told him some of the things I'd seen in Rainbow Lake and wanted to know if he thought they would happen or not. He said one of us would be dead within weeks."

"Why didn't you tell us?"

"You didn't have enough warnings? Spencer, Yangchen, Wandus, even you came back from the future to tell you. Didn't you see things in Rainbow Lake?"

"Yeah, but what's real? It always changes."

"Exactly. And I wish I'd told you because Spencer was so certain, but I thought he was just trying to scare me into agreeing to use violence."

"I understand."

"He told me he couldn't be sure which one of us. He's seen futures with the change from each of us. But I thought it would be me. I wanted it to be me." Amber cried.

"Why?" I put my arm around her, and she took a deep breath.

"You have to live, Nate. This is your time. You're the leader."

I shook my head. "I'm no leader."

"Not yet, but you will be. And I knew you could never forgive yourself if something happened to Linh, and Linh would be devastated without Kyle, so I'm the one that doesn't matter."

I silently shook my head, mourning the loss of Amber. My words choked, unable to escape.

"I'm okay with that." She sniffled. "I thought I would die for you, and that's the meaning my life would have."

"No, Amber. No, I need you. You can't die, I wouldn't be here without you." I cried as if she were already dead.

Amber hugged me. "I know. Me too."

We held each other for a moment.

"There's something else too."

"More?"

"Yangchen told me about another mystic. He's difficult and dark, but he can communicate with the dead and knows how to bring them back."

I stood up. "Where is he?"

"We may not want to find him."

"Why?"

"Because no one knows for sure if he is good or bad."

"Let's get back to Taos and find Yangchen. I want to know everything about this mystic and, most important, where he is."

"Didn't you hear me? He may not be good."

"How can a mystic not be good?"

"Stuff like this always has a catch."

"In the movies, but mystics are here to help me. The Old Man said I would meet fifteen, and so far I've counted ten. I must be close to the third stage. We'll find this mystic. We'll bring my dad back, and Kyle, Crowd, Lee Duncan, whoever else we need to beat Lightyear. I wonder if he can bring back Hibbs and Clastier." I was almost dancing.

"I don't think you should count too much on this, at least until you talk to Yangchen. Finding Calyndra is more important."

"We'll do that, too."

Later, we were served a fabulous vegan dinner on the veranda. Booker knew how to do food, or rather how to hire a staff to do it. He also knew how to break the tension that existed between everyone.

"Remember we're all on the same side here." He raised his glass of water. "There's not a helluva lot we can count on these days, but of that I'm sure. Let's stay focused on our objective and not let the petty differences of a few days jeopardize the work of lifetimes." We half-heartedly raised our glasses as we shyly glanced across the round table.

"Tomorrow, the real fun begins," he added. "And, Nate, you get to see Storch's face in person—I'd love to see his reaction."

Linh stammered a confused "What?" No one had told her yet. Another hurt look. "Why are you going?"

"It's critical Nate speaks to Storch tomorrow."

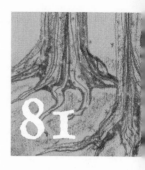

81

L inh and I walked down the beach to watch the sun dip into the ocean. Her long pleading rant about me not meeting Storch ended with the words "If you die too... I'll find death, and he'll take me to you." She was trembling.

"When I died at Outin, Kyle was waiting for me."

"You saw him?"

"Yes, and talked with him. He said it wasn't my time and wanted me to go back."

She was speechless.

"You know something? I didn't want to come back," I said. "I wasn't worried about you and Amber, my mom... no one. It's like when you're dead, the human world becomes trivial."

"That's because most of it is trivial."

I nodded. "Except the soul-connections..."

"What else did he say?"

"Linh, he was happy and beautiful—radiating, seriously radiating. He told me to tell you that he was always with you."

"I know souls never die. It's just I miss Kyle so much."

"But you still have him. His soul is connected to us, but his personality is like the clothes he wore." I paused. "When I came back, there were two things I couldn't get out of my mind."

"What were they?"

"There are many causes I would die for. There is not a single cause I would kill for. Nonviolence is a weapon of the strong."

"Who said that?"

"Gandhi."

 She nodded. "And the other thing?"

"I would not look upon anger as something foreign to me that I have to fight... I have to deal with my anger with care, with love, with tenderness, with nonviolence."

"Thich Nhat Hanh."

"How'd you know?"

"I lived with Kyle, remember?"

"Kyle somehow gave those quotes to me when I saw him. I've been wrestling with how to stop Storch and Lightyear ever since we met Yangchen. Spencer thinks it's impossible to win without fighting but, from beyond death, Kyle has told us that nonviolence is the only way."

 Her eyes filled, "Okay."

"And if I die—when I die—we'll be together again, don't worry."

"I want to be together now." Her look was like she'd been waiting for my return after two years at sea. It opened me. We stared at each other for so long that a silent conversation resumed. The origins of it could be traced back centuries. Its exact beginning eluded me, but I knew it would continue for many more lifetimes. After several minutes sharing Outviews of our times together, I kissed her. Our tongues and lips danced like the surf playing with starlight.

 When we said good night. Linh handed me a poem.

> It has taken me far over time, mountains,
> oceans, trees, stars, dimensions...
> Handheld warmth and whispers
> sitting together but not touching,
> dreaming but not sleeping.
> I am talking low and sad
> out to the end of your breath
> and the begin of my music
> between my ears, love,
> this easy disturbance

turns and tumbles,
rough edges soften in its wind
and rain sharpens instinct

this place, deeply burrowed and
fresh, replaces every piece of
scent and matter my body
contains, and my skin
disappears in enigmatic
magic where clouds and dirt sing.
Oh, I cannot take this pause,
this simple exchange of eye
and hand, no, simplicity and
reoccurrence is not the manifesto
in this tryst.

If you die too... I'll find death and
he'll take me to you, Love, he'll take
me to you. And I will scream and
scratch into the world where your
breath springs and drink the essence
of your life. I, too, remorse not for the
living. I, too, see your wake and
pleasure in its circumference... we
are that eternal voice, feel me,
vibrating in everything you touch,
                and see and do.

While falling asleep, I replayed every touch; the sighs and stirrings of the heated passionate exchanges with both girls mingled and confused my drowning mind.

I woke just before dawn from a bad dream about Fitts. He was a regular guest in my nightmares, but this one had the added twist of featuring both Ren and Fitts. They ran at me from opposite directions. Fitts wielding an oversized syringe while Ren twirled a samurai sword above his head. Sleep would not be returning. Today we would release the evidence against Lightyear, and I was going to confront Storch.

There was an incredible fruit spread being prepared when I entered the kitchen. A sweet old Cuban woman made me a tray. We spoke in Spanish about her kids, who were my age, and she wanted to know if I was on vacation from school. I was surprised when she said it was May 1st. My seventeenth birthday had come and gone, lost forever in a portal or an Outin Window. I asked her if anyone else was up. She pointed to the veranda. "Sólo Spencer, como de costumbre."

I found him, staring into the dim ocean awaiting the sun. "What happened with Ren?" I asked, sitting next to him and offering him some fruit.

"He's still at Cervantes. He doesn't know."

"Are you sure?"

"Yes. He's spending a lot of time with Wandus."

"So, he's staying within the Movement."

"All souls are welcome."

"Seems risky."

"None of us are without a past. The shame of what we're capable of—what we've done in our past lives—could crush a personality, and often just a glimpse of it, through Outviews, nightmares, déjà vu, intuition, whatever, can shatter a person, and they never know why."

"I obviously can't argue with that, but Ren's past was only a few months ago when he tried to kill me and Dustin… and he killed my dad."

"You know it wasn't Ren."

"Depends on how close to the surface his soul is. It just seems a frightening coincidence."

"There are always frightening coincidences to contend with. Today isn't the day to worry about Fitts. As Wandus would say, 'you've spent that worry already.'"

"I'm happy to know Wandus is still free. How are they finding mystics? How do they even know about them?"

"As you know, they've been tracking me for years. Storch knows there are many people who have advanced beyond the limitations of the human world. He sees them in two ways, as a threat or a potential tool to be used in his schemes."

"Like Rose?"

"It's possible for any of us to fall, Nate. Remember, there is a dimension out there right now where you're happily helping Lightyear."

"That's hard for me to believe. Because if that's true, then what is the point of this life, this dimension?"

"This is the one *you* are in. It's the one that matters. This is the only real moment."

"Where did you go when you left Marble Mountain?"

"Cervantes."

"Before that?"

He hesitated. "I went to Wizard Island."

The news surprised me. "To try and save Kyle?"

"Yes."

"But you missed him?"

More hesitation. I studied him as he reworked his answer several times. "No. I got there before him."

I gasped. "Did you know he was going to die at Outin? You must have—that's why you went. How could you let him through?"

Spencer took a deep breath. "I told him not to go to Outin and explained he would definitely die if he did. But, Nate, he knew you were going to die during the battle. And—"

"Oh my God," I said, already piecing it together. "He allowed himself to get killed so he could be there to greet me when I died. Oh Spencer, tell me that's not true."

He shook his head.

"Please, Spencer." I was crying. "Say he didn't sacrifice himself so I could live. Why did you let him do that?"

"He was intent."

"What do you mean? You're a freakin' wizard, Spencer. How hard did you try? You didn't try hard because it was the only way to save me. Did Kyle really come by that knowledge on his own or did you spoon-feed him?"

"Nate." He took me by the shoulders and caught my eyes. "He knew. Kyle was no ordinary boy. Don't you know that by now? It's not just you. Dustin, Kyle, Amber, and Linh—you're

all special old souls. It's no accident the five of you came together in this lifetime. You have all been working on this
longer than history exists. You've done the same for each of
them in past lives. Kyle understood. He did not hesitate. I
could have physically restrained him, but I have too much
respect for his soul. I discussed it with him. He understood
what he was doing."

"And there was no other way? There's always another
way!"

"Yes, there is always another way, but this was the best
way. The next closest left both the girls dead... and isn't that
what you've been trying to avoid most of all?"

"I don't know, Spencer. Choose between the girls and
Kyle. Choose between Amber and Linh, the kids in the mall
and my friends, Crowd or me. I'm seventeen, how am I supposed to make decisions like this?"

"Even a hundred-year-old person can't make decisions
like that. Don't let it bury you. Kyle knew what he was doing.
You saw him. Did he look to be suffering or even regretful?"

"No, he looked like a flower blooming in the morning
sun. But it was Outin. I never know if what I see there is real."

"Yes, it's wise to remember Outin is another dimension,
and some things you see or think while in another dimension
don't translate exactly the same in this one. But dimensions
overlap and share much. So it's usually only subtle differences.
Kyle is dead. I felt his change. And when we die we move
closer to the pure love that we are... and there is complete
joy in that."

"Am I going to die today?"

"The question is, are you ready to die today? Every day
we should be ready to die, not become attached to this human
world we're playing in. If we're true to our soul, then every
day is a good day to die."

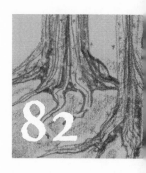

82

Every major newspaper and news website in the world had the scandal; Booker's team had done well. Washington was in a frenzy. Video of Storch saying, "If you insist on fighting us, I'll blow up a mall or an airplane... and I'll blame it on you," was running side-by-side with footage of the Mall of the America burning. There were pictures of the dead along with Storch's statement, "People are expendable— do you know how many are born every day? We're sure as hell not running out of them." One conservative news channel floated the theory that perhaps I did the mall attack so I could frame Storch and Lightyear, but with Lee Duncan's evidence and the affidavits from the IMers at Marble Mountain, there was little doubt.

The FBI, three foreign governments, and four different members of Congress announced investigations. Indictments and imminent arrests would take time. But under extreme pressure, the president asked the state department to revoke the passports of Storch and eleven other Lightyear officials. There was no other news. Calls to exhume Fitts' body gained steam until it was learned he was cremated. The explosion of attention and scrutiny was so great that Spencer delayed my trip to see Storch. For the next three days, we watched as the story ratcheted up beyond every past Washington scandal, including the infamous ones involving presidents— Watergate,

Iran-Contra, Monica Lewinsky. And then reporters began asking if it might reach the top of the current administration. "How could the president not know of such a powerful group within the CIA?" It was spectacular.

Once the media got a full grasp of the psychics' capabilities within Lightyear, special news shows were created to do nothing but follow the story, and even plans for an entire cable channel were discussed. Storch had remained in seclusion, but with calls for the resignation of the CIA director at a fever pitch, and congressional subpoenas for Storch, it was about to get even uglier. I avoided being alone with either of the girls, heeding Booker's advice to pick one, and because that was too difficult, I chose not to decide.

"We might even be able to go home," Linh said.

"Do you think Nate will ever be able to go home?" Amber said.

"They say the whole administration may come down," Linh said. "Our families may be released any day."

"Soon, at least everyone will know you're not a terrorist," Amber said.

"Nate, it's time to go," Spencer whispered, as he entered the room where we were watching the coverage.

"Why does he still have to go? Everything is falling apart for Lightyear," Linh asked.

I looked at Spencer. There was urgency in his eyes.

"I'll be back before you even have a chance to miss me."

Amber glanced at Linh then said, "I miss you already."

"Why do this? You could die," Linh said.

"When I die, it won't be today."

Thirty minutes later, Spencer and I were in the wooded mountains. I saw the portal forty feet above the ground near a trickling waterfall even before he stopped the jeep.

"After Washington, when you return to Wizard Island, take the portal to Cervantes. We'll be there." I'd once seen a future where Lightyear seized Cervantes, and I never returned. The future had changed again, and would again.

"Okay. Any more insight as to why I'm seeing Storch?"

His concerned expression softened. "I'm looking forward to you telling me why when next we meet."

I Skyclimbed up and then dove into the portal. I came out a few miles from Crater Lake. Although it was May, it was still cold at that elevation, particularly coming from tropical Cuba. I expected to come out on Wizard Island and knew Spencer was concerned about the time. I moved fast across the treetops toward the magic lake and looked for the Old Man. When he didn't appear, I sprinted across the water. He was waiting for me at the top of the cauldron.

"Thought I heard some noise in one of the portals. Then I felt a warm salty breeze. Where you coming from, boy?"

"Cuba."

"Good place to hide. Where you heading?"

"Washington."

"Still letting that foolish streak of yours have some control?"

"I'll be all right."

"Maybe you will, maybe not." He looked down into the portal. "Odds are still against you."

"Thanks for the pep talk."

"The closer death gets to you, the more you need to be aware. Do you know what I'm saying?"

"No."

"Keep your brother alive."

"I've been trying."

"You think so? Foolish boy. Better get to your very important meeting in the cap-it-toll."

"See you, Old Man." I jumped, holding the address and information about Storch's office in my mind.

A moment later, I was staring at a startled Storch from the other side of his desk.

"What the hell are you doing here?" he asked, as I glanced nervously around his large office. We were alone.

"I was hoping you could tell me," I said, careful not to move out of the portal.

"Yeah, I'll tell you. I'm going to have you killed." His eyes glared at me. Who was he? I felt close to knowing, but something was blocking the recognition. That must be why I was here. I needed to know who he was.

Three monitors to the side of me showed the developing scandal. No doubt more information was coming across the three additional screens on his desk.

"Are you filming this, too?" he sneered.

"Everything that has ever happened is always there, always retrievable. Energy doesn't die." I recognized the painting behind his desk. It was mine.

"Oh my God, you actually think you're some kind of prophet," he growled. "I'll show you about dying." He picked up his phone. I studied him, trying to figure out his soul's identity, ready to duck away. I knew from Spencer that the back of the portal would protect me from being seen or attacked. They would have to come around and get me from the front. Storch didn't have a gun, or he would have shot me already. Before he could speak into the phone, his face lost color and filled with terror. He dropped the receiver.

An unwelcome person had entered the room. Two tiny-sized darts suddenly hit his neck. He looked at the intruder and then at me, so full of fear that I closed the portal in rapid retreat. But in that last split second with our eyes still locked, his guard dropped, and I saw the reason for my trip, I saw the identity of his soul, and as I landed back on Wizard Island, I was hysterical.

The Old Man sat with me. "You kind of wish *you* had died, don't you?"

I couldn't speak.

"Death is easier than some things, ain't it?"

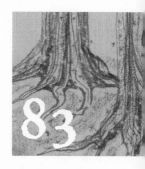

## 83

I stayed with the Old Man that night. I didn't care about missing the news of Storch's death because I knew the truth. My most evil enemy still lived through another person. Storch had ordered my father killed and had been trying to destroy me for almost a year. The mass murderer behind the mall attack and greatest force against the Movement was a soul that I knew well and loved dearly. If I hadn't seen their common soul in Storch's eyes myself, I never would have believed it.

The Old Man and I stayed in the cauldron, warmed in a weather dome of his making. The questions were so numerous that they remained lodged in my head for hours before I could ask, "Does Dustin know?" It was the first and most pressing question; all the others depended on the answer to this one.

"I'm not like Spencer, I don't have never-ending insights into your life. But I do know something of this because of an unrelated matter. Your brother does know well of his simultaneous incarnation as Luther Storch."

"Oh, God!" I'd been wrestling with that possibility since my return from Washington and arguing with my intuition, which said he knew.

"Dustin is a powerful soul. In a prior life he was one of his generation's seven. And this time, for many reasons known only to him, his torment is great."

"Maybe he was the betrayer of the original nine entrusted."

"Now you're talking above my pay grade. Perhaps he's trying to help you, or maybe he's intending harm. But either way, trusting him should be done very carefully, the way one would treat a grizzly bear as a companion."

"The fact that he has known and not told me, not let us use it to our advantage, not done something to help get our mother and the others released, tells me all I need to know."

The Old Man was silent.

"And who killed Storch?"

"Spencer may be able to help with those answers."

"There was a painting on Storch's wall called 'Endure.' It was given to me by the artist, an old friend of mine named Trevor."

"Surely, Lightyear has removed all your belongings from your house."

"But the painting wasn't at my house. Only Trevor knew it was mine and was keeping it for me, on his boat... Oh, wait, I showed it to Dustin when Trevor took us both to Cervantes. That's how Storch knew. Dustin must have turned Trevor in." I went on the astral but couldn't find Trevor; it was the same for Dustin, Rose, and Spencer. They must have all been using some form of Kellaring. I only hoped someone was blocking me from contacting Trevor, and silently added him to the long list of people who had either died or were in prison because they helped me. Sitting in the darkness of night, dazzling starlight visible through the craggy rim of the ancient volcano, surrounded by one of the great energy vortexes, I vowed to free every one of those still living from the hold of Lightyear. What must Trevor be going through while held in confinement after his lifetime in the concentration camp?

The Old Man was a wise mystic and listened more than he talked. After hours of my theories and speculations, he sent me on my way with these words: "You will never find what you need until you stop searching. You will never be who you must be until you let go of who you think you are. You will never discover all the answers until you understand the questions. Be well, boy. I hope we meet again."

The portal opened onto the dark beach of Cervantes. A familiar voice, one I most wanted to hear, greeted me as I stepped out: Wandus.

"You have journeyed long since we last met, my friend. To death and back, to love and betrayal, anger and elation, peaceful victory and violent defeat... yes, you are old in your eyes now."

"I feel old. I'm lost and confused."

He smiled. "That is when the greatest treasures are closest."

"Kyle is dead, my aunt is alive and helping Lightyear, Dustin *is* Lightyear, and I no longer have the ability to know who to trust or what to do."

"Come." He walked to the surf and began wav-o-tating.

"It's too dark," I yelled from the sand.

"The dark is only your perception. An abundance of light is always there."

The sun, which was still hours away, rose seemingly minutes later, but my meditation could have been so deep that hours might actually have passed. When we returned to the sand, I felt as if I'd slept for days and had energy enough to Skyclimb for a week and clarity like I'd been soaking in the fifth lake of Outin for a month. What I didn't know was how soon I was going to need these reserves.

84

A plane landed just as I reached the main house. One of Booker's employees who I remembered from my last visit told me someone was meeting the plane and that Booker and my friends would be there in about ten minutes. He offered me breakfast—a feast of fruit, vegan pastries, and miso soup filled with baby Brussels sprouts that I ate too fast. The girls rushed in.

"Are you really okay?" Linh asked.

"When the news broke of Storch's suicide, we thought you could've been hurt," Amber said.

"Luther Storch did not kill himself," I said matter-of-factly, as Booker and Spencer entered.

"I suspected as much," Booker boomed.

"I was there. He was assassinated."

"Why?" Linh asked.

"To keep him quiet. He knew too much. And to make him appear guilty," Booker said. "No trial, no naming names, no mess."

"What happened?" Amber asked.

"I only had a moment before he was killed..." I hesitated, unsure how much to share, but when Spencer asked if I now knew the reason for the trip, it seemed right to tell everything. I described each disturbing second of our encounter. Then, before anyone could react fully, Booker took an urgent call and everything changed.

"That was Garcia in Cuba. The house has been raided. Not more than thirty minutes after we left, a SEAL unit came in. They, of course, found nothing, but the breach is critical. Cuba is untraceable to me. It is far more secure than Cervantes. We must go immediately."

Everyone was given assignments; mine was to gather the IMers. The weight limit on Booker's plane meant only a portion of them could get out with us; the rest would have to wait several hours for another flight.

I found the IMers on my favorite stretch of beach, a slice of white powder cradled by jungle on one side and a crescent curve of coast on the other. The energy had always been good for training there. Seventeen were practicing, only five could come with us and Spencer had given me a list of the lucky ones. Ren was on it.

I ignored him and found another I remembered from Marble Mountain. He was concerned about the prospect of leaving so many of the best IMers behind. "How are they finding the centers?" He asked the exasperated question we'd all been working on.

I looked over at Ren. "Obviously, a Lightyear agent has infiltrated the upper levels of the Movement."

"Someone on this island?"

I nodded silently, watching Ren. "There isn't much time. Tell everyone what's happening and get the ones on this list to the airstrip. The others can wait in the main house until the next plane arrives. I'll tell Ren."

Ren seemed happy to see me. "Another center has been raided, where I just left."

"How do they know?"

"You tell me Ren," I sneered.

"Do you think?" he stood back. "I've done nothing to harm the Movement."

"How am I supposed to believe that when you share a soul with Lightyear's most violent agent?" I shouted.

Several IMers came toward us.

"What do you mean?"

"You pretend not to know, but you must. I cannot believe a coincidence this great exists and that it could go unnoticed by an enlightened guy like you."

"Please, what are you talking about?"

"You and Sanford Fitts share a soul!"

Gasps from onlookers. Ren coughed and fell backward into the sand. "Why do you say this lie?"

"I'm not lying. You know I'm not. You're how Lightyear keeps finding the centers and catching mystics. They're killing people, friends of mine. Do you know how close I've come to getting killed?"

"It's not me, Nate. This is not true!" He scrambled to his feet, but I knocked him down again with Gogen. "Why are you against me? I've done nothing."

My fury was building, all my pent up rage at Fitts was finding an outlet. All the IMers were gathered round. Some had confused expressions, as they obviously liked Ren. Others were afraid for their own safety and saw Ren as the scapegoat. "You need to admit what you've done, admit who you are. Tell us what they know."

"I know nothing. This is wrong," He tried to get up again. This time I sent him sailing back toward the water. He tried to run. With Gogen, I easily pushed him into the waves without moving. He fought and clawed as they broke over him. "Tell me the truth," I screamed, ready to toss him farther.

"Nate! Stop."

Spencer and the girls were running toward us. Ren was still tumbling in the surf. Spencer must have used Gogen, because Ren suddenly flew out and landed softly next to him. I raised my arms, ready to correct his mistake, when suddenly it went completely dark, as if a giant black tarp had been wrapped around the sun. Not even my night vision worked. The ocean still sounded the same; the air continued to move. All the IMers were whispering and calling out.

"Nate, Ren is not Dustin."

"I know who Ren is," I yelled back, trying to conjure light from somewhere, but there was no trace.

"He didn't know. You're misplacing your anger about Dustin. We don't have time for this."

"This has nothing to do with Dustin. Ren is the traitor."

"No. You're blaming him because Dustin isn't here to blame."

I could not immediately respond. Either Spencer could be trusted, or he could not. I had to admit to myself that, even with all our differences, one thing was certain: I did trust Spencer and always had. Even when he withheld information, or prevented me doing what I thought best, he had never done anything other than earn my trust since the moment we met. Tears broke the silence of my contemplation. Ren was sobbing softly at first but then uncontrollably. In the absolute darkness, while twenty other people listened, Ren whimpered and sobbed. He had just discovered his greatest enemy was himself. He could not escape.

Spencer was right, I was using Ren to vent my frustration with Dustin. Ren didn't know about Cuba, but Dustin did. Ren didn't know about Trevor, but Dustin did. Dustin alone knew Kirby and Baca. Dustin had access to all the centers through his earlier time on Cervantes with me. And Dustin was Storch, who had been alive all this time. Fitts was dead before the raids and mystic arrests began. As much as I didn't want to admit it, everything pointed to Dustin being the traitor, and that meant we needed to escape Cervantes in the next few minutes.

"Ren, please forgive me," I said, as light returned. I went and helped him to his feet. "I'm sorry."

I nodded to the girls, but stayed with Ren as golf carts arrived to take us to the plane. Less than ten minutes later we were in the air. The other twelve left behind would not be so lucky. It would be weeks before we confirmed it, but within forty minutes of our departure, half were killed and half were taken into custody.

85

Ren sat next to me on the first part of the flight until Book-er asked him to trade places. "Nate, the initial success of our attempts to discredit Lightyear have hit some serious re-sistance," he whispered. "It seems that they're claiming the affidavits are fake and that you have several body doubles. In other words, you were in Minnesota for the mall attack. They now claim that even the Storch film, although authenticated, was part of a sting operation. They say that Storch merely said those things so you would believe the CIA wanted to recruit you, that it was all part of the feds' plan to arrest you."

"And his suicide?"

"You did that too and made it look like suicide."

"Incredible. Our families?"

"They'll remain incarcerated indefinitely."

"How do they explain the deaths of the eleven Mont-gomery Ryders? Did I somehow do that as a twelve-year-old?"

"No, they blame that on a rogue agent and cite it as your initial motivation."

"Great. What now?"

"Well, they've begun freezing my assets."

"You're kidding, are you broke now?"

He laughed. "No, no, they'll never find it all, but things will be a little more difficult from here on out."

"They've been pretty damn difficult until now. I'm not looking forward to more difficult."

"Don't worry. This has hurt them a lot more than they're letting on."

"Where are we going?"

"I'd rather not say right now. But I'll not be going with you to your final destination. I have to take every precaution, for both our sakes. But you're headed to the safest place on earth. Somewhere so isolated and secret, I can't even get there without Spencer."

"How is Lightyear surviving this?"

"The president has just signed an executive order consolidating all the investigations into Lightyear's activities because of national security concerns. Not one member of Congress is disagreeing; there is a power here beyond Luther Storch."

"What? Who?"

"It's always about money. See where the money goes, and you'll find the answer. Who benefits from the way things are?" The captain called Booker to the cockpit.

Amber slid into his seat. "We heard most of what Booker told you. Linh's upset about her parents."

"We'll get them out, Linh," I said, leaning over Amber. "I'm not waiting for the government to figure this out. We're going to fix it ourselves. First, we have to stop Dustin from causing any more damage."

"Why would he do this?" Amber asked. "Is he that jealous of you?"

"No, this goes back lifetimes."

"Can't you get him back on our side?" Linh asked.

"Who knows? I still can't believe what I could have learned in Clarity Lake, but he didn't want me to go back in. Now I know why. He knew I'd learn his great secret: he and Storch are the same. Outrageous! It's hard to say whether we'll ever get back to Outin."

We drifted off to sleep. When I awoke, Wandus was sitting next to me. I looked over and saw Amber asleep next to Linh. "Where have you been?" he asked.

"In a dream I was in Kyle's room, but he wasn't there. After wandering around for a moment, remembering our good times, I saw someone else in the room—a man standing over a table, fitting the last piece into Kyle's 5,000-piece white puzzle. It was Travis Curry, the guy who wrote the Mayan book, one of the nine."

"It wasn't a dream."

"No, of course it wasn't."

"What did he say to you?"

"He looked at me with Kyle's eyes and told me that the Mayans weren't wrong, that we just misinterpreted their calendar's meaning. It is actually just another prophetic marker of the shift, the end of hatred and lies and the beginning of love and truth."

"You must help with this."

"Help with the shift? I don't even know how to stop Lightyear."

"All through human history people have sought power from external sources—magic rings, swords, castles, weapons, wealth. These are all possessions, but there is no real power there. All the power is within. It's inner power… thus the Inner Movement."

"I can stop Lightyear and help bring the shift through IM? In case you haven't noticed, we're on the run. The Movement is crumbling."

"It needs a leader."

"How do I lead the Movement? That's Spencer's thing."

"Spencer is not a leader; he knows this. He has prepared the Movement for you. All this means is that you will to show them. They will teach themselves."

"I don't know how."

"We've talked of this before, my friend. It is the Outviews you must use. They are your soul's experience. Your soul-powers are from a different place; they seem alien in this world. But the Outviews are all of this human plane."

We landed a few minutes later on an abandoned airstrip. Booker told us we were in southwestern Arizona. Two Suburban SUVs were waiting. Booker and his people hastily took one and headed in the opposite direction. Ren and the four other IMers, Wandus, Spencer, the girls, a driver, and me bounced along a rutted dirt road for half an hour before finding pavement. I leaned up to Spencer in the front, "Are we going anywhere near Taos? I'd like to see Yangchen."

"That's exactly where we're going, but tonight we're sleeping at a ranch Booker owns, near Silver City, New Mexico."

"Do you know if Trevor is alive?"

"I haven't seen his change. I believe he is, but I have no idea where."

"Dustin will know."

"It's possible."

"How did you not know about the Dustin/Storch connection?"

"Dustin was blocking it. He's powerful."

"He has access to all the Windows of Outin. That's power!"

"The Windows are extraordinary."

"We should protect them."

"We protect one thing."

"Isn't it time you returned it to me?"

"Tonight, when we stop."

"Why not now? I thought we could trust Ren."

"Tonight."

That night, after Spencer announced more centers had been raided, he and I went for a short walk into the Gila National Forest, which bordered Booker's land. He handed me the Jadeo. "This is the thing, above all else. I should not have to tell you this. You're choosing not to remember."

"I get it."

"Then forget the Windows, Outin, friends, relatives, whatever. They all come a distant second to this."

"This does not mean we have to abandon everyone else."

"No," he said, shaking his head, "but it means we know our priorities."

"More centers falling. They're overwhelming us. Isn't there someone in the government? The FBI? Somewhere? How deep is the corruption? Who have they made? Who do they own? How big is Lightyear? I mean I feel like this is becoming a dystopian world."

"It's not Lightyear. It's Omnia."

"I've been afraid of that since I discovered the documents in Hibbs' safe."

"Omnia controls the world using Lightyear, corporations, and governments, in that order of importance. It's already a dystopian world."

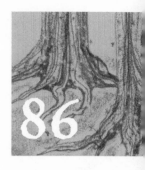

I n dejected terror, I sat alone in an observation tower Booker had built onto the side of his cabin in order to view distant ridges. We were all on standby, as the authorities seemed to know everything the Movement was doing. I needed to find Dustin and make him stop. Because I couldn't get to Outin, I explored the outer reaches of the astral and suddenly he was there.

"Dustin, or should I say Storch? How could you? I'm your brother."

"Nate, it's not like that."

"No, I guess not. You killed Dad, so what's a brother after all... just another problem in your way."

"Just because we share a soul doesn't mean I'm working with him, and it sure as hell doesn't mean I am him."

"Then why didn't you tell me?"

"Because I knew you would react this way. I knew you wouldn't believe me."

"I don't believe you."

"See."

"See? Screw you, Dustin. Do you know—" We lost contact. Two minutes later we connected again.

"Are you tracking me right now?" I asked.

"I wouldn't even know how."

"You think I believe that. I've got some of the greatest mystics the world has ever known helping me, and not one of them could show me how to project the Storch movie. Who are you really?"

"I could do that because I was Storch."

"Whatever. Dustin why are you denying this? I'm not coming for you. I'm just telling you that we're no longer brothers. I don't ever want to see or talk to you again."

"We're always brothers, Nate. From this life and many others. Pretending something isn't so doesn't make it not so… brother."

"My brother wouldn't kill our dad. Or do you want to deny that too? How about Kirby and the other mystics they've arrested. Moab, Marble Mountain, Cervantes, and all the others. How did they find those and Cuba? Only you knew about Cuba!"

"Not true, Nate, there have been raids and arrests that I knew nothing about. Only one person knew everything, and it wasn't me. I'm not the traitor in this life…"

"Oh yeah, then tell me who is. Who knew all these things? Spencer? Do you think I'd believe Spencer is a double agent?"

"No."

"Then who?"

"You won't believe me."

"Who?" I yelled.

"You, Nate… You are the leak!"

"What? That's the best you've got? Me? If we were talking on the phone, I'd hang up on you. I suppose I just forgot calling in details to Lightyear."

"You don't have to. Someone else is doing it for you."

"Really? Ha! The fairy tale gets more complicated."

"Nate, there's an open channel out of you."

"I can tell you're just making this up as you go along."

"I'm not. You just don't want the truth."

"Fine. Stop the suspense."

"Ever since you've been using advanced Kellaring, the person who you traded energy with so that he is tracked instead of you, is that person. If he knows what he is doing, that person can also monitor all your thoughts."

"Wow, that's your big theory? Dustin, I traded with Mom."

"Exactly."

I was quiet as my mind raced with reactions and implications.

"You know I'm right, Nate."

"No, you're just pushing your paranoid delusional anger at Mom onto me."

"Am I? Why don't you ask her? A young wizard like yourself ought to be able to get the truth from a simple lady like Mom."

"I may come for you after all, Dustin." I ended the connection.

I needed to think; meditation was impossible. I thought of finding Wandus, but I worried time was too short.

It took almost an hour to reach Mom.

"Nate, my God, how are you?"

"Mom, will you tell me the truth?"

"The truth? Nate, are you okay? Of course I will."

"Have you been helping Lightyear?"

She was quiet for a moment. "Yes... but Nate, I've been doing it to help you."

"Help me? Mom, they want me dead."

"No, sweetie, that's not true. They want to clear all this up. They know you're a good kid."

"How did they get you to believe this stuff? I've been blaming Dustin and Rose."

"Turn yourself in, and you'll see I'm right."

"No. You're tracking me now, aren't you? I'm so stupid. Mom, Kyle is dead!"

"I know. You need to surrender before they get you."

"I hope you've got a good enough deal that you'll be freed soon because I'm done using Kellaring with you anymore, and you'll not be hearing from me again."

"No, Nate, don't do that. You'll get yourself killed if you keep running. Don't—"

Less than a minute after we lost contact. Amber yelled, "Nate, we have to go. They may know we're here."

87

Seven hours later, we arrived in what could only be described as an organized junkyard— old buses, shelters made from appliance boxes, duct tape, tin foil and car hoods, old trailers and stripped RVs. It was a turmoil of crude cul-de-sacs out of a bad sci-fi flick. Among the wreckage, of whatever "civilization" this was, were people who could have stepped out of the Star Wars bar scene. "What planet are we on?" Amber asked.

"Planet Taos." Spencer laughed. We're about forty-five minutes from Taos."

"Why aren't we going to Greater World?" Linh asked. The familiar Sangre de Cristo Mountains were visible out to the east, but the landscape where we found ourselves, in the middle of the vast sagebrush volcanic desert that bordered Taos to the west, seemed as far from the modern world as one could get.

"They're watching it. This place is off the map and not an IM center, but we've got friends here."

"If they have Greater World under surveillance, isn't it risky being this close?"

"It's risky everywhere right now. Besides, the best place to hide is in plain sight. They'd never expect us to be this close a center."

I hadn't spoken since we'd left Silver City. The girls had tried, but Spencer left me alone. I suspected he knew about my mother's betrayal, but either way, I wasn't ready to talk

about it. I'd switched Kellaring to my only other living relative—Dustin. There were probably a hundred reasons this was
a bad idea; it gave Dustin a channel to me, it made finding
Outin easier for Lightyear, it put Dustin in jeopardy... my
brain had been burning for hours trying to figure all the ramifications and alternatives, and it came down to the fact that
there was no other choice. If Dustin was bad, I was not likely
to survive much longer. He could have killed me at Outin, but
maybe there was a reason for him to have kept me alive longer.
To lead them to Spencer? To all the mystics? It was exhausting,
impossible work trying to understand the depths of my crisis.

Someone opened the car door from the outside, and I
stumbled out onto the ground. Yangchen pulled me to my feet.
I was crying.

"Did you tell him?" she asked Spencer as he got out.

"He knows. Nate can feel the change, too."

"What is it?" Amber asked, as I sunk to my knees.

"His mother is dead," Yangchen said.

"Oh, Nate." Linh was suddenly kneeling next to me.

"I did it. I killed her, too."

"No, Nate."

"I took Kellaring from her, so Lightyear killed her."

"It wasn't Lightyear," Yangchen said quietly.

"What?" I leapt to my feet, accidently knocking Linh back.

"Good God, Yangchen, this is not the time," Spencer said.

"It's too late now, isn't it Spencer?"

"Tell me," I demanded.

Spencer waved the IMers in the direction of a sheet
metal shanty. "It's nicer than it looks," he told them and then
ushered us to a "building" constructed of cinder block, tarps,
chicken wire, and fiberglass roofing. Inside it was quite different—roomy, furnished like a real house, and clean.

Amber and Linh sat on either side of me, on what
seemed to be the plush leather backseat of a 1970s Cadillac.
Yangchen sat across from us in a La-Z-Boy. Spencer stood with
one leg perched on a wooden bench. "Tell me," I repeated,
"who killed my mother?"

Spencer sighed, as Yangchen began. "It was IF, a faction within the Movement that advocates violence. IF stands for Inner Force."

"What is this, a comic book?" I asked, repulsed. "Where are they? Take me to them."

"We don't know who they are," she said.

"I bet he does," I said, pointing to Spencer.

"I don't believe so," Yangchen said.

"Nate, I'm sorry about your mother, and although I agree it was likely the work of IF, I cannot be certain. And I have no knowledge of the identities of who supports IF within the Movement."

"Come on, Spencer, you advocate violence."

"Not like they do."

"There are several factions within the Movement. We may all agree on most of the goals, but we often differ on the methods," Yangchen confirmed.

"We'd like to find them, but our energies have been elsewhere," Spencer said.

"Why would they kill my mother?"

"She was helping Lightyear. She was the main supplier of information on the centers and your whereabouts."

Linh gasped.

"Mom didn't know what she was doing. They had her convinced that it was the only way to save me."

"Well, karma and time will reveal the truth, whatever it may be," Yangchen said.

"It was the Kellaring that gave her the access, and now I've given it to Dustin. He may be more dangerous."

"Don't worry about Dustin right now. He is unable to harm you at present."

"Who can we trust?" Amber asked.

"Yangchen," I said, ignoring Amber, "Will you take me to find the dark mystic?"

"Jesus!" Spencer shouted.

"Please, Yangchen."

"The dark mystic is not someone you're ready to deal with, Nate. Believe me when I say that," Spencer said.

"Quit trying to control me."

Spencer closed his eyes and shook his head.

"He's right," Yangchen replied. "The dark mystic has reached a place of such knowledge that is hard to know... Well, let's just say there are places where good and evil are seen from different angles, and the difference is a matter of perspective. It's in those places that the dark mystic dwells."

"Take me."

"Nate, I beg for your trust, and in exchange, I will promise you the knowledge needed to find the dark mystic... when you're ready." Her unblinking stare held a flickering purple light that pulled me. I could not refuse.

After a long silence, Spencer spoke. "Enough of IF, the dark mystic, and Lightyear. Time is overwhelming us. Nate, you now know that Lightyear is yet another pawn of Omnia, who is at this very moment using is limitless resources to dismantle Booker's empire. Lightyear will simply be moved from the CIA building over to NSA and renamed. Those agents will still search for anyone connected to the Movement, the soldiers will still track you, and the girls are the next to die."

I stared at Spencer. "Somehow I'm supposed to defeat the most powerful government and advanced military the world has ever known... with peace and love?" I thought of the night Spencer told me he'd looked into a thousand futures and had never seen a way.

"There is a way," Yangchen said, gazing out the yellowed plastic window at a stand of juniper trees before turning back to me.

I stared into her wise, calm eyes, seeing hundreds of lifetimes and something startling. I suddenly realized it might really be possible to keep the girls alive and defeat Omnia.

"Oh my God," Linh gasped.

I turned to see two silhouettes and was both frightened and amazed as Clastier and Rose entered the shack.

## END OF BOOK TWO

❧

# Acknowledgements

Writing is a solitary journey. Preparing a book for publication involves many – Thank you to my first readers Roanne Lewis, Barbara Blair (my mother), Harriet Greene, Marty Goldman and Kate Black, all of you have done so much more than read and find errors. Continued gratitude and respect for my friend, Mike Sager. Deep appreciation to all my friends who have helped get the word out about the *Inner Movement*, and thanks again to the readers who bought my debut novel and are now holding this one! And finally to Teakki, who patiently waited, often in full superhero costume, until I finished writing each day.

# About the Author

Brandt Legg, a child prodigy who, after the tragic death of his father and crippling migraine headaches, at age ten turned an interest in stamp collecting into what became a multi-million dollar business empire. National media dubbed him the "Teen Tycoon" but by his early twenties, the high-flying Legg became ensnarled in the financial whirlwind of the junk bond eighties, lost his entire fortune... and ended up serving time in federal prison for financial improprieties. Legg emerged, chastened and wiser, one year later and began anew in retail and real estate. From there his life adventures have led him through photography, magazine publishing, newspaper writing, FM radio, CD production and concert promotion.

Made in the USA
Lexington, KY
23 June 2013